The Campus History Series

CARSON-NEWMAN COLLEGE

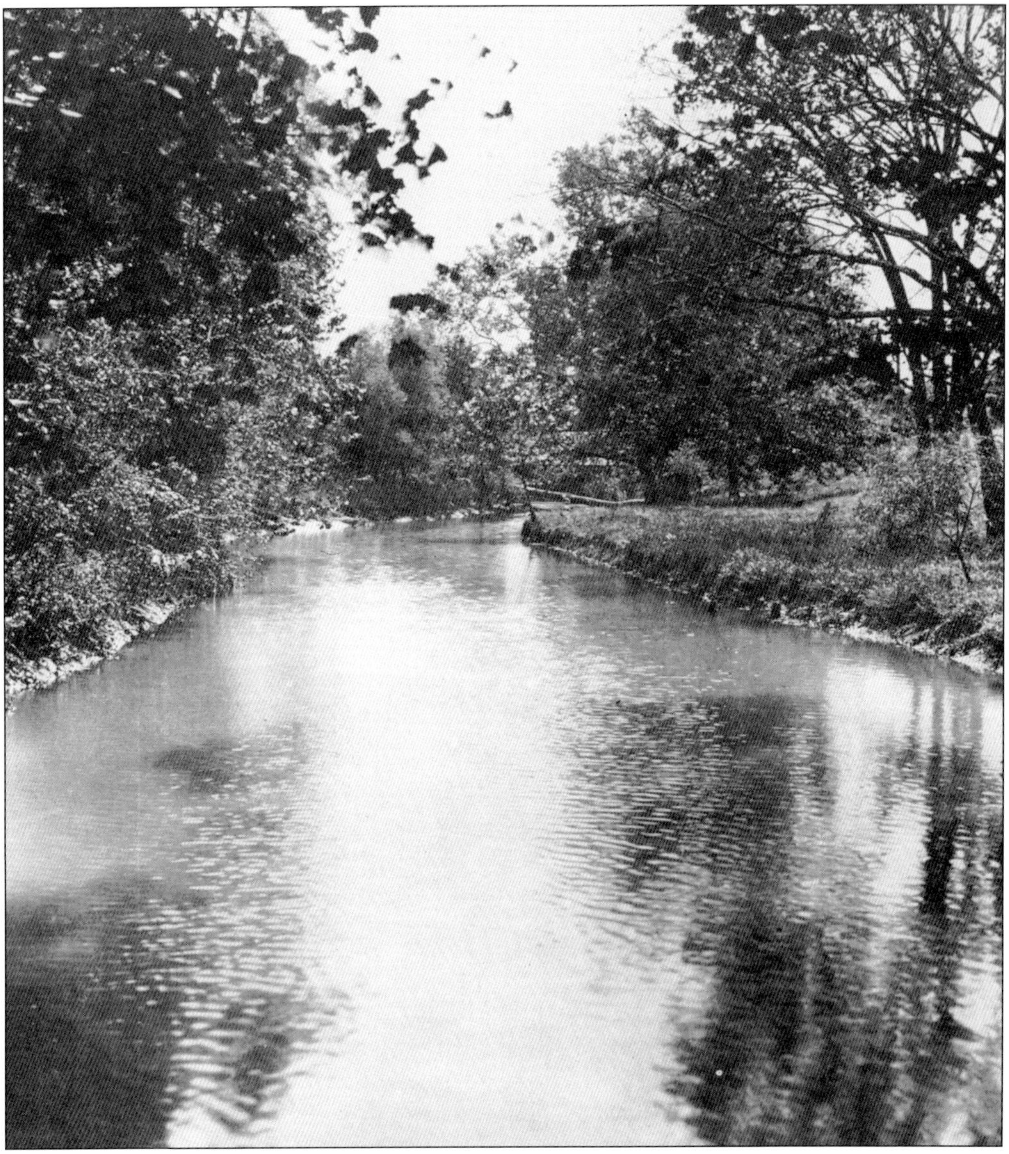

Mossy Creek. At one time providing the name for the town now known as Jefferson City, Mossy Creek is a five-mile waterway that winds its way northeastward to meet the Holston River. Cherokee Dam was constructed just downstream from this point. On its east bank, Carson-Newman had its beginnings in 1851, where it initially offered classes in the local Baptist church's building. The next year, the school moved across the creek into its own newly built structure on the original two-acre campus. (Courtesy of the Mildred L. Iddins Special Collections' College Archives.)

On the Cover: Class Lets Out. As the trees begin to bloom in this early spring photograph from the 1950s, class lets out and students proceed to chapel services in First Baptist Church, Jefferson City. The decade proved to be eventful as the campus experienced a flu epidemic, new female and male dormitories were opened, the Baker Building and Holt Fieldhouse were constructed, and the college celebrated its centennial. (Courtesy of the Mildred L. Iddins Special Collections' College Archives.)

The Campus History Series

CARSON-NEWMAN COLLEGE

LINDA T. GASS AND ALBERT L. LANG

ARCADIA PUBLISHING

ISBN 978-0-7385-9374-6

Published by Arcadia Publishing
Charleston, South Carolina

Printed in the United States of America

Library of Congress Catalog Card Number: 2011945486

For all general information, please contact Arcadia Publishing:
Telephone 843-853-2070
Fax 843-853-0044
E-mail sales@arcadiapublishing.com
For customer service and orders:
Toll-Free 1-888-313-2665

Visit us on the Internet at www.arcadiapublishing.com

For Charlie and our four Carson-Newman graduates:
Michael, Brian, Patrick, and Brent.

To Cindy, Harper, Maggie, and Gracie Li:
You are God's biggest blessings to me.

CONTENTS

ACKNOWLEDGMENTS

It has been a privilege to produce a work such as this for Carson-Newman. We are indebted to many wonderful people, not only for help with the book, but also for constant encouragement.

We would like to extend our gratitude to our provost, Dr. Kina Mallard, and vice president for advancement, Danny Nicholson, without whose commitment and support this project would not have been possible.

We express our thanks to Frieda Self and Imogene Brewer for their editorial assistance. We are grateful for the help of Charles Key with the presidential images and graciousness in letting us use any of his work we needed. We are indebted to Mark Brown not only for use of his photographs but also for allowing us to borrow from his narrative work on Carson-Newman's web pages. We are also grateful to Ricke Hester and the *Standard Banner* for permission to use their photographs. Thanks to faculty professor emeriti James L. Pethel and Dr. John Lee Welton for the images and materials they have provided the college archives over the years, as well as Dr. Earl Cleveland for his technical assistance with several images and historical contributions. We are thankful to current faculty member Dr. Eric Thorson for the numerous images he has given the archives documenting the music department's history, particularly A Cappella Choir. Thanks to Don Elia for the images, statistics, and information documenting wrestling at Carson-Newman.

Over the years, the special collections have received innumerable gifts from donors, several of which are used in this book. We are thankful for all those who have shared their treasures. We are grateful for our colleagues here at Carson-Newman, especially those who we are blessed to serve with in the Stephens-Burnett Library under the leadership of our ever-supportive dean, Bruce Kocour.

This book is the product of images available to us in the college archives. We acknowledge that it is not comprehensive and is only a sampling of the people and events that have made Carson-Newman the unique and wonderful place it is. Unless otherwise noted, all images appear courtesy of the Mildred L. Iddins Special Collections' College Archives.

As a faith based archives, we believe that in preserving materials documenting the history of Carson-Newman, we are keeping a record of God's gracious work in the lives of His people. As David wrote in Psalm 22:30: "Posterity will serve him; future generations will be told about the Lord." We hope this project will accomplish that.

For Charlie, Michael, Brian, Patrick, and Brent, thanks for your support and enthusiasm for this project.

I cannot say thanks enough to my wife, Cindy, who is always in my corner, and to my children Harper, Maggie, and Gracie Li, who are always a constant source of joy and encouragement.

INTRODUCTION

After initial discussions in the early 1840s, the East Tennessee Baptist Educational Society applied in 1850 for a charter to establish an institution of higher learning. Making use of the town's Baptist church until they could construct their own building, Mossy Creek Missionary Baptist Seminary offered its first classes in August 1851 under Pres. William Rogers. The Tennessee legislature granted the school's charter in December of that year. Unfortunately, the first of several tragedies to befall the college occurred in November as Rogers died from typhoid. He was succeeded by R.R. Bryan, a dedicated teacher and one of the early visionaries.

As noted in their founding documents, the founders possessed a twofold intent: "to promote education in general, and among the ministry in particular." Over time, that ideal has become the institution's DNA of Christian service as evidenced in student volunteers as well as in the lives of alumni. The institution produced its first graduate, Richard Scruggs, in 1855. Manifesting the ideal of "education in general," Scruggs went on to become a physician. The following year, the second graduating class reaffirmed the school's mission by producing a lawyer and a minister.

The year of 1855 also witnessed the first of several name changes, as the school became Mossy Creek Baptist College under Pres. Samuel Anderson. By the end of the decade, enrollment was up to 160 young men and prospects looked bright. However, the Civil War loomed on the horizon and the college was forced to close. Records show that no classes were held between 1861 and 1868. Federal troops occupied the campus and the damage was significant. Years later, the college received $6,000 in reparations from Congress.

After the war, the college found itself in significant debt when it reopened in 1868, once again under the leadership of R.R. Bryan. The next year, Jesse Baker assumed the presidency and went on a legendary 3,500-mile horseback trip that raised over $5,000 and pulled the college out of financial distress.

Efforts in female education took significant strides on the local front as an institute was established in the Masonic Lodge. The Masons then approached several of those with close ties to Mossy Creek Baptist College to assist with running the school. By 1879, the college assumed operation of what would eventually become Newman College.

During this period, the college purchased the 35-acre Mountcastle estate. The mansion would be utilized for classes and administrative offices. Over the years, it would provide housing to female and male students. In 1880, the college changed its name once again, becoming Carson College, named in memory of longtime trustee and founding father James Harvey Carson.

In 1889, Carson and Newman Colleges joined. Led by future governor Ben Hooper, the students conducted a "marriage" ceremony to celebrate the union. The merger of men's and women's institutions made Carson-Newman an early entrant in coeducation in the region. Plans for expansion were developed and in 1892, classes were offered in the newly constructed administration building, locally referred to as "The College."

Tragedy struck again though, with the first of two fires that would devastate the campus. In 1916, a faulty flue led to the complete destruction of the main building, destroying classrooms, administrative offices, the library, and literary society halls.

The college rebounded quickly and the John T. Henderson Memorial Hall was built on the same location, opening in 1919. Unfortunately, this building too would be destroyed by fire as the result of arson in 1974. It was replaced by the Henderson Humanities Building, a testimony to the college's resiliency.

In 1918, Carson-Newman officially entered into an agreement with the Tennessee Baptist Convention, a relationship that continues today. The early 1920s saw male and female athletic teams take on the monikers Fighting Parsons and Parsonettes, respectively. A decade later, they would adopt the current Eagles name.

World War II opened another chapter in Carson-Newman's history. The college entered into a relationship with the military, hosting a Navy V-12 officers' training program. While doing its part in the war effort, the college was also able to offset the loss of many students to active duty.

The year 1948 marked the start of one of Carson-Newman's longest serving presidents, Harley Fite. Known as the "Great Builder," over 20 structures were built during his tenure. Three years later the college celebrated its centennial, punctuated with various events including reenactments and a pageant.

The school continued to grow and was successful in all arenas. It won national championships in baseball and football, as well as debate. Academic programs were nationally recognized for excellence and Carson-Newman was also proudly recognized for its development of student leaders.

Unanimously elected by Carson-Newman trustees, J. Randall O'Brien officially took over presidential duties in 2009. Borrowing from Carson-Newman's rich history, he reinforced the foundational belief that giving back to God through diligent study and serving His creation should combine to make the double helix of the Carson-Newman experience. That heritage is tailor-fit to Dr. O'Brien's vision: "C-N's future will be built on the twin pillars of academic rigor and Christian excellence." Carson-Newman students learn to think, write, read well, and to present and enter into the give and take of argument so as to become educated citizens and worldwide servant leaders. Under his leadership, the board of trustees voted in the spring of 2012 to pursue the school's mission as Carson-Newman, a Christian University.

Servant leadership programs abound on campus, the effects of which are staggering. Appalachian Outreach and its volunteers have provided more than 2,200 weeks' worth of home repairs in 25 years. Baptist Campus Ministries sends out more than 200 fall and spring break volunteers annually, Bonner Scholars provide approximately 10,000 hours of service per year, and Community Connections offers a student-run agency that matches area needs with helpers. Global education and broadening students' horizons are staples of the Carson-Newman experience. Scores of international students study at Carson-Newman each year while others travel from campus to study abroad. Efforts have included a two-week study trip to South Africa, archeological excavation in Jordan, earthquake relief work in Haiti, a focus on health care in South Korea, and ministry in Zimbabwe.

In March 2012, the school received the highest federal recognition possible to denote an institution's commitment to community service. The Corporation for National and Community Service and the US Department of Education presented the Presidential Award in the 2012 President's Higher Education Community Service Honor Roll to Carson-Newman at ceremonies held in Los Angeles.

Throughout its history, the institution has instilled a deep commitment to service in its students. The fruits of its labor—its alumni—have filled schoolrooms, courthouses, hospitals, boardrooms, pulpits, and mission fields the world over in spreading the lessons of Carson-Newman's motto of truth, beauty, and goodness.

One

A Dream Fulfilled
Foundations and Builders

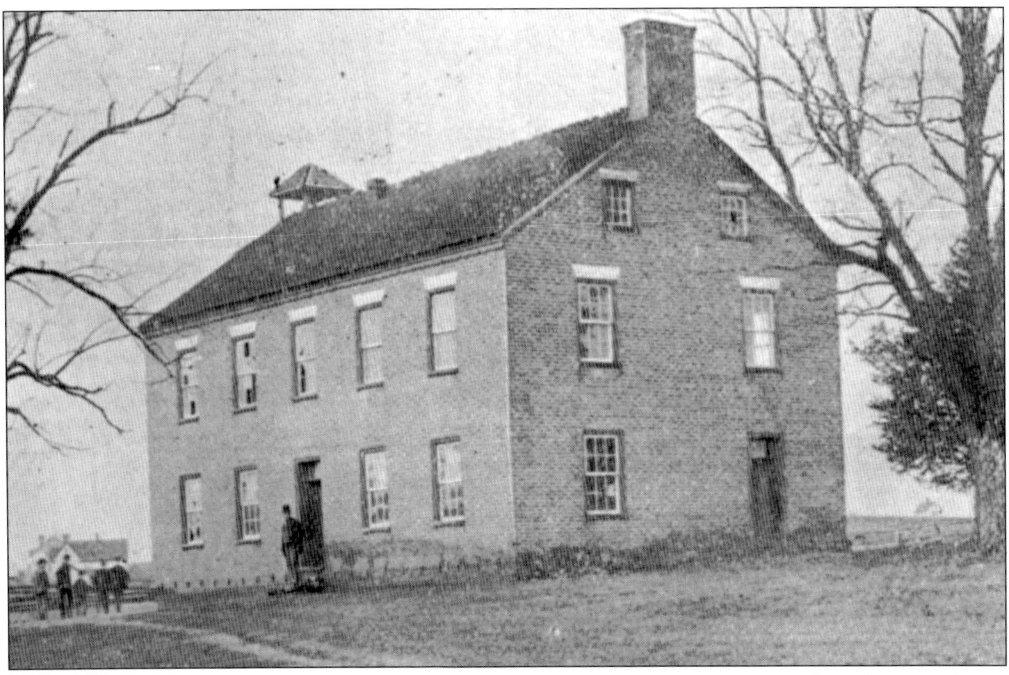

Mossy Creek Missionary Baptist Seminary. Two years after the founding fathers' organizational meeting, the fledgling institution opened its doors for its first session in September 1851, in the Mossy Creek Baptist Church building. William Rogers was named president but tragically died in November of typhoid. Prof. R.R. Bryan stood in the gap and the next year the school moved into its own building on a two-acre lot on the creek's west side.

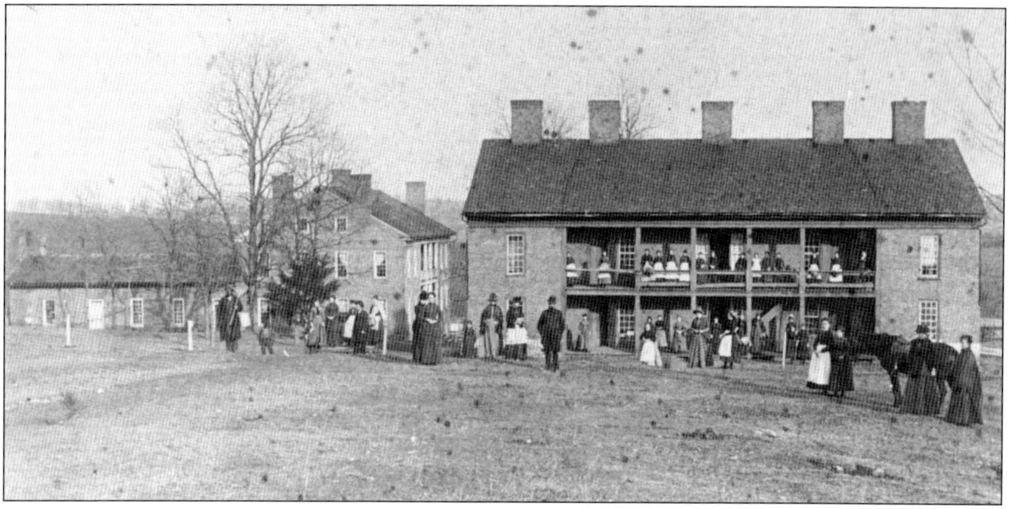

Mossy Creek Baptist College. In 1855, the school changed its name to Mossy Creek Baptist College and by decade's end boasted an administration building and Newman dormitories numbers one and two. Enrollment was around 150 students, including 75 in the preparatory department. Four faculty taught all courses and tuition ranged from $10 (preparatory) to $18 (senior). Much of this first campus is now covered by the Silver Diamond Baseball Complex.

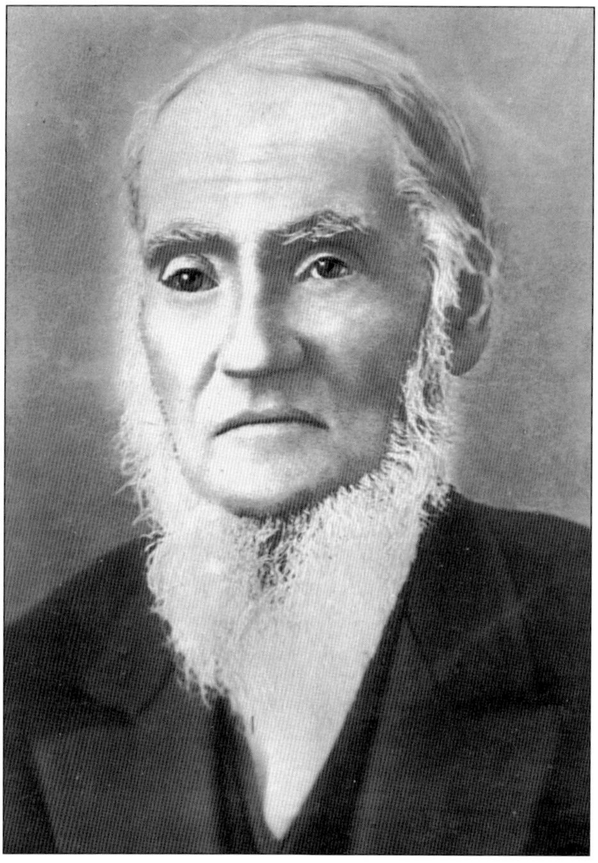

William C. "Uncle Billy" Newman. One of the original "Oak Tree Five" who met in 1849 to discuss the need for a Baptist institution of higher learning, Newman was a resident of Mossy Creek and deacon in the Mossy Creek Baptist Church. In 1855, the trustees purchased land and planned for the construction of two dormitories, charging him with overseeing their fundraising and construction. He advanced the school over $10,000, which was never repaid due to financial struggles but which he graciously counted as a donation. He also worked with his brothers to establish Newman College for girls.

Isaac M. Newman. Another of the "Oak Tree Five," Isaac Newman was present at the 1849 meeting. Along with his brothers Maj. Jonathan Nelson Newman and William C. Newman, he also acted as a visionary in the establishment of the all-female Newman College, which bore his family's name. A native of Mossy Creek, he was an active member of the Mossy Creek Baptist Church. In addition to giving of his time and creativity, Newman also made significant financial contributions. (Courtesy of Glenmoor Garrett.)

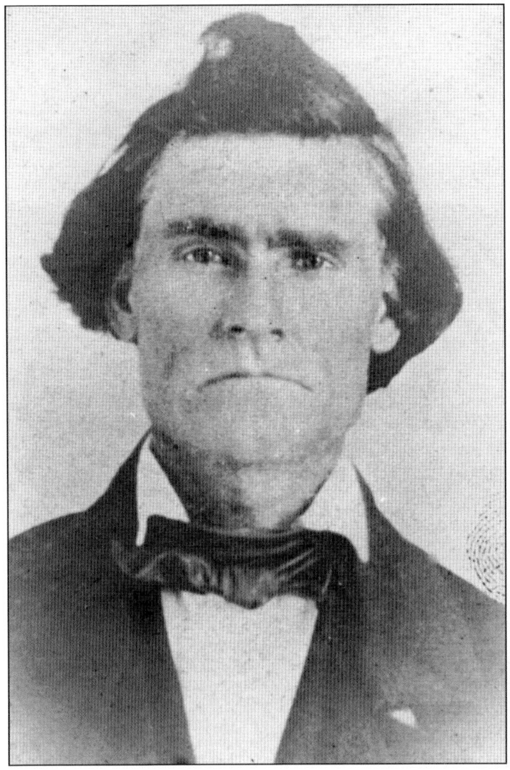

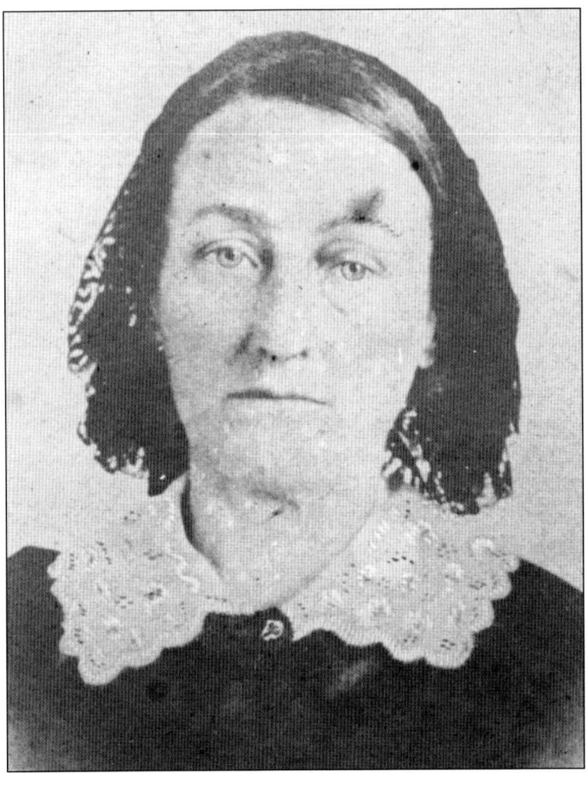

Sallie Underwood Newman. The wife of Isaac M. Newman, Sallie Newman was a faithful sympathizer and supporter of her husband's work. The Newman family gave considerably of their time and resources for the construction of the early Mossy Creek Missionary Baptist Seminary and Newman College. (Courtesy of Glenmoor Garrett.)

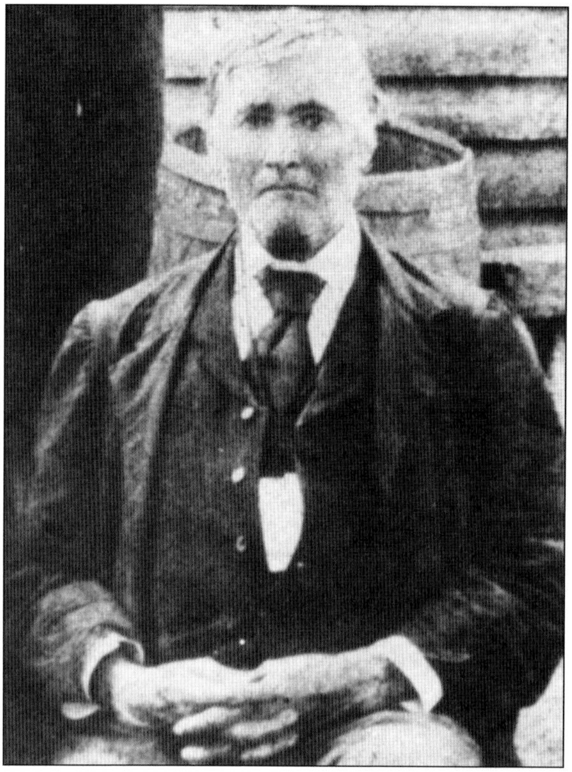

MAJ. JONATHAN N. "UNCLE NELSON" NEWMAN. Brother to Isaac and William, Major Newman was another of the region's early educational visionaries. A strong believer in a Baptist liberal arts education, Jonathan contributed his support and financial backing to the development of the new Baptist seminary. He served as a trustee and was also committed to female education, as he was instrumental in establishing Newman College.

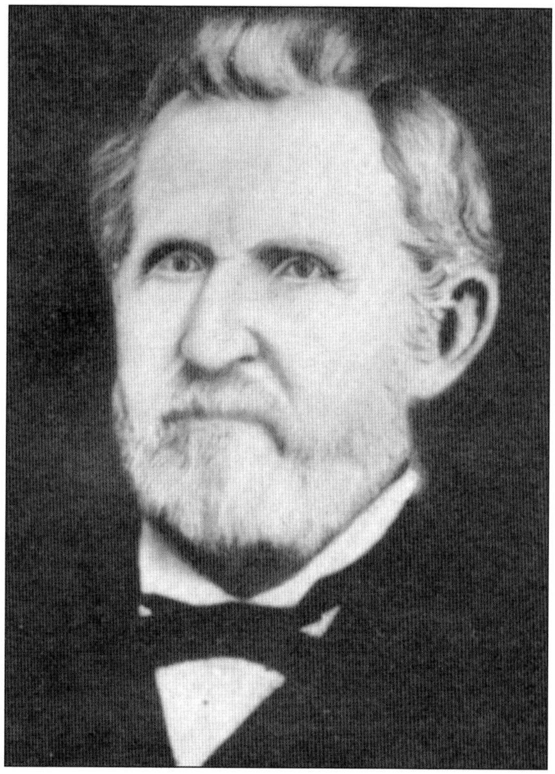

JAMES H. CARSON. A devout layman from Dandridge, Tennessee, Carson was one of the early organizers of Mossy Creek Missionary Baptist Seminary. He served as a trustee for most of the period from 1851 to 1880 and was a faithful financial contributor. Upon his death, he left the school $25,000, its largest gift to that point. The board of trustees honored him by renaming the school Carson College in 1880.

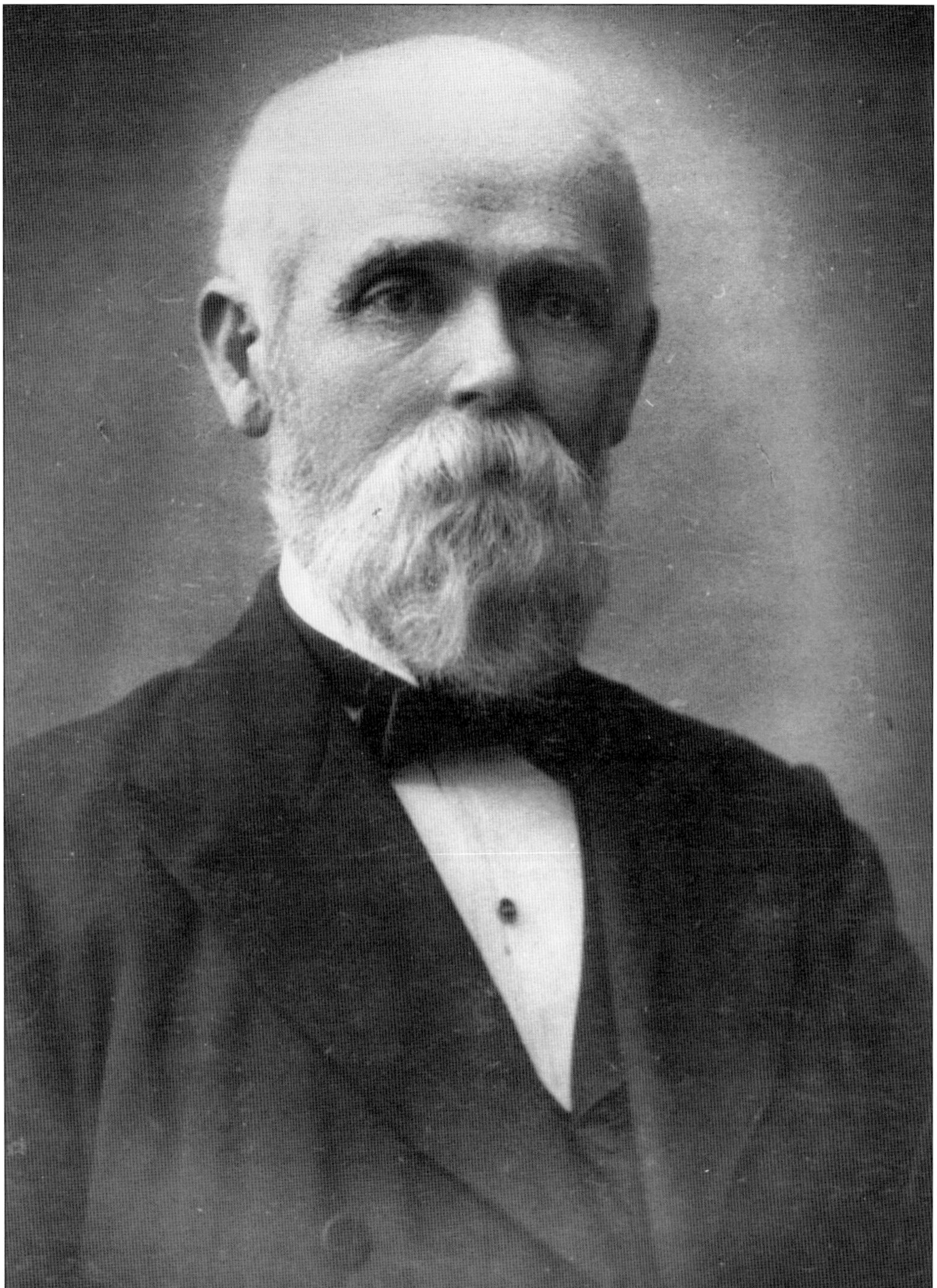

Richard Scruggs. Scruggs, whose mother was a first cousin to Davy Crockett, holds the distinction of being the college's first graduate. Receiving his Baccalaureate degree in the 1855 commencement ceremony from Mossy Creek Baptist College, he went on to attend Jefferson Medical College. He became a practicing physician in Sweetwater, Tennessee, until his death on December 28, 1903.

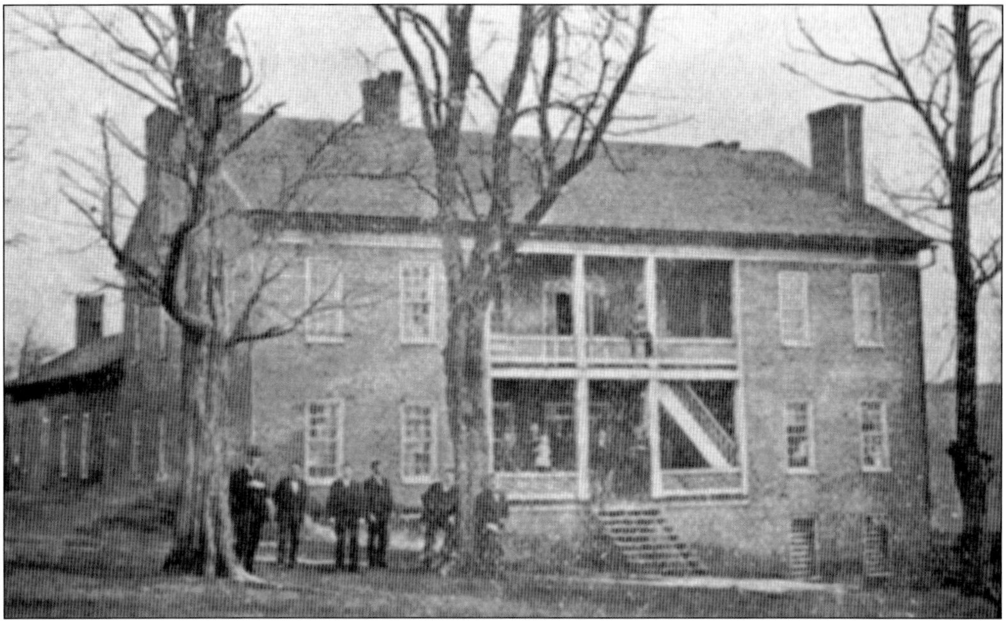

Newman Dormitory No. 1. During its first four years, the college housed all of its students in community homes. This policy was discontinued and two dormitories were commissioned in 1855. By 1857, they were ready for occupancy and together they housed 84 men. This building also had an attached dining room and kitchen and contained a partial basement.

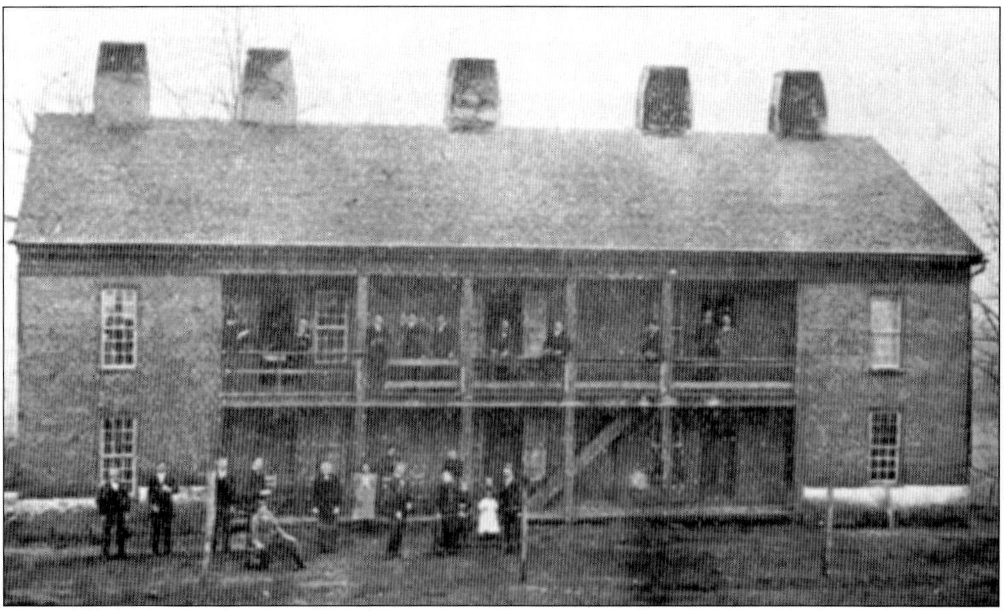

Newman Dormitory No. 2. This was the second dorm built by the Newman family and was also a two-story structure heated by open fireplaces. Mossy Creek and a local spring provided water for the new residents. During the Civil War, both Newman dormitories were occupied by federal forces and badly damaged. The college submitted a claim for financial compensation to the government, which it received years later.

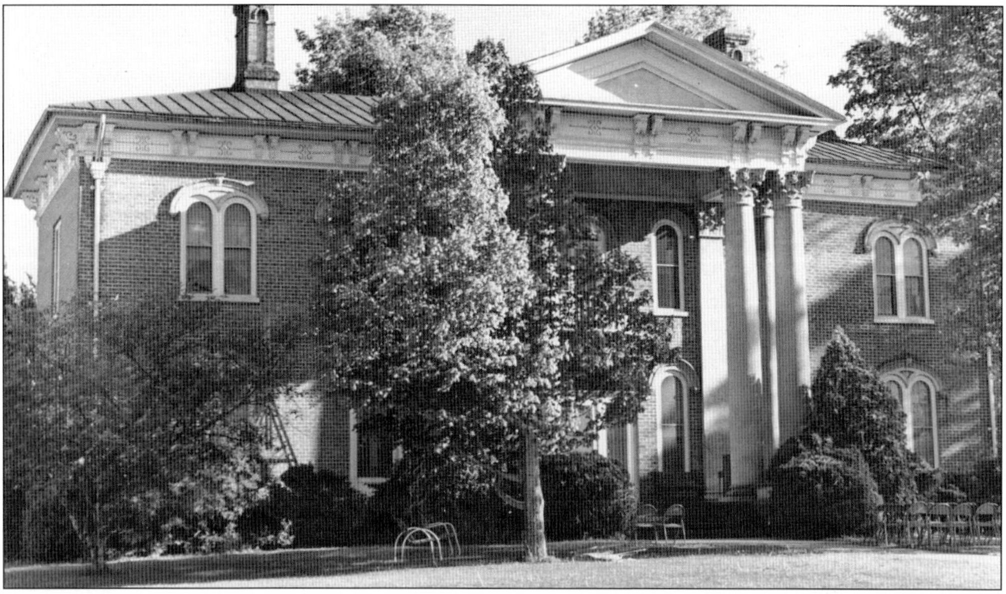

Carson College. In 1876, the trustees purchased the 35-acre A.J. Mountcastle estate, through which Highway 11-E now runs. While the preparatory department stayed behind on the original Mossy Creek campus, the stately Victorian mansion was converted into college classrooms, a library, and a laboratory along with an attached kitchen. A boardwalk was built to connect the old campus. In 1880, the school was renamed Carson College. The property was sold to Jefferson City in 1917 and used for an elementary school. Later, after several private ownerships, the mansion was finally razed in 1987.

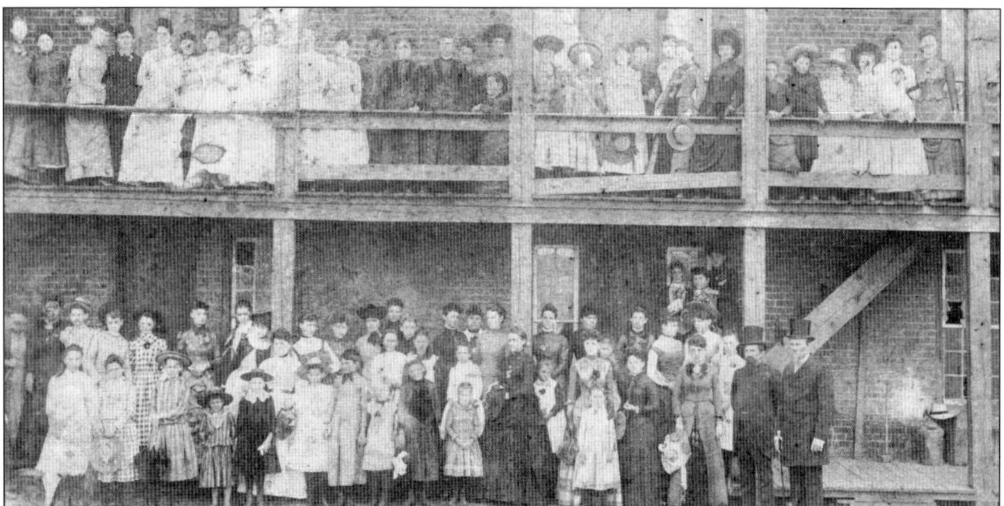

Newman College. The trustees and supporters of Carson College saw the need for a girls' school and assumed control of the Mossy Creek Masonic Female Institute in 1879. In 1882, efforts were made to convert the buildings vacated by the college's relocation to the Mountcastle property for occupancy by the newly renamed Seminary for Young Ladies. In 1885, the school was chartered as Mossy Creek Female Academy, but later that year, the trustees named it Newman Female Seminary to honor the Newman family who had given so much to help establish both institutions. By 1886, it was referred to as Newman College.

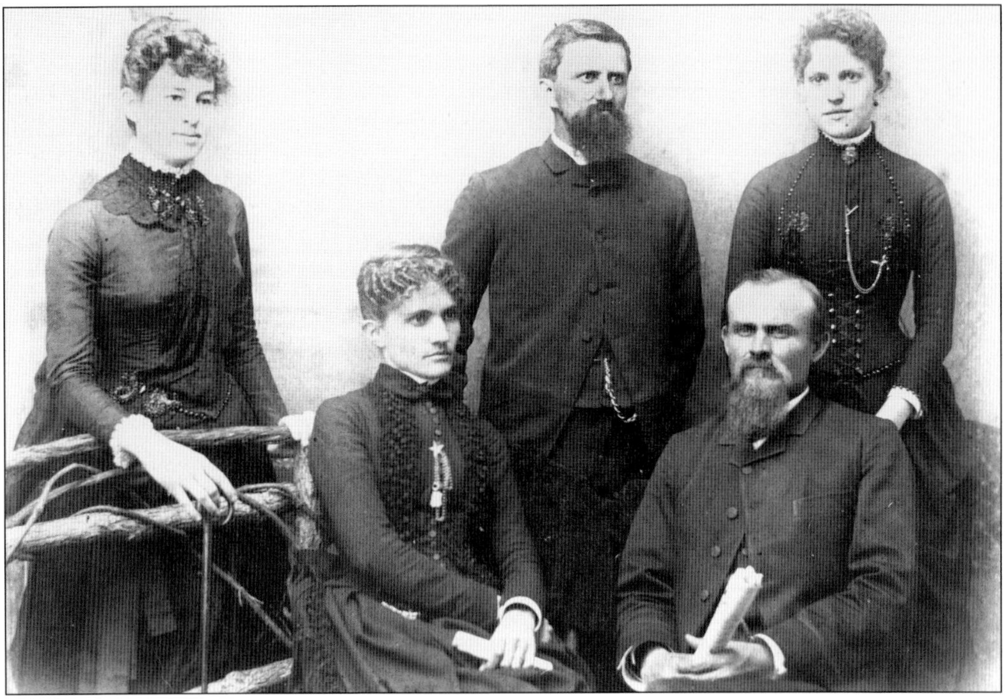

Newman College Faculty, 1886. The college offered three divisions that included primary, college preparatory, and collegiate courses. Among the faculty were, from left to right, (seated) Mrs. W.N. Brown, principal of preparatory school; and W.T. Russell, president and professor of metaphysics and pure and applied mathematics; (standing) Emma Sue Knox, principal of instrumental and vocal music; S.N. Newman, professor of natural science and Latin; and Ella Williams, professor of French, German, and English literature.

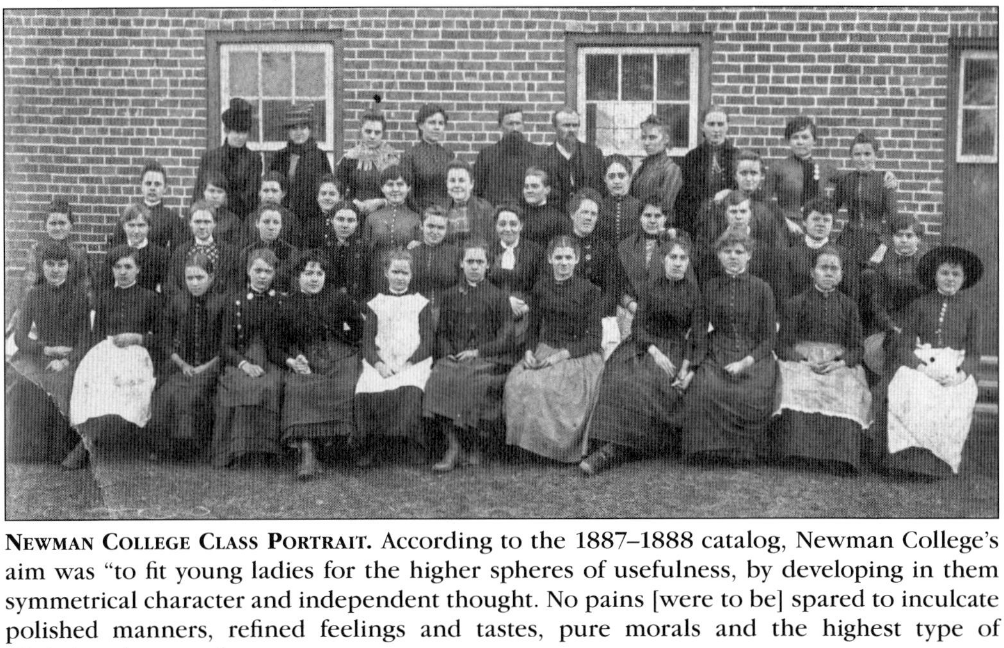

Newman College Class Portrait. According to the 1887–1888 catalog, Newman College's aim was "to fit young ladies for the higher spheres of usefulness, by developing in them symmetrical character and independent thought. No pains [were to be] spared to inculcate polished manners, refined feelings and tastes, pure morals and the highest type of Christian character."

54TH CONGRESS, } HOUSE OF REPRESENTATIVES. { REPORT
1st Session. } { No. 771.

TRUSTEES OF CARSON-NEWMAN COLLEGE.

MARCH 13, 1896.—Committed to the Committee of the Whole House and ordered to be printed.

MR. GIBSON, from the Committee on War Claims, submitted the following

REPORT:

[To accompany H. R. 6708.]

The Committee on War Claims, to whom was referred the bill (H. R. 6708) for the relief of the trustees of Carson-Newman College, at Mossy-creek, Tenn., submit the following report:

It appears from the evidence that some time in the spring of 1864 the Twenty-third Army Corps was encamped at Mossycreek, Tenn., in the immediate vicinity of this college, and while thus encamped Gen. H. M. Judah, commanding the Second Division of the said Twenty-third Army Corps, ordered a portion of his command to go to said college and obtain plank, lumber, and other materials, and that his men proceeded to the college and tore up the floors and sleepers, and took from the buildings nearly all the woodwork in and about the same and the fences around them, for the purpose of making and improving quarters for their officers and themselves, and for firewood. The weather being extremely cold, and the troops totally without tents or other shelter, fuel had to be used wherever found, and the college buildings and fencing suffered as a matter of course and necessity. The injury thus occasioned to the buildings and grounds is alleged to have been $8,000.

It was the custom of the War Department to place churches and school buildings in the same condition as when they were taken possession of by the United States, natural wear and tear excepted, or allow a reasonable amount in money in lieu of such repairs. A number of claims were presented to the War Department from States and districts declared to be in insurrection during the late war for the suppression of the rebellion. The Quartermaster-General decided that they were precluded from favorable consideration by the President's proclamation of July 1, 1862 (12 Stat. L., p. 1266), and by subsequent legislation of Congress (14 Stat. L., p. 397). In accordance with precedent, it seems to be the policy of Congress to pay for the use, occupation, and damage to institutions of this character.

Gen. Joseph A. Cooper, then an officer in the said Second Division Twenty-third Army Corps, says he was, "at that time encamped at Mossycreek, and an eyewitness to the facts, and that it was necessary to use the material in said buildings, the fences, and shade trees for the purposes of making tenable their quarters and for firewood."

Your committee is of opinion that the trustees should be paid the sum of $6,000, and recommend the passage of the bill with the following amendment:

In line 7 strike out "eight" and insert in lieu thereof "six."

○

CIVIL WAR REPARATIONS. Enrollment began to drop in 1861 and the college eventually closed from 1862 to 1868. Due to federal occupation, the campus suffered severe damage. An initial claim for $2,000 was submitted to Congress in 1880 but was denied. Rep. Richard Henry Gibson took up the fight and between 1896 and 1901, he worked to get the college's claim passed by the Committee on War Claims, the House of Representatives, and finally the Senate. Originally seeking $8,000 in damages, Carson and Newman finally received approval for $6,000 in February 1902. (Courtesy of HeritageQuest Online-US Serial Set.)

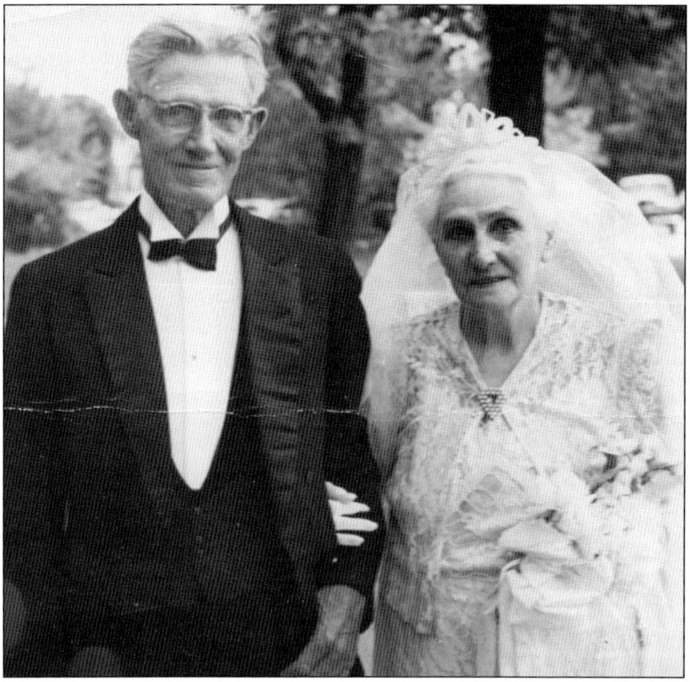

Carson and Newman College Wedding. On April 3, 1889, the two boards of trustees met and unanimously agreed to consolidate the schools. Male students reacted by staging a memorable mock wedding to celebrate the occasion. In the fall of 1889, Carson and Newman College opened its doors with an enlarged academic program. During 1950–1951, the college celebrated its centennial. A reenactment of the wedding was conducted with professors W. Powell Hale and Tennessee Jenkins playing the bride and groom.

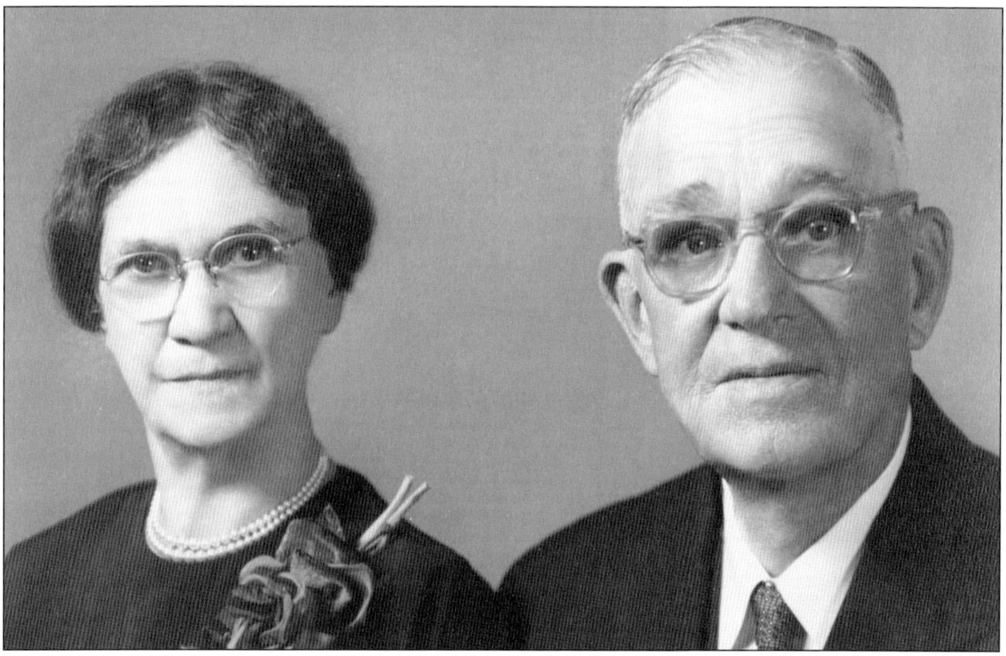

Mr. and Mrs. D.L. Butler. Both graduates of Carson-Newman, the Butlers served the school throughout their lifetimes, giving their time and money. Their generosity helped construct numerous buildings, including the Henderson Administration Building, Dougherty Science Center, Kathleen Manley Infirmary, Maples Library, Butler-Blanc Gymnasium, and Alumni and Bertie Maples Butler Residence Halls. He served 42 years on the board of trustees and 41 years on the executive committee, and was president of the alumni association. Bertie Maples Butler taught piano for a time in the music department. (Photograph by Tallent Photography.)

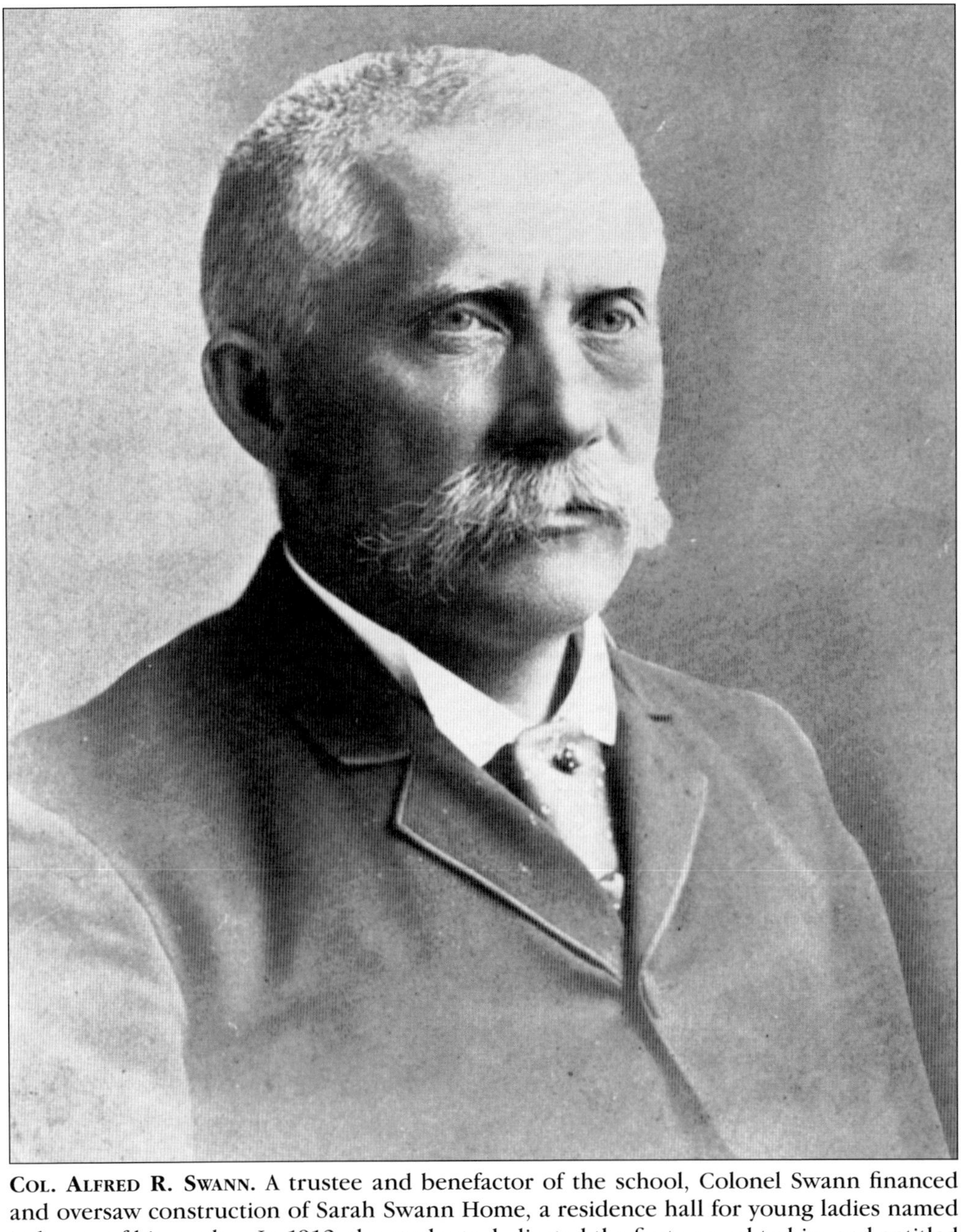

Col. Alfred R. Swann. A trustee and benefactor of the school, Colonel Swann financed and oversaw construction of Sarah Swann Home, a residence hall for young ladies named in honor of his mother. In 1912, the students dedicated the first annual to him and entitled it the *Swann*. Due to its great expense, the administration did not allow another official annual until 1917.

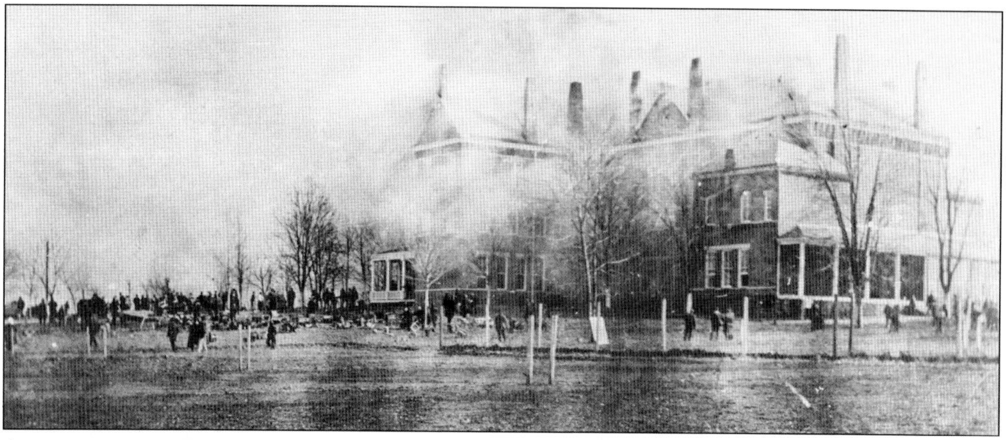

Administration Building Fire. On December 13, 1916, the first of two devastating campus fires took place, completely destroying the administration building. There were no injuries, but library, laboratory, art and business departments, admissions records, and the beautiful Philomathean and Columbian literary society halls were lost. The campus united, classes resumed, and plans were quickly drawn up for another structure.

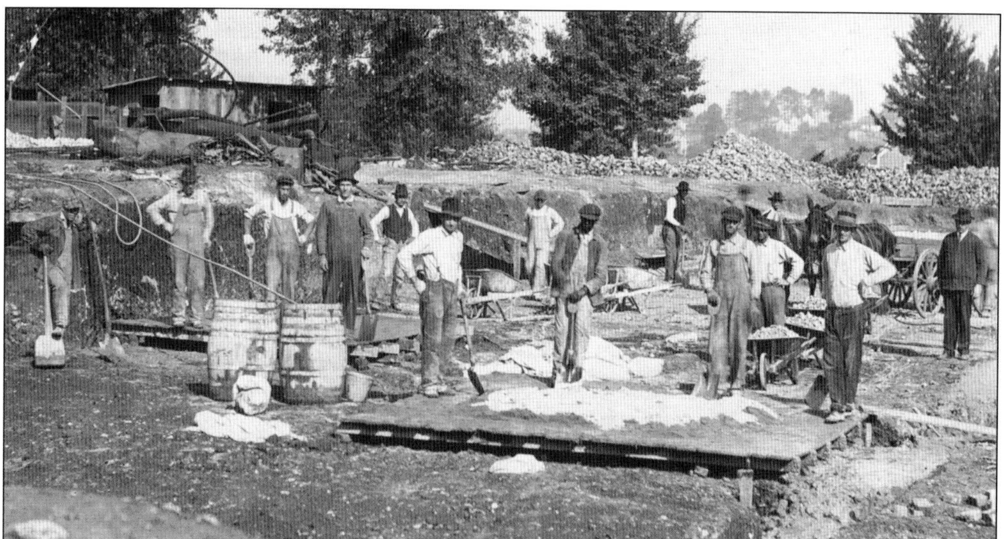

Building the John T. Henderson Memorial Hall Administration Building. After the institution's main building was destroyed by a fire that was thought to have been caused by a faulty flue, a new and more modern facility was designed combining Georgian architecture with Corinthian columns. Construction was completed in time for the beginning of the 1919–1920 school year. Built at a cost of $100,000, catalogs from that time proudly stated that "few colleges and universities in the entire country can boast of as magnificent an administration building."

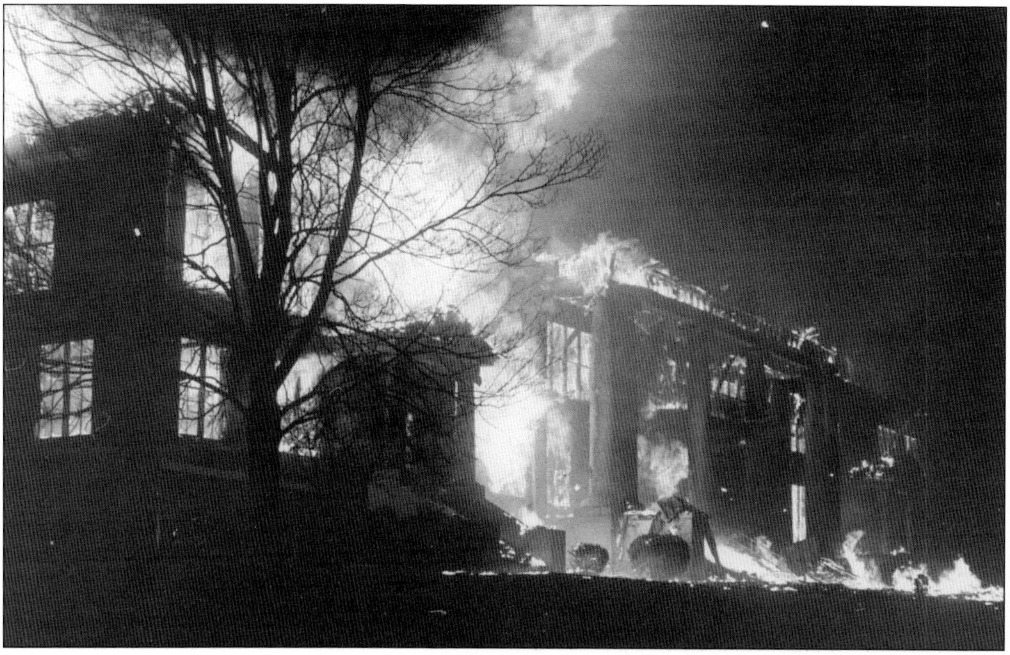

JOHN T. HENDERSON MEMORIAL HALL ADMINISTRATION BUILDING FIRE. The oldest campus building at the time, Henderson housed faculty offices and Gentry Auditorium, as well as the departments of religion, foreign language, speech, drama, and English. The 48,000-square-foot building was also home to the society halls of the Calliopeans, Hypatians, Columbians, and Philomatheans. On Wednesday morning, January 16, 1974, fire was spotted in two different locations. After a third fire broke out, the predominantly wooden building was rapidly destroyed. Very little was saved and institutional as well as personal losses were incalculable. Arson was suspected. Classes were relocated to First Baptist Church and other campus locations.

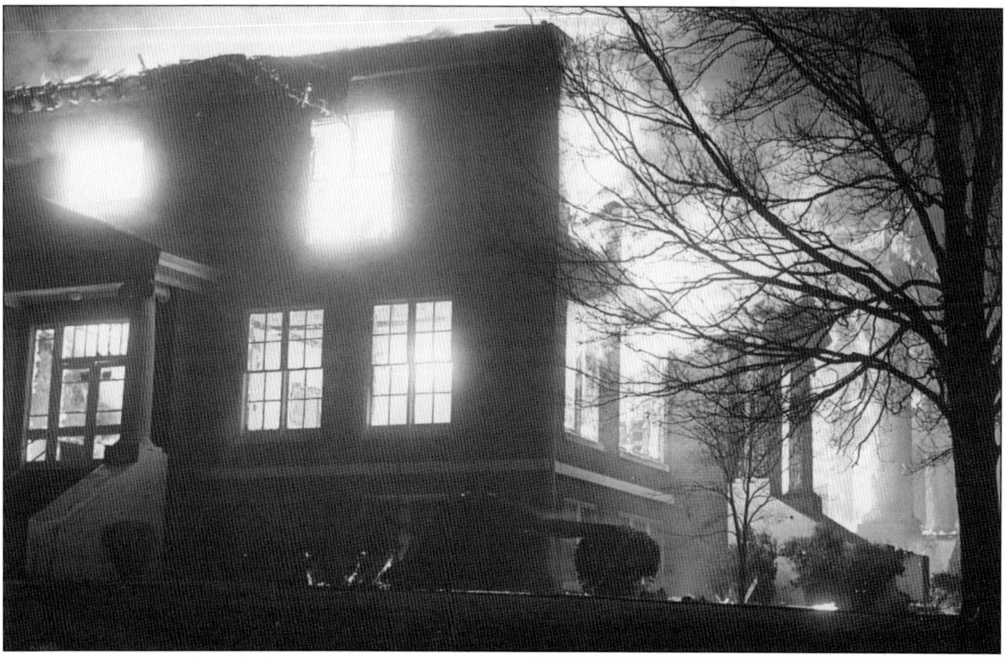

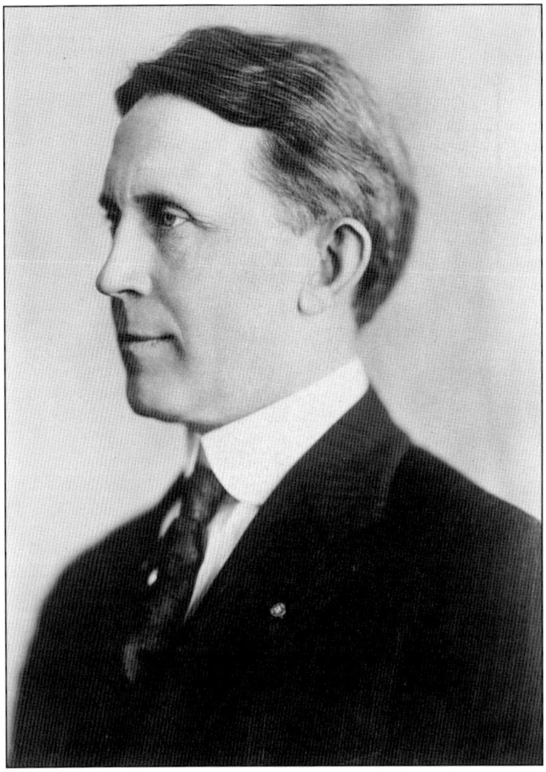

BEN HOOPER, TENNESSEE GOVERNOR. Hooper, an 1890 graduate, had a rough start. Born to Sarah Wade on October 13, 1870, in Newport, Tennessee, he was raised without a father. Sarah fell on hard times and placed Bennie, as he was called, in St. John's Orphanage in Knoxville. His real father, Dr. L.W. Hooper, heard of his plight and adopted him. He had married a girl from North Carolina and they had no children. Ben went to public schools in Newport and graduated from Carson-Newman, became a lawyer, and entered the world of politics. He eventually became governor of Tennessee, winning over both famed Taylor brothers, Alf who was a Republican and Bob the Democrat. (Courtesy of Library of Congress, Prints and Photographs Division, reproduction number, e.g., LC-B2-1234.)

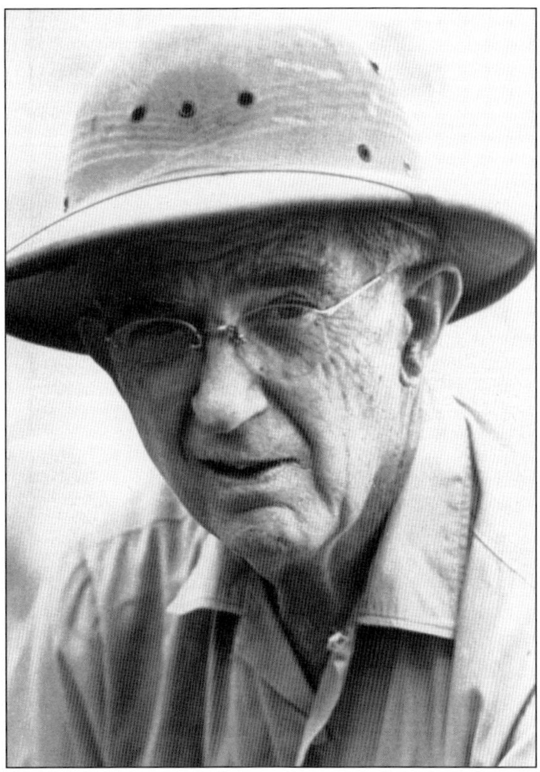

T.B. MASTON. Maston was born on November 26, 1897, and grew up in New Market, Tennessee. He graduated from Carson-Newman in 1920 and later received an honorary doctorate in 1958. Maston received his master's and doctorate in religious education from Southwestern Baptist Theological Seminary, where he later taught for 41 years. He later received another master's from Texas Christian University and his doctorate in philosophy from Yale.

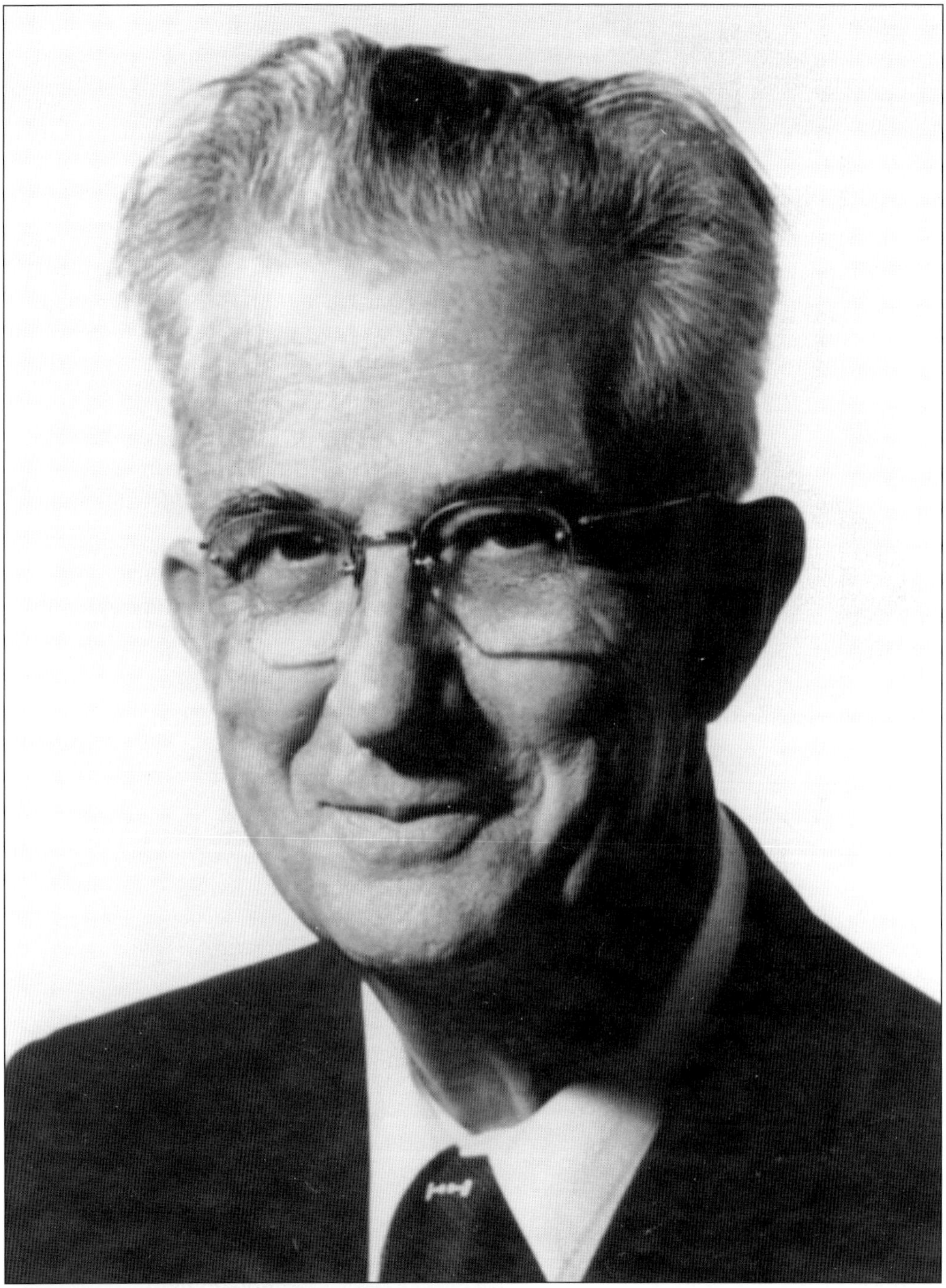

T.B. MASTON, ETHICS PIONEER. Referred to as the "Conscience of Southern Baptists," Maston became a pioneer in the field of Christian ethics and worked to lead the denomination into racial desegregation. The author of 23 books and hundreds of articles on Christian ethics and Christian development, Maston influenced innumerable ministers and laymen. His influence continues years after his passing on May 2, 1988. Each spring, an annual lecture named in his honor is sponsored by the Center for Baptist Studies Steeple Committee.

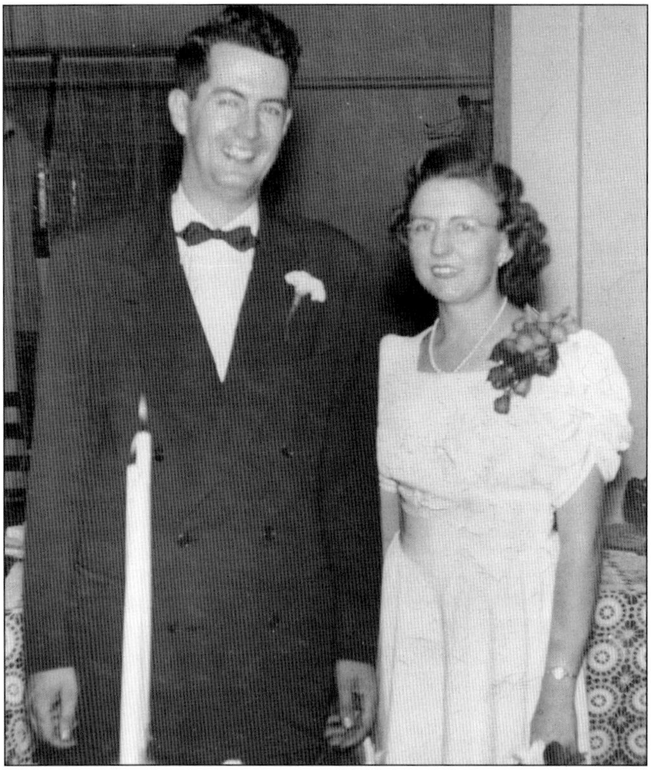

James Earl Stallings. A 1943 graduate of Carson-Newman, Stallings became pastor of First Baptist Church in Birmingham, Alabama, in 1962. As part of that city's reconciliation committee, he worked with seven other ministers for racial harmony despite strong opposition. He was pictured on the *New York Times* front page shaking hands with three African American visitors during Easter services in 1963. Martin Luther King Jr. mentioned him by name in his famous *Letter from a Birmingham Jail* for his stand on the side of justice. He went on to serve as director of Christian Ministries for the Southern Baptist Convention Home Mission Board. In 2003, Carson-Newman honored him with the Distinguished Alumnus Award.

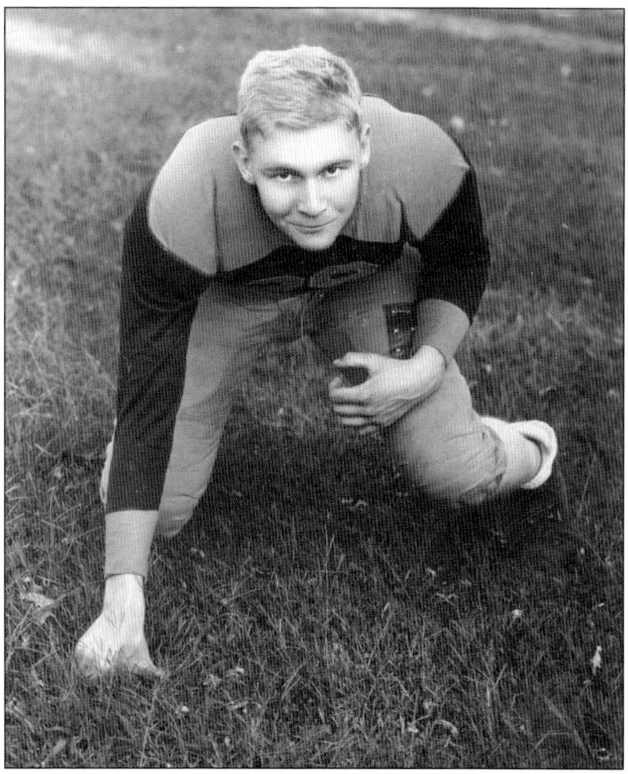

Carlyle Marney, Student Athlete. Leonard Carlyle Marney was born on July 8, 1916, in Harriman, Tennessee. He received his AB from Carson-Newman in 1938, having entered on a football scholarship in 1933. He returned with a firm calling to the ministry after taking a year off to work. He earned his master's of theology in 1943 and doctorate of theology in 1946 from Southern Baptist Theological Seminary. He also received honorary degrees from the University of Glasgow in Scotland, Wake Forest University, Johnson C. Smith University, and Kalamazoo College.

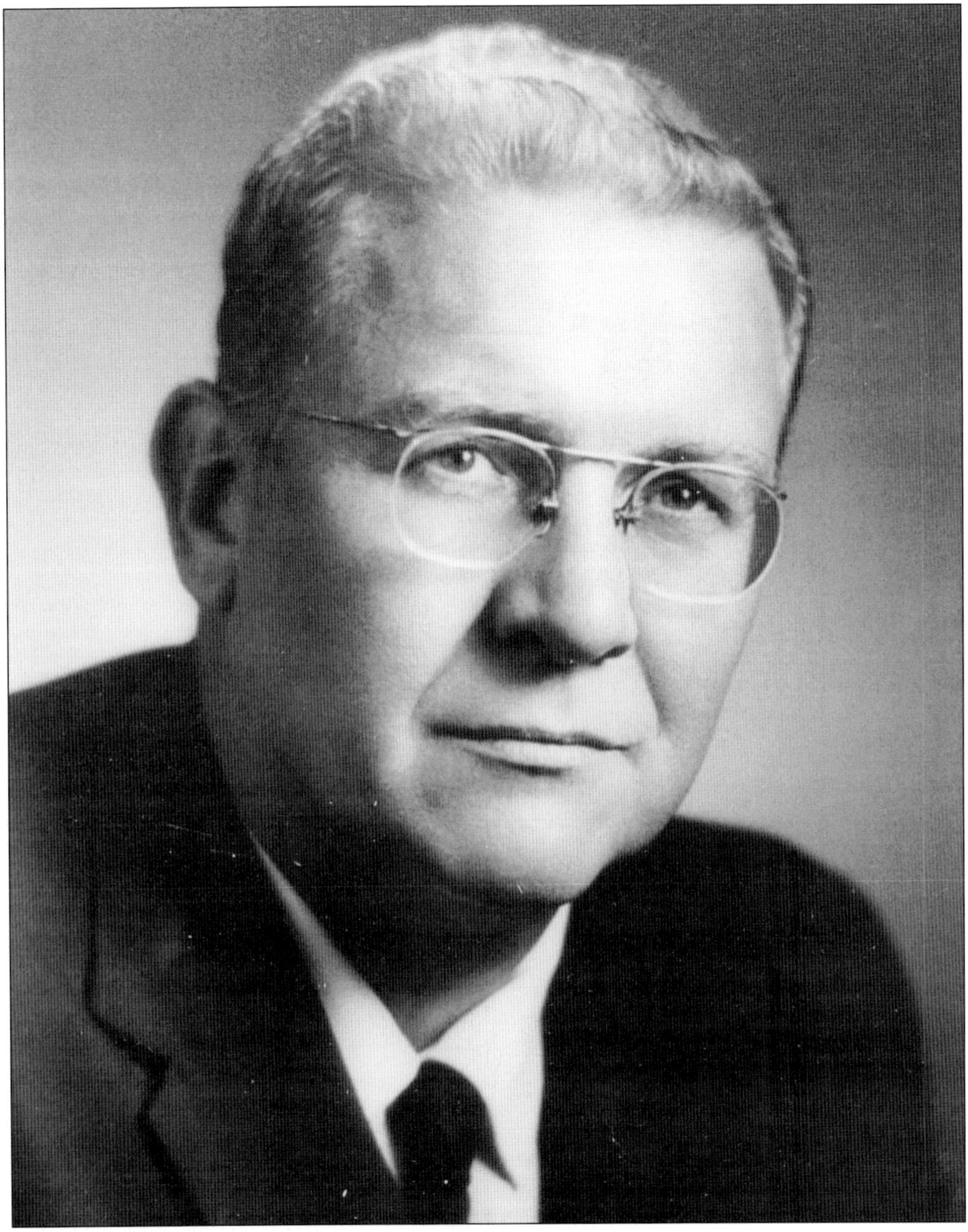

CARLYLE MARNEY, PASTOR. After briefly pastoring churches in Fort Knox, Beaver Dam, and Paducah, Kentucky, Marney pastored First Bapstist Church in Austin, Texas, from 1948 to 1958, and served as professor of Christian ethics and Westervelt lecturer at Austin Presbyterian Seminary. From 1958 to 1967, he was the senior minister at Myers Park Baptist Church in Charlotte, North Carolina. He resigned to establish Interpreter's House, an ecumenical study center for clergy and laity at Lambuth Inn, Lake Junaluska, North Carolina. The author of numerous books and articles, Marney died suddenly of a heart attack on July 3, 1978. The Center for Baptist Studies Steeple Committee sponsors an annual lecture series in his honor.

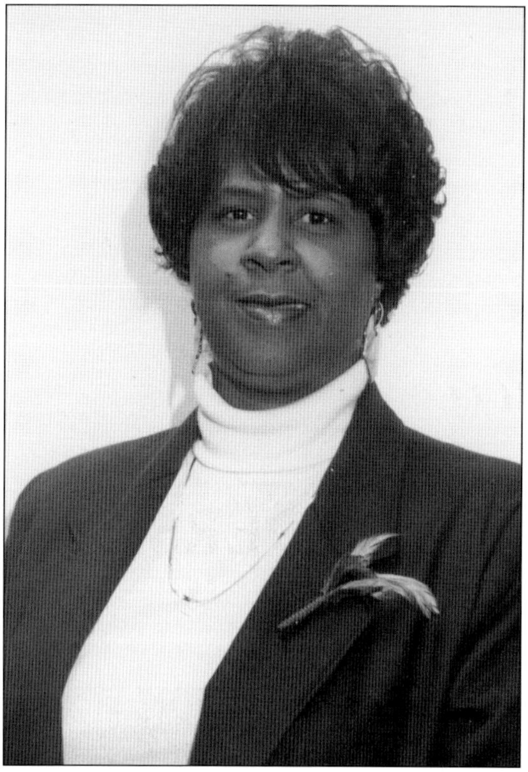

Patricia Crippins. In 1968, Crippins became the first four-year African American graduate of Carson-Newman. Her grandparents, John Sheets and Gertrude Sheets, served the college for many years. Crippins went on to become the manager of the East Knoxville Community Action Committee Neighborhood Center. In 1997, she became the Knox County administrator of elections, retiring in 2003. She received the Community Service Award in February 2008 from the Greater Knoxville Community during the Martin Luther King Jr. holiday observance. Crippins passed away on October 6, 2011.

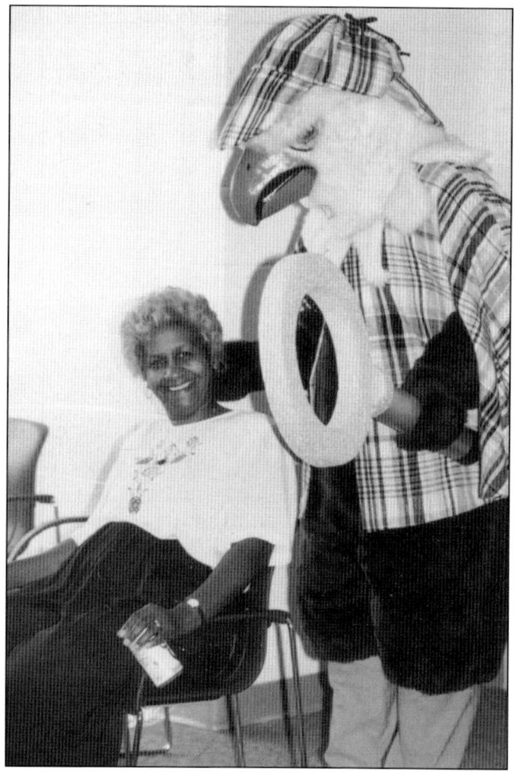

Gladys Sheets Clay. Clay was Carson-Newman's first full-time African American professor. She grew up in Jefferson City and spent much of her time on campus where her parents worked. At the time of her graduation from Nelson Merry High School, African Americans were not permitted to enroll at Carson-Newman. She received her bachelor's of science from Knoxville College and her master's in English from Union College. Joining the faculty in 1992, she served eight years in the field of developmental education and tutoring. After a five-year hiatus, Clay returned in 2005, retiring in 2007 as assistant professor of English and education and director of academic skills development.

Two

PORTRAITS OF LEADERSHIP

THE PRESIDENTS

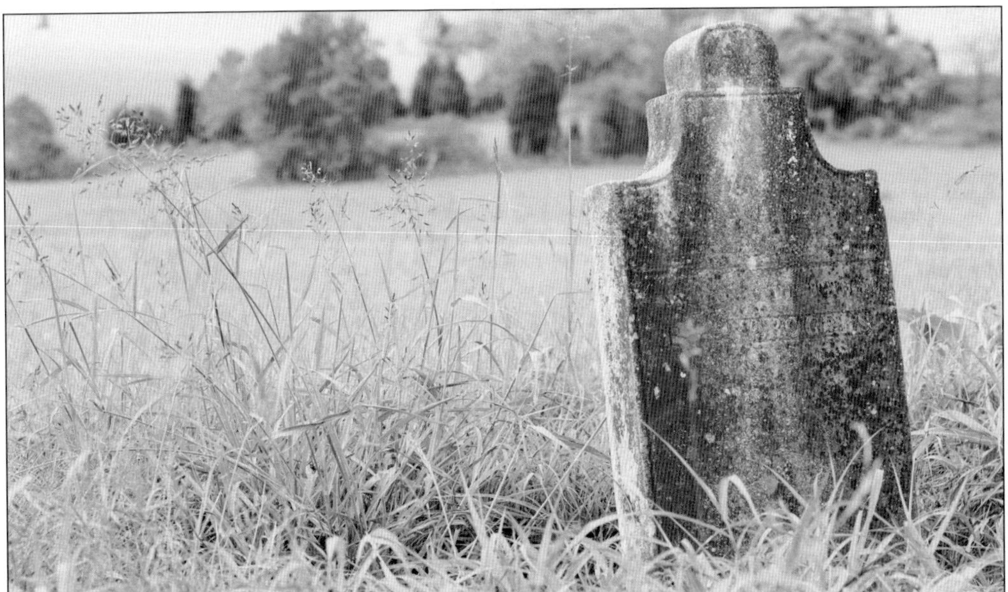

WILLIAM ROGERS, 1851. Educated at Maryville College and East Tennessee College (later University of Tennessee), Rogers pastored the Dandridge Baptist Church. It was here that the Education Society of East Tennessee met to discuss the need for an educational institution in 1849. In February 1851, he was appointed one of two financial agents for the newly established Mossy Creek Missionary Baptist Seminary and in August was unanimously elected its first president. Tragically, Rogers died of typhoid fever in November. His tombstone reads in part: "A useful minister of the gospel, humble and persevering in the cause of Christ. He sacrificed property, health and life for truth's sake." (Photograph by Charles Key.)

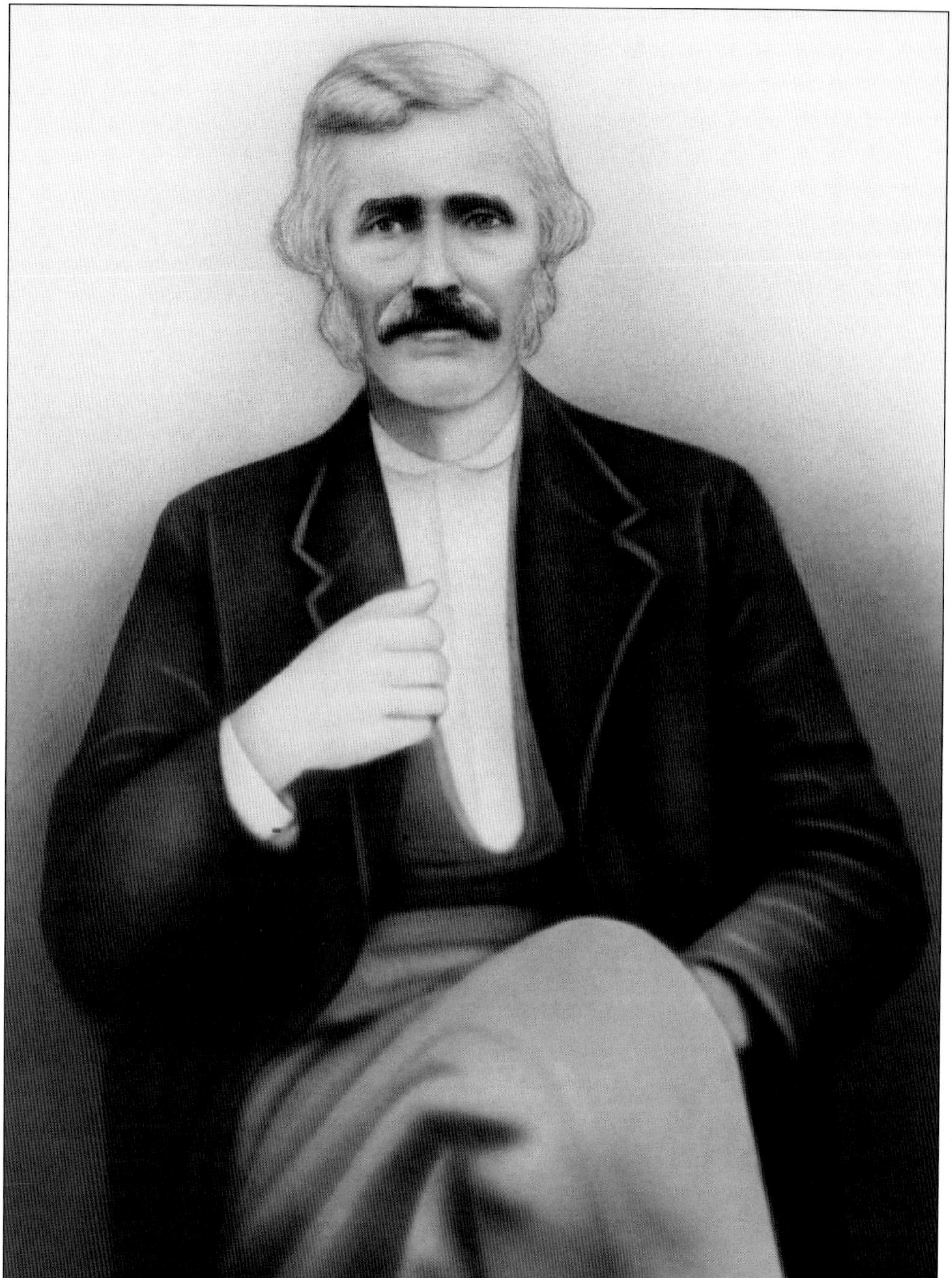

ROBERT REEDY BRYAN, 1851–1853, 1866–1868. One of the founding fathers, Bryan's love was teaching, specifically the natural sciences. He became the second president of Mossy Creek Missionary Baptist Seminary when William Rogers died from typhoid fever. He served again as the sixth president and worked tirelessly to help get the school back on its feet after the devastating effects of federal occupation. Fellow president N.B. Goforth noted that Bryan's legacy was the "monuments of immortal minds" he had helped nurture.

Board of Trustees.

Rev. E. MORE, *President.*
J. H. CARSON, Esq., *Treasurer.*
Rev. N. B. GOFORTH, *Secretary.*
" W. BILLUE.
" T. J. LANE.
" MAT. HILLSMAN.
" J. MANNING.
" J. QUARLES.
" G. G. TAYLOR.
" W. M. BURNETT.

Doct. R. BIRDWELL.
" J. CARSON.
" W. M. F. HELM.
J. MULLENDORE, Esq.
E. ALLEN, Esq.
W. C. CARSON, Esq.
C. M. WITT, Esq.
C. M. ORE, Esq.
W. C. NEWMAN, Esq.
W. PHILLIPS, Esq.

T. TITTSWORTH, Esq.

Faculty.

Doct. SAM ANDERSON, A.M.,
President—and Professor of Mathematics, Mental and Moral Science.

R. R. BRYAN, Esq.,
Vice-President—and Professor of Natural Philosophy, Astronomy and Chemistry.

Rev. N. B. GOFORTH, A.B.,
Professor of Latin, Greek and Hebrew.

J. A. RUSSELL,
Tutor in Mathematics.

E. E. McCROSKEY,
Tutor in Latin and Greek.

JAMES C. BOWERS, Esq.,
Steward elect for the ensuing Collegiate year.

SAMUEL ANDERSON, 1853–1857. Anderson was elected president of Mossy Creek Missionary Baptist Seminary in 1853 and in 1855 he led the school's first commencement exercises. That same year, the school changed its name to Mossy Creek Baptist College. Two years later, the first dormitory was completed and the Columbian and Philomathean literary societies were chartered. Anderson returned to his alma mater, Tusculum College, but returned to teach in 1860 before the college closed its doors due to the Civil War. He would later serve as superintendent of public instruction for Jefferson County from 1873 to 1878.

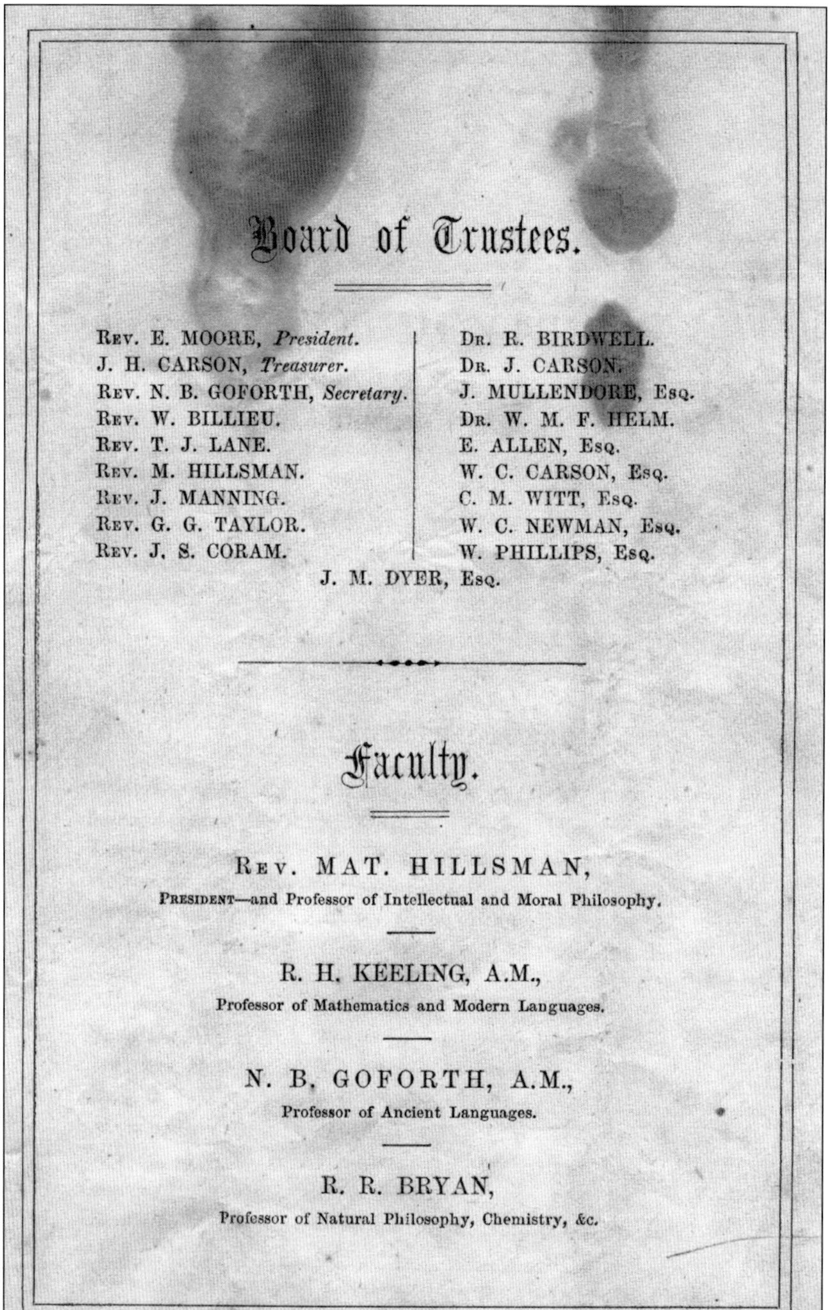

Board of Trustees.

REV. E. MOORE, *President.*	DR. R. BIRDWELL.
J. H. CARSON, *Treasurer.*	DR. J. CARSON.
REV. N. B. GOFORTH, *Secretary.*	J. MULLENDORE, ESQ.
REV. W. BILLIEU.	DR. W. M. F. HELM.
REV. T. J. LANE.	E. ALLEN, ESQ.
REV. M. HILLSMAN.	W. C. CARSON, ESQ.
REV. J. MANNING.	C. M. WITT, ESQ.
REV. G. G. TAYLOR.	W. C. NEWMAN, ESQ.
REV. J. S. CORAM.	W. PHILLIPS, ESQ.

J. M. DYER, ESQ.

Faculty.

REV. MAT. HILLSMAN,

PRESIDENT—and Professor of Intellectual and Moral Philosophy.

R. H. KEELING, A.M.,

Professor of Mathematics and Modern Languages.

N. B. GOFORTH, A.M.,

Professor of Ancient Languages.

R. R. BRYAN,

Professor of Natural Philosophy, Chemistry, &c.

MATTHEW HILLSMAN, 1857–1859. Over his lifetime, Hillsman pastored churches throughout Tennessee. Always a leader in Baptist work, he also founded and edited the Knoxville based *Baptist Watchman*. Upon coming to Mossy Creek Baptist College, Hillsman taught ancient languages, logic, rhetoric, and intellectual and moral philosophy. He went on to become corresponding secretary of the Bible Board of the Southern Baptist Convention. Hillsman served 27 years as vice president of Tennessee's Foreign Mission Board, as well as a trustee for Southern Baptist Theological Seminary.

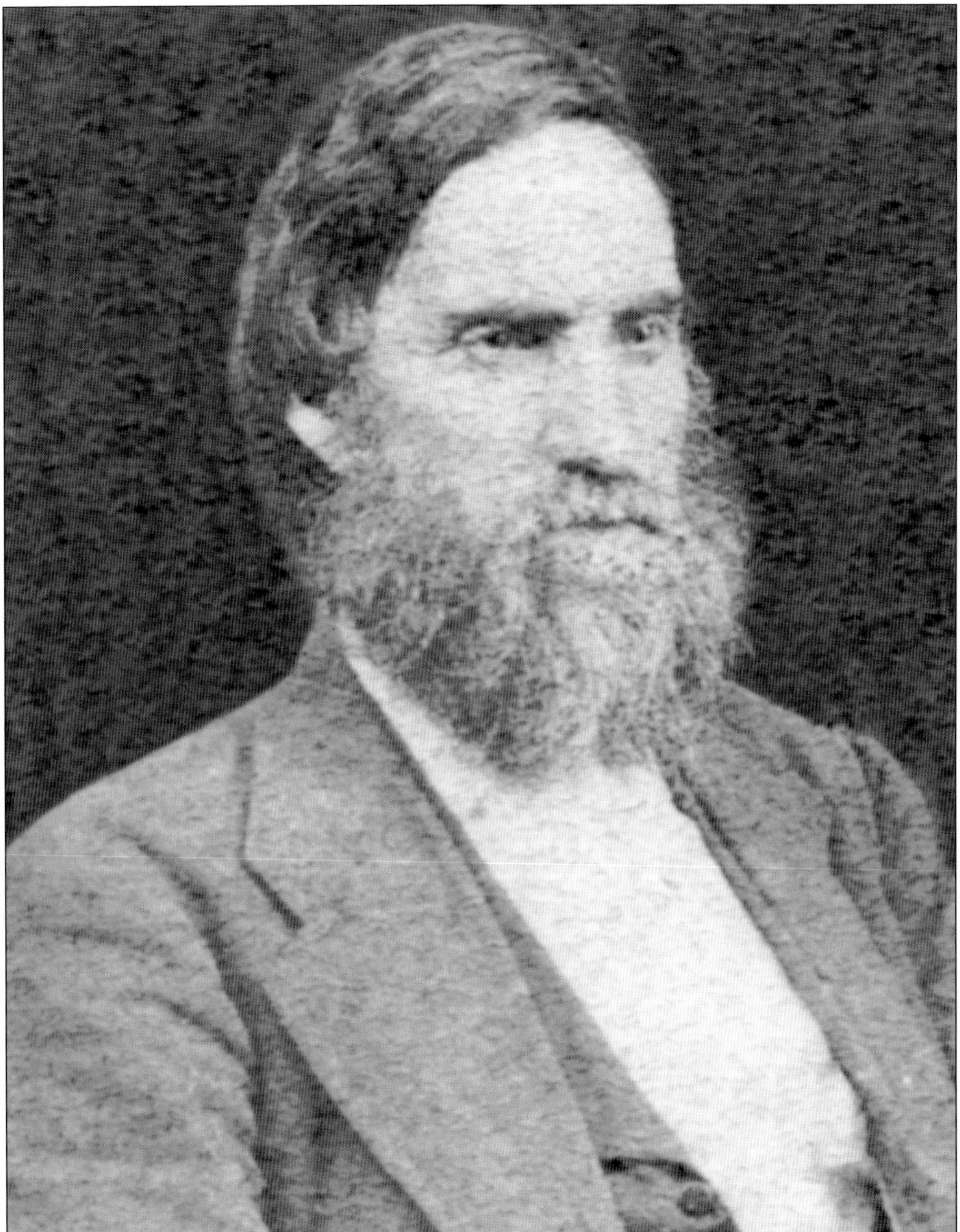

Napoleon Bonaparte Goforth, 1859–1862, 1870–1882. Goforth attended Maryville College and later received a master's degree and honorary doctoral degree from Mossy Creek Baptist College. In 1855, he became chair of the Mossy Creek Baptist College's languages department as well as a teacher of moral science. Four years later, he became president and served until the Civil War forced the institution to close in 1862. During his presidency, he was ordained at Boyd's Creek Church and pastored the Mossy Creek Church. Goforth returned for a second presidential term, during which the growing college purchased the Mountcastle estate and changed its name to Carson College.

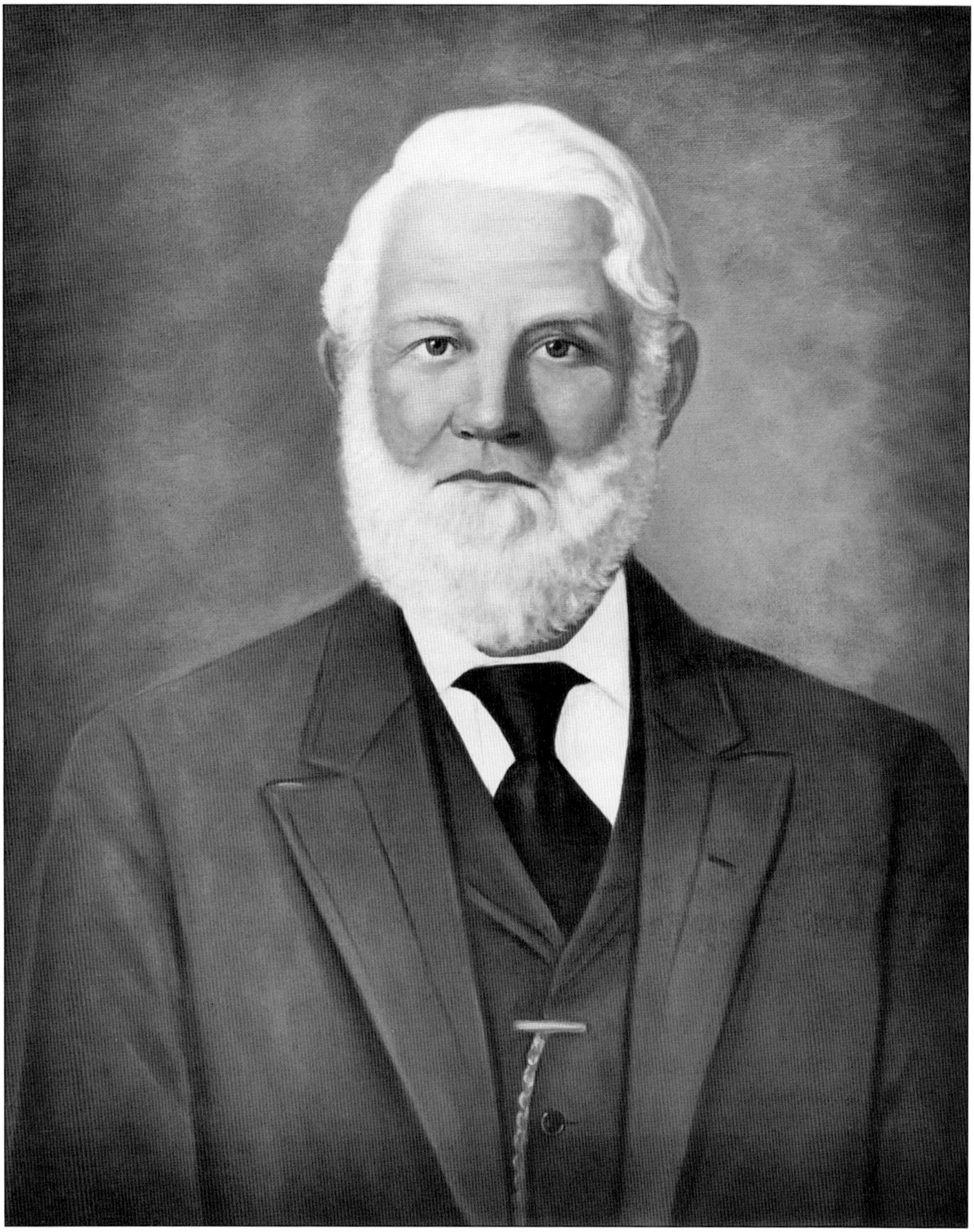

Jesse Baker, 1869–1870. Baker attended Mossy Creek Baptist College from 1855 to 1859. During that time he was ordained, and after graduation went on to pastor several churches, including Mossy Creek Church, where he baptized over 500 people and was present for the 1870 revival. He came back to help R.R. Bryan reestablish the college after the devastation of the Civil War and then served as president. He is best remembered for his 10-month, 3,500 mile fundraising campaign that brought in over $5,000 to pull the institution out of debt. In 1882, he was awarded the honorary doctor of divinity degree.

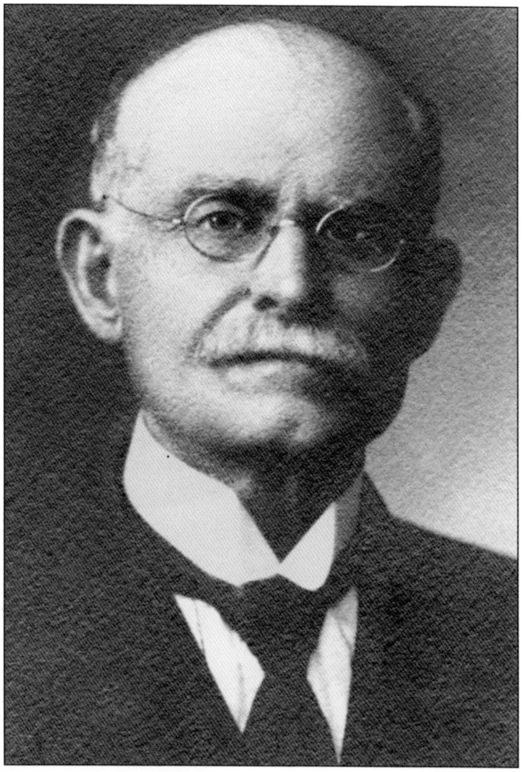

William Thomas Russell, 1882–1889. A graduate of Mossy Creek Baptist College, Russell returned to teach mathematics and mechanical philosophy. For a short time, he was editor of the Knoxville based *Baptist Beacon*. In August 1882, he became the first and only president of Newman College and taught metaphysics as well as pure and applied mathematics. After the union with Carson College in 1889, he served as vice president and professor for the coeducational institution in addition to being a member of the board of trustees. Russell was also the first mayor of the newly incorporated Jefferson City (formerly Mossy Creek) from 1902 to 1903. (Photograph by Knaffe and Brakebill.)

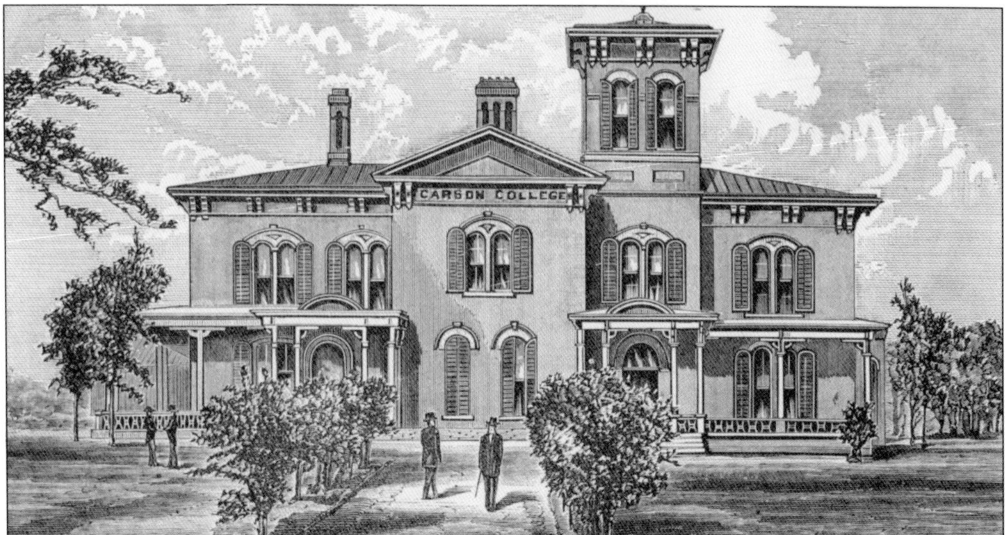

Birdwell Gibson Manard, 1882–1883. Active in education, Baptist life, and journalism, Manard received an honorary doctorate of divinity degree from Mossy Creek Baptist College in 1873. Nine years later he was elected president. That same year the college welcomed the women of Mossy Creek Masonic Female College to its original campus location on the creek as Carson College moved into the Mountcastle Estate. The female institute changed its name to the Seminary for Young Ladies and by mid-decade became Newman College. Winter brought a smallpox epidemic, which greatly affected both the town and campus.

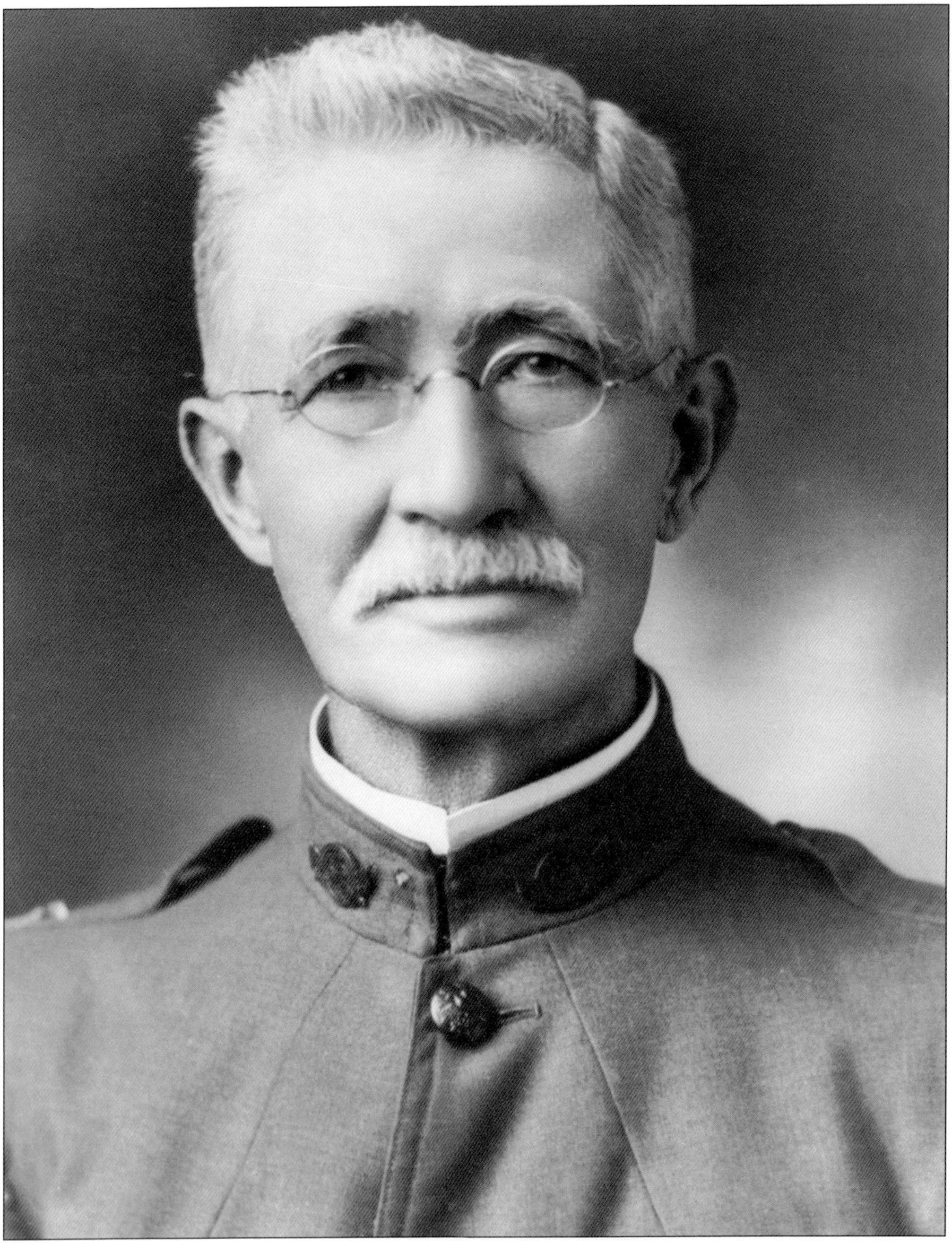

Samuel Watson Tindell, 1883–1888. A veteran of the Union army, Tindell was ordained a Baptist minister in 1874. He served as professor of ancient and modern languages at Carson College and continued to teach when he became its president. Tindell also wrote numerous books on church history and was a crusader for temperance. During his presidency, a theological department was established to focus on ministerial training and course offerings were increased. In Tindell's first term, 20 Native American men were enrolled by the Commissioner of Indian Affairs, four of whom lived in his home. He was also awarded the honorary degree of doctor of divinity.

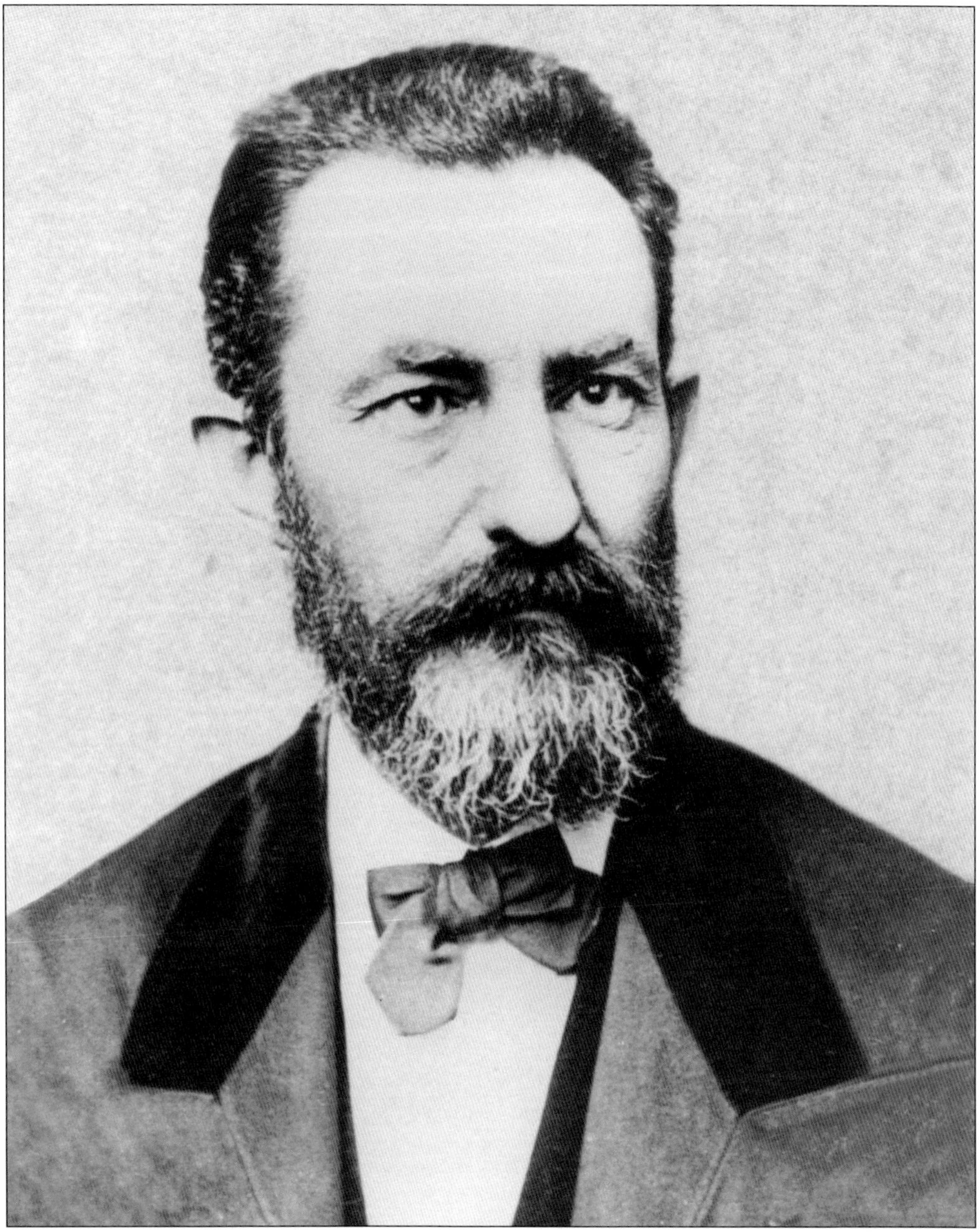

WILLIAM ALLEN MONTGOMERY, 1888–1892. A lawyer and a preacher, Montgomery served as a chaplain in the Confederate army. He pastored several churches in the southeast and served as secretary of state missions. In 1870, Montgomery was awarded the doctorate of divinity title by Carson College. While president, he taught metaphysics and theology. During his tenure, Carson and Newman colleges were joined and the first administration building was erected. Montgomery also served as associate editor of the *Tennessee Baptist* and the *Religious Herald*, and was a staff correspondent for the *Baptist and Reflector*, Tennessee's state Baptist newspaper.

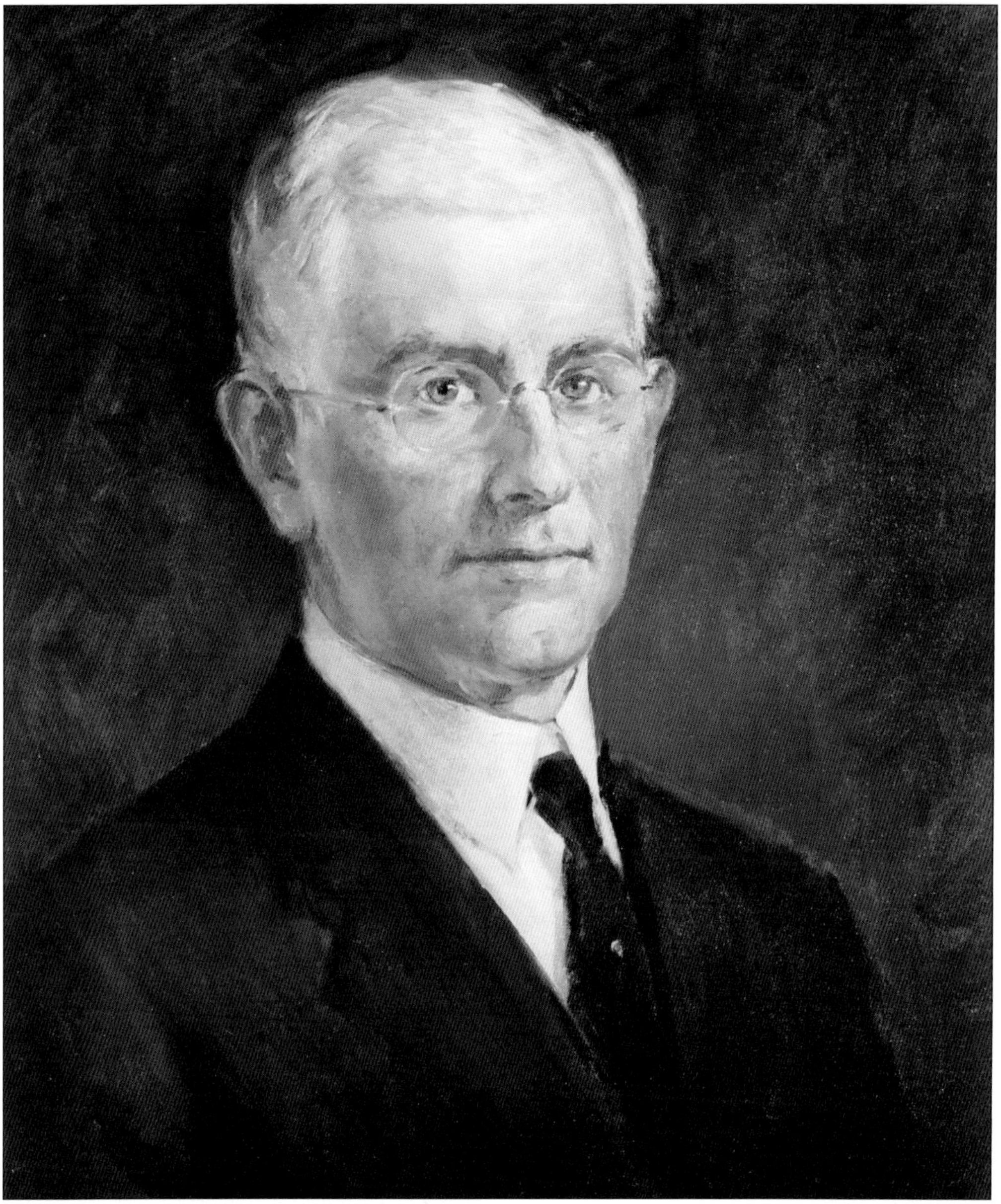

John Thompson Henderson, 1893–1903. Another graduate of Carson College, Henderson returned in 1883 to become the principal of the preparatory department and professor of mathematics. He also served as treasurer, financial agent, librarian, and later a trustee. The school was greatly improved academically and administratively under his leadership. In 1917, he was awarded an honorary doctor of literature degree. The current humanities building is named for him as was the second administration building, which burned in 1974.

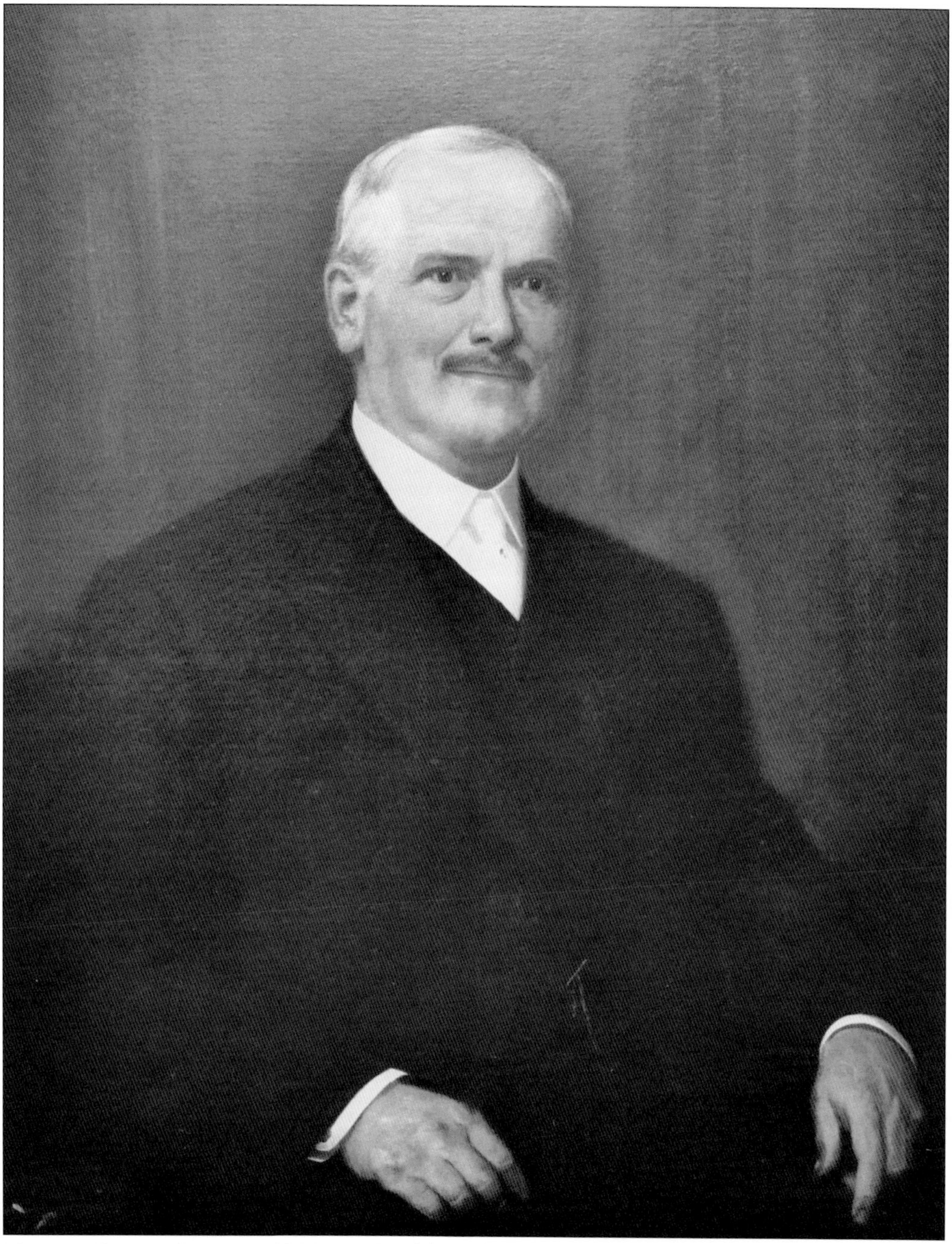

MILLARD DUDLEY JEFFRIES, 1903–1912. Although a medical school graduate, Jeffries followed his seminary training and had been in the ministry for almost 20 years before becoming president and financial agent. He was pastoring Broadway Baptist Church in Knoxville when called to Carson and Newman. He taught philosophy and under his administration both enrollment and the endowment increased. Davis Hall for young men was completed, along with the Sarah Swann Home for women.

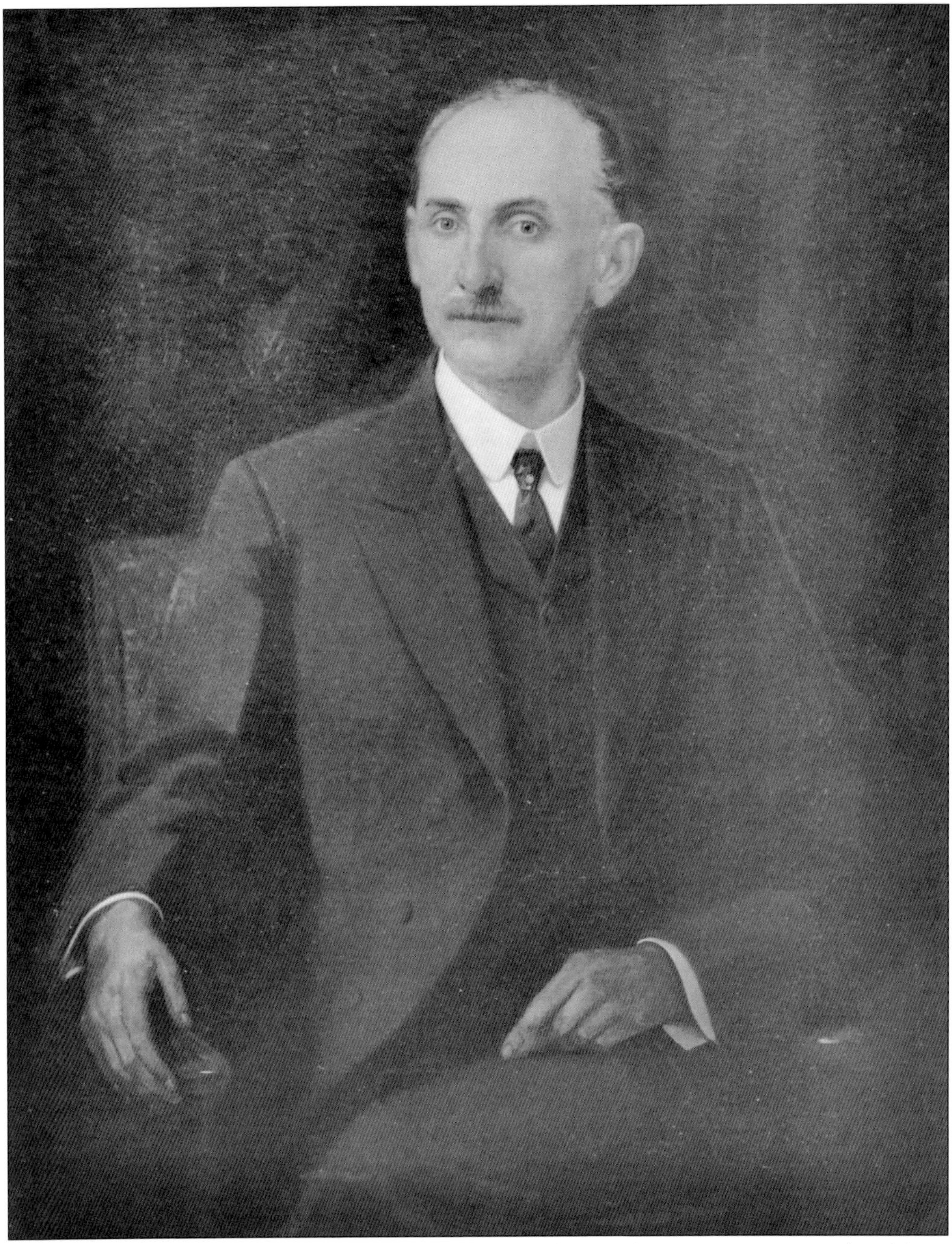

JESSE MCGARITY BURNETT, 1912–1917. A professor of foreign languages since 1894 and later of philosophy, Burnett became chairman of the faculty and was then elected president. He was a graduate of Carson College's preparatory school and later went to seminary. During his five years, the first yearbook (the *Swann*) was published and the greatest campus tragedy to that point occurred with the burning of the administration building in 1916. After leaving Carson and Newman, he pastored the First Baptist Church in Belton, South Carolina, for over 20 years and then become editor of the *Greenville Baptist Courier*. Burnett Residence Hall is named in his honor.

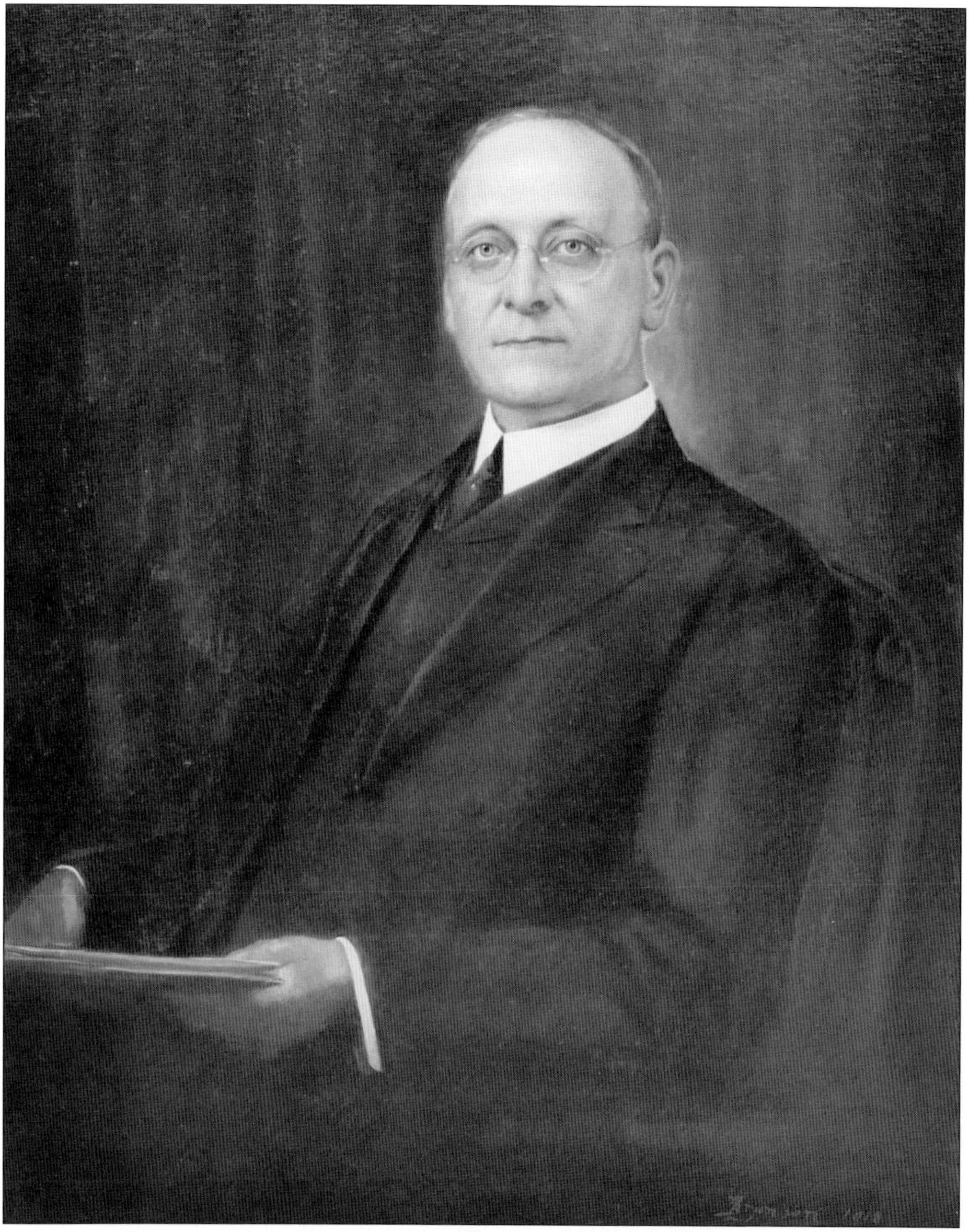

William Lee Gentry, 1917–1919. Gentry came to the college in 1906 and taught education, English, and mathematics. He later served as dean. His inauguration came on the same day the cornerstone was laid for the new Henderson Hall Administration Building. During this time of reconstruction, Gentry fought to keep the college from being moved to Morristown, Tennessee. After a four-year hiatus, the annual was revived and named the *Larker*. The first edition of the *Orange & Blue* was also published. During his last year in office, a formal relationship with the Tennessee Baptist Convention was established. The current auditorium in the Henderson Humanities Building bears his name. In 1919, he was awarded the honorary doctor of literature degree.

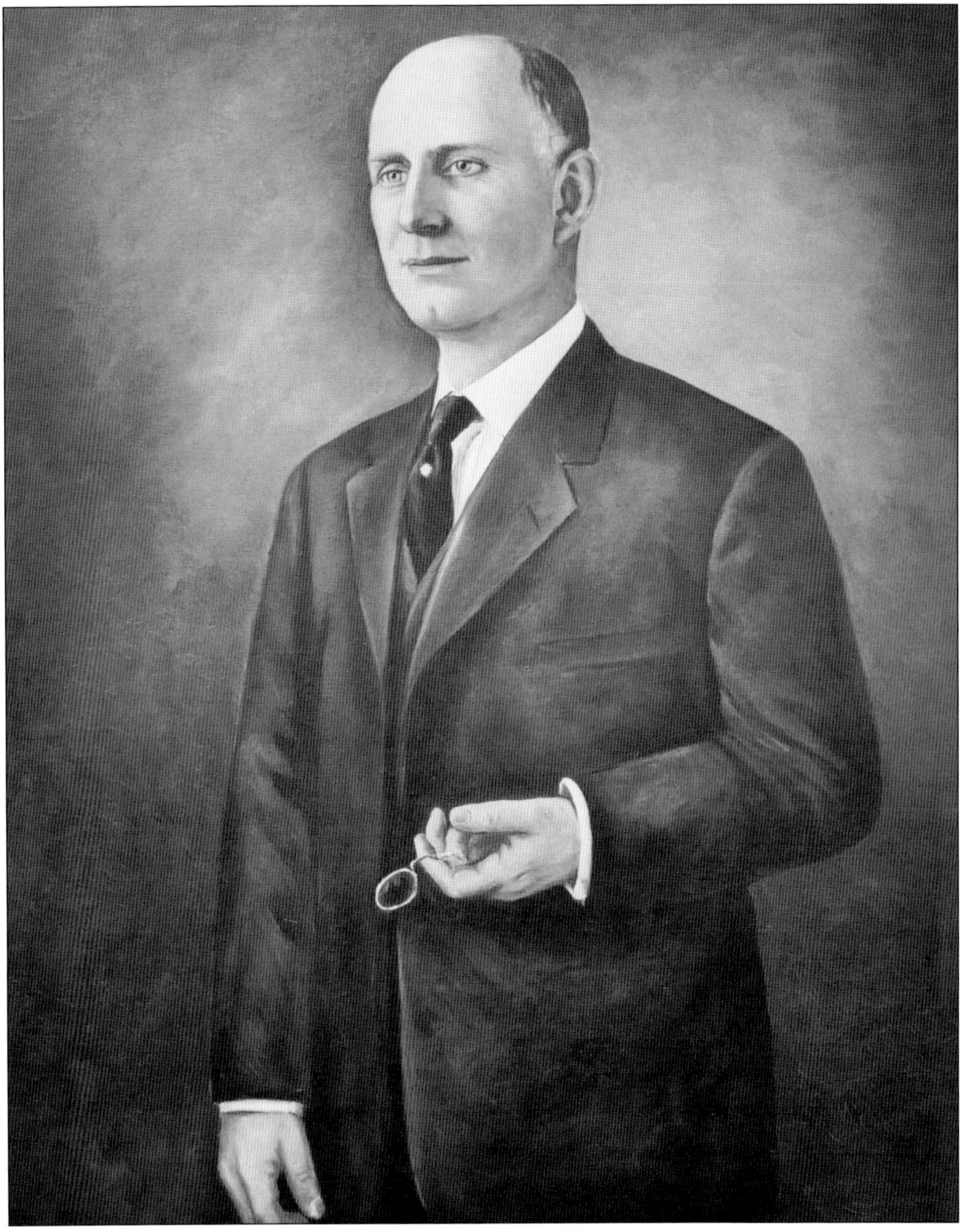

Oscar Ernest Sams, 1920–1927. Sams came to the presidency from his pastorate at Central Baptist Church in Johnson City, Tennessee. He received the honorary doctorate of divinity degree from Carson and Newman College in 1919. Under his leadership, the Butler-Blanc Gymnasium was completed, as was Blanc Hall for young men, being an addition to the existing Davis Hall. Athletic teams played under the new moniker of the Fighting Parsons. After publication of the *Grenade* and the *Wanehi* yearbooks, the *Appalachian* was finally settled on as the permanent name for the school's annual. The preparatory department was eliminated but college enrollment increased and significant curriculum improvements were made.

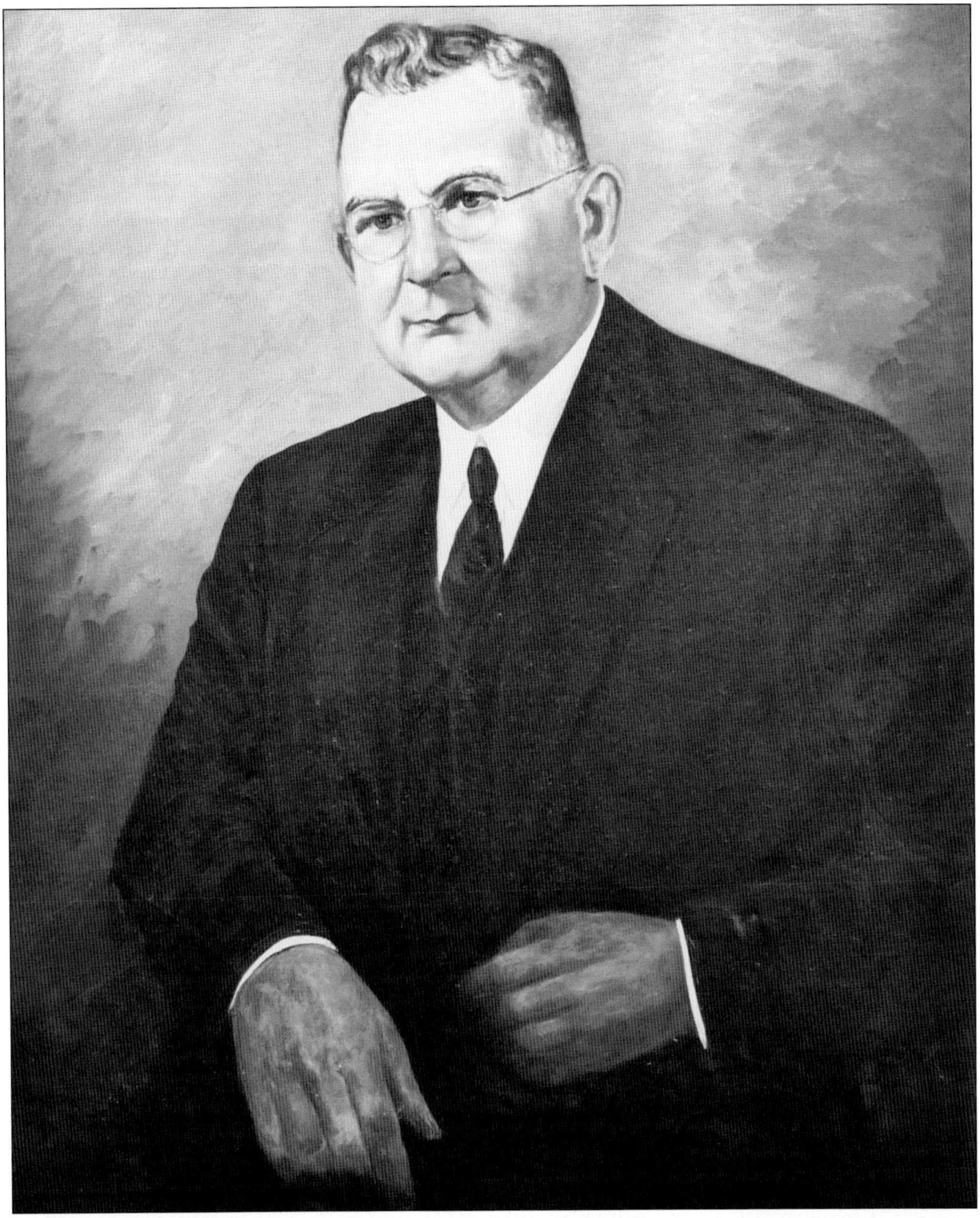

JAMES THOMAS WARREN, 1927–1948. Under Warren's administration the college's name officially became Carson-Newman. The new science (presently art) building was completed and named for him, an infirmary building was acquired, the Burnett Home was renovated as a residence hall for young women, and a central heating plant was completed. The Fighting Eagles replaced the Fighting Parsons as the college's moniker. During World War II, Warren helped negotiate a contract with the Navy for its V-12 pre-officer training program to be housed on the college's campus. Resolutions expressed by faculty following Warren's untimely death from cancer gave appreciation for his raising of the academic standards of the school, efficient financial management that brought the school through the Depression, and "contagious enthusiasm for Christian education."

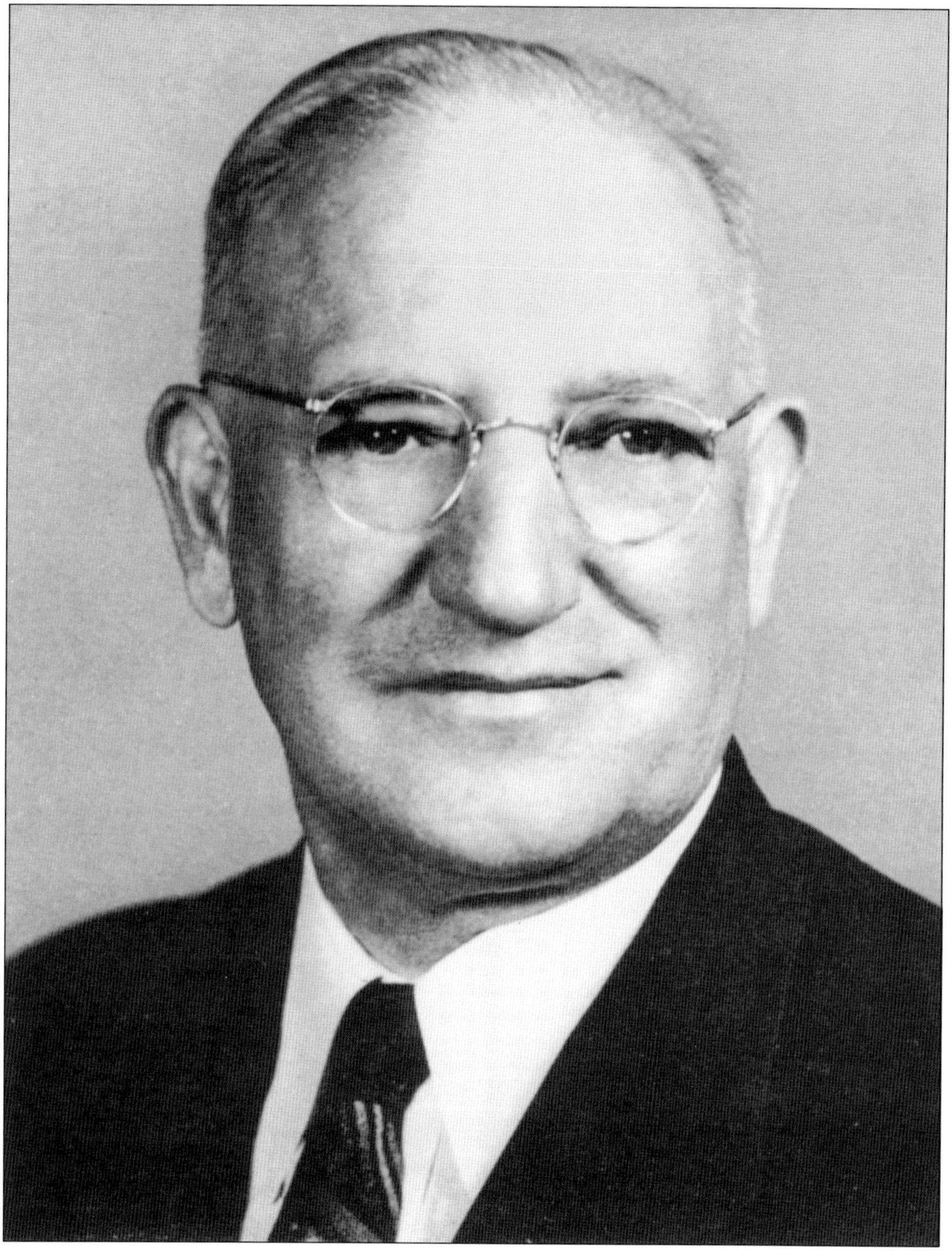

Isaac Newton Carr, 1948. Carr graduated from Carson and Newman College in 1916 and was a veteran of both world wars. He returned in 1945 as professor of history and political science. The college awarded him an honorary doctorate of literature degree in 1940. In 1947, he became dean of the college and served in that capacity until his retirement in 1957. After the death of President Warren, Carr was elected acting president from January to October 1948, when Dr. Fite took office. After his retirement, Carr was commissioned by the trustees to write the *History of Carson-Newman College*, which was published in 1959.

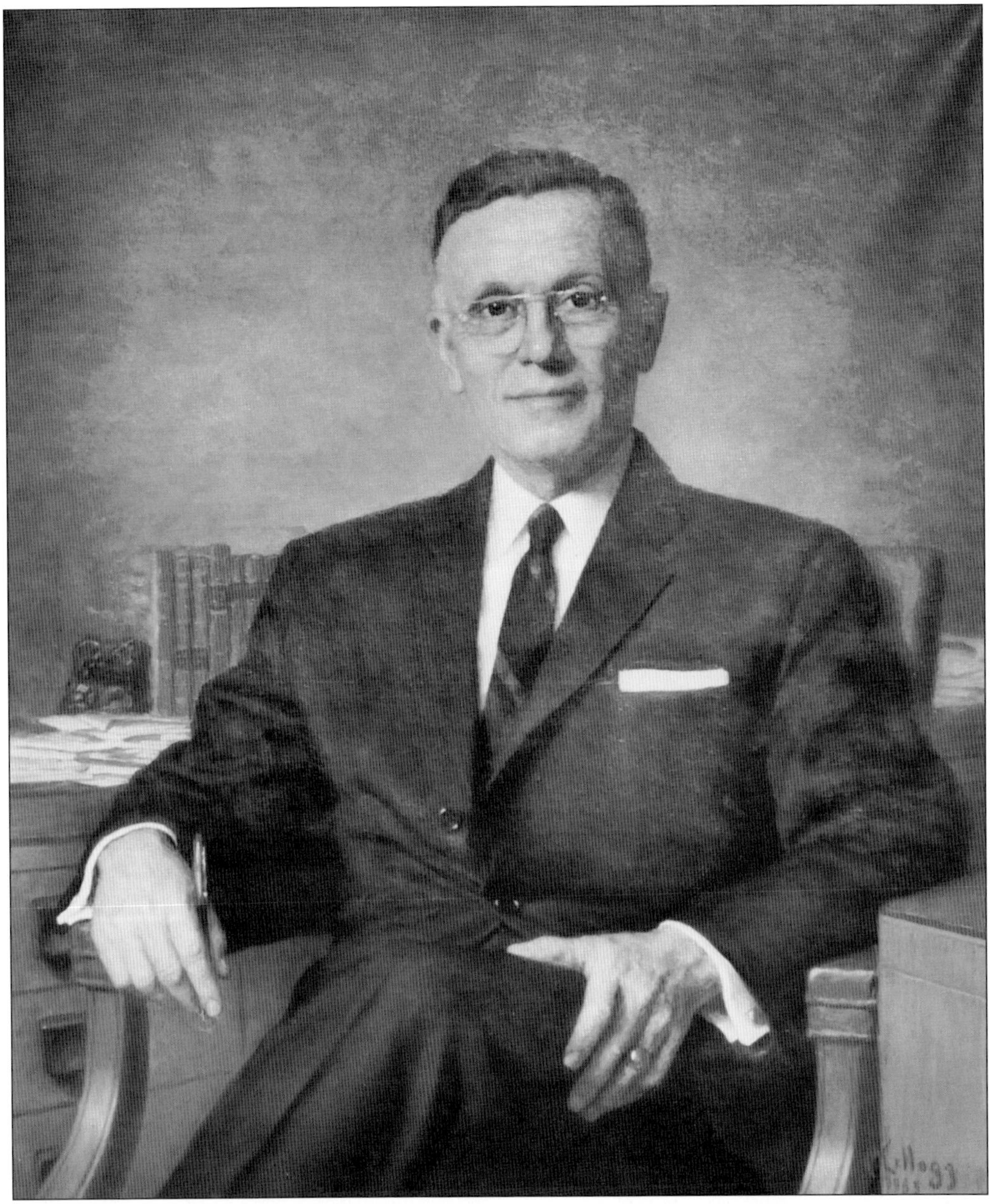

DANIEL HARLEY FITE, 1948–1968. The third longest serving president, Fite was known as the "Great Builder." During his tenure, more than 20 buildings were constructed. The academic program underwent significant development and expansion. Eight majors and 26 new programs were added. Carson-Newman celebrated its centennial during Fite's tenure, along with national championships in baseball and debate in 1965. The current administration building is named for him.

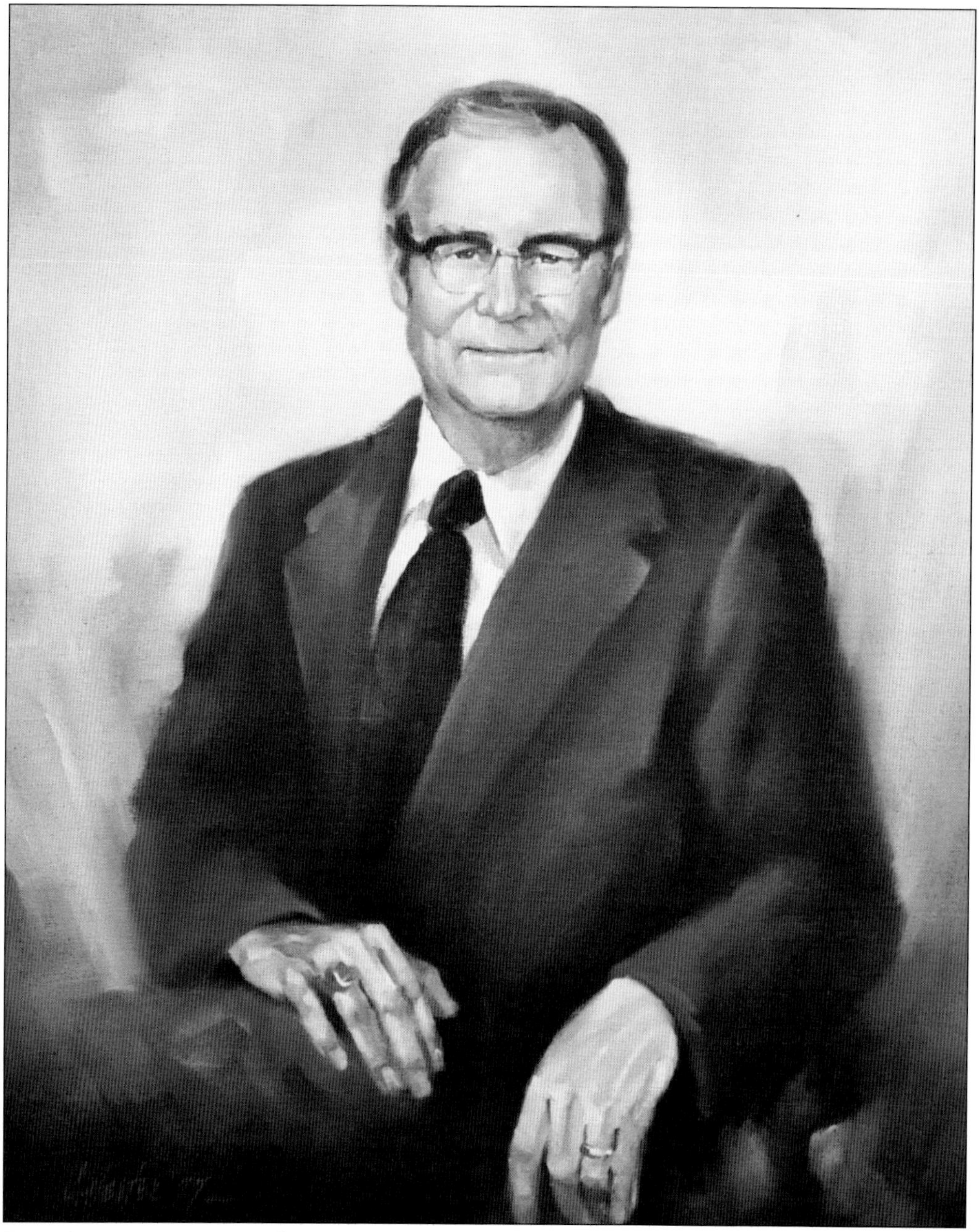

John Albert Fincher, 1968–1977. Fincher was the first to occupy the presidential home known as "The Columns." The ROTC program was added and dancing was allowed on campus, finally putting a controversy to rest. Work was finished on an addition to the library, the Dougherty Science Center was completed, and renovations were made to the Warren Building. In 1974, the school suffered its second fire with the burning of the Henderson Hall Administration Building. The new Henderson Humanities building was completed the year Fincher retired.

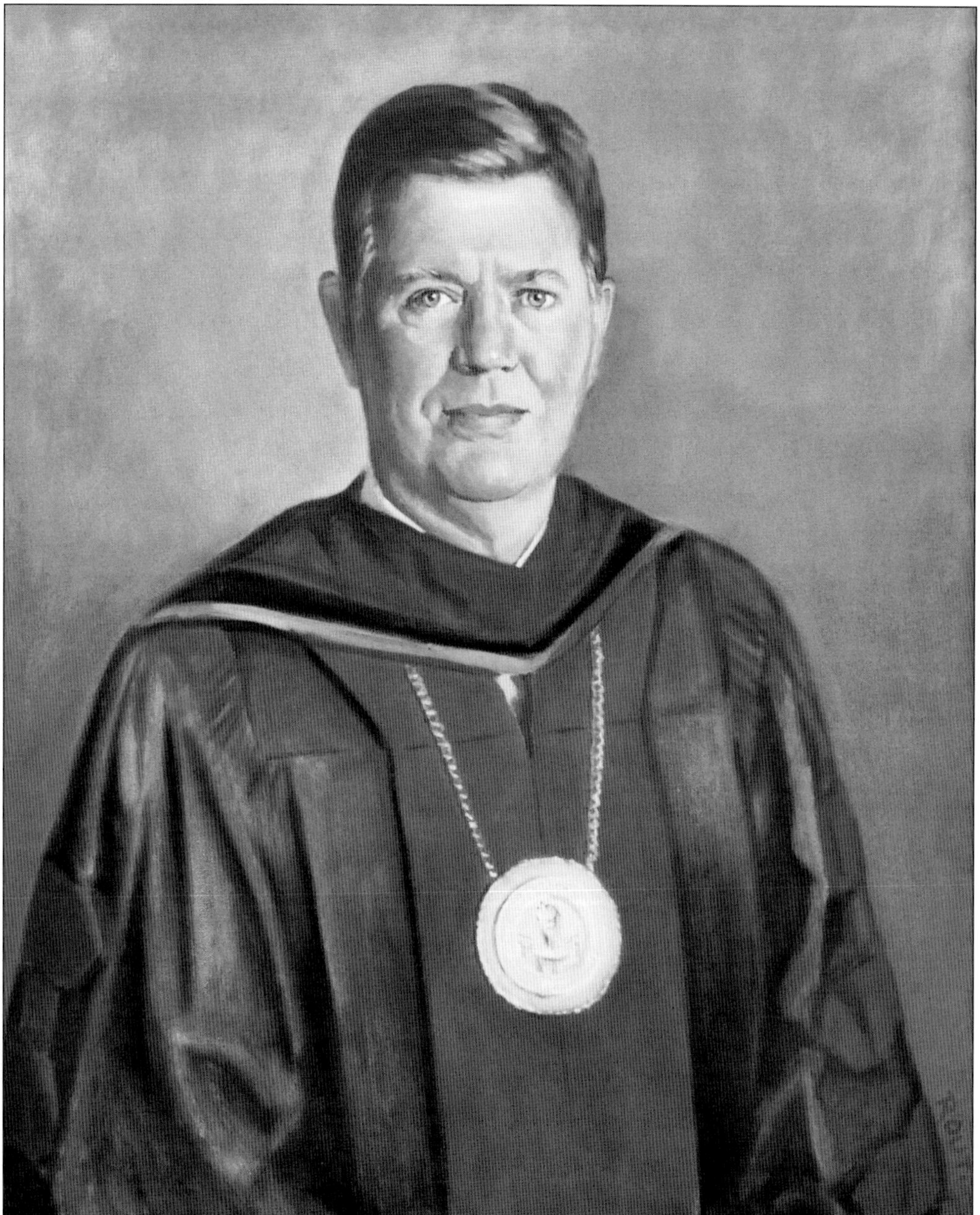

JESSE CORDELL MADDOX, 1977–2000. The college's 20th president, Maddox helped to increase annual financial contributions from $1.5 million in his first year to almost $6 million at the end of his service. A graduate program was reestablished, and the college's first strategic plan was designed. Carson-Newman was recognized by several national publications and the football team won five NAIA national championships. During the school's longest presidential tenure, a new music building and student activities center were completed, the latter named for Maddox.

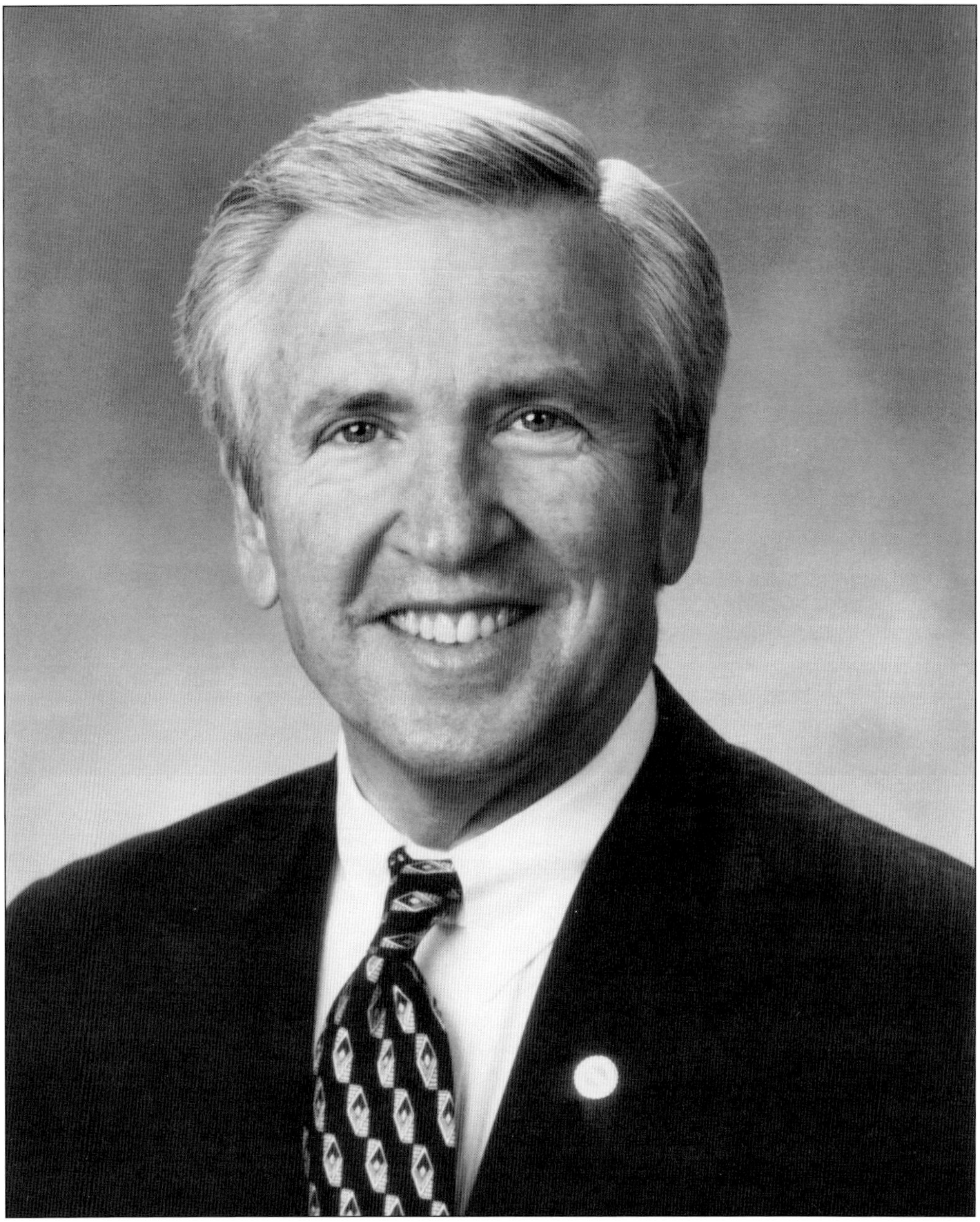

JAMES SIDNEY NETHERTON, 2000–2007. Netherton led the college into a new century, celebrating its sesquicentennial in 2001. The campus grew during his tenure as the Appalachian Commons residence halls, Blye-Poteat Hall and the new Burke-Tarr Stadium were all completed. Following renovations of Sarah Swann and alumni halls, the college broke ground on the new Ted Russell Hall for the school of business. In the fall of 2011, the Netherton Gates were dedicated at the Russell Avenue entrance to campus. (Photograph by Ricke Hester.)

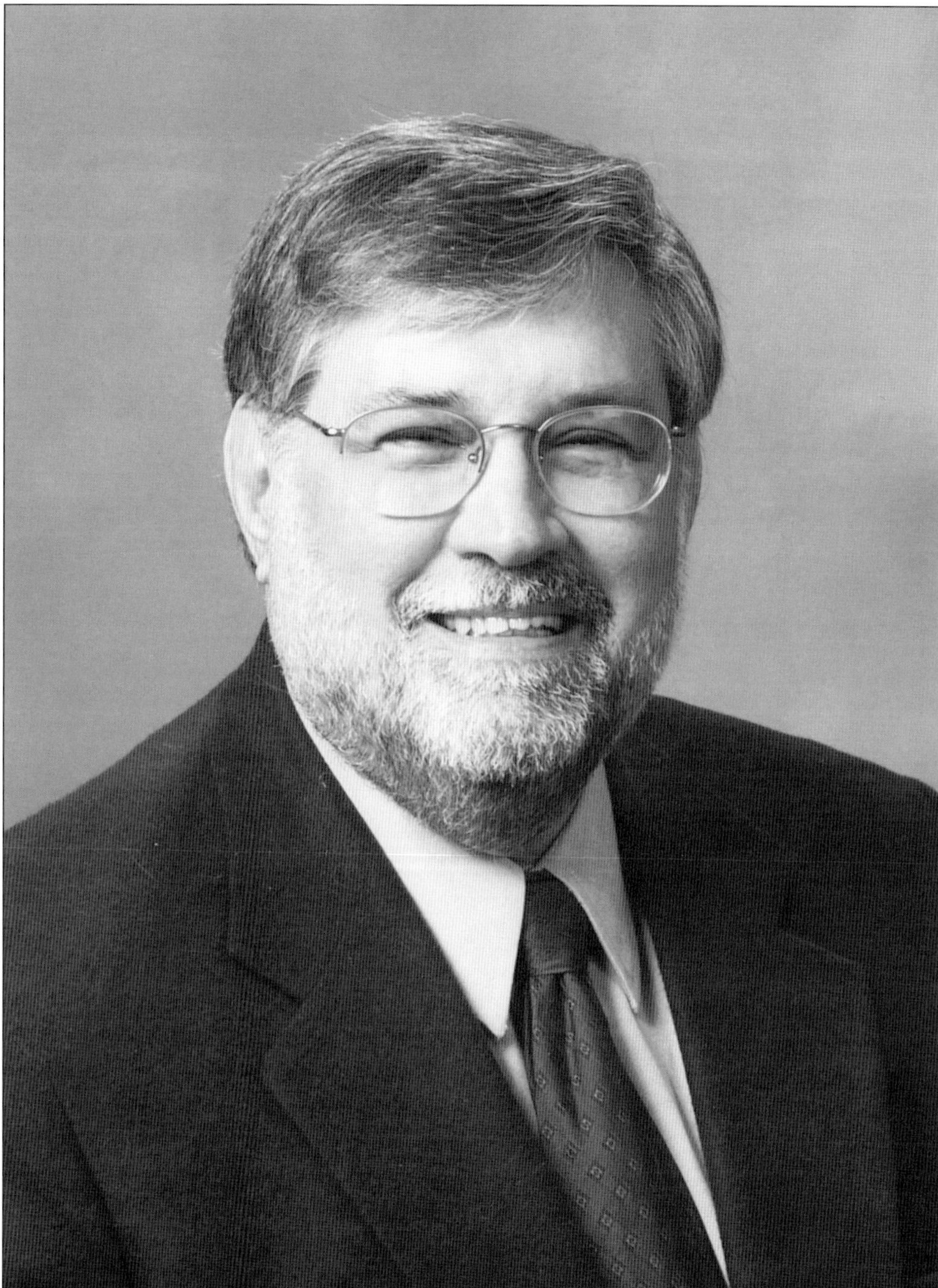

JOE BILL SLOAN, 2007–2008. A 1967 graduate, Sloan served 38 years as associate professor of political science and later as provost. Asked by the trustees to serve as interim, he provided leadership in the areas of facility fundraising and pension plan restructuring. During this time, he also oversaw the transition of the academic structure moving from divisions to schools as the college followed the university model. (Photograph by Ricke Hester.)

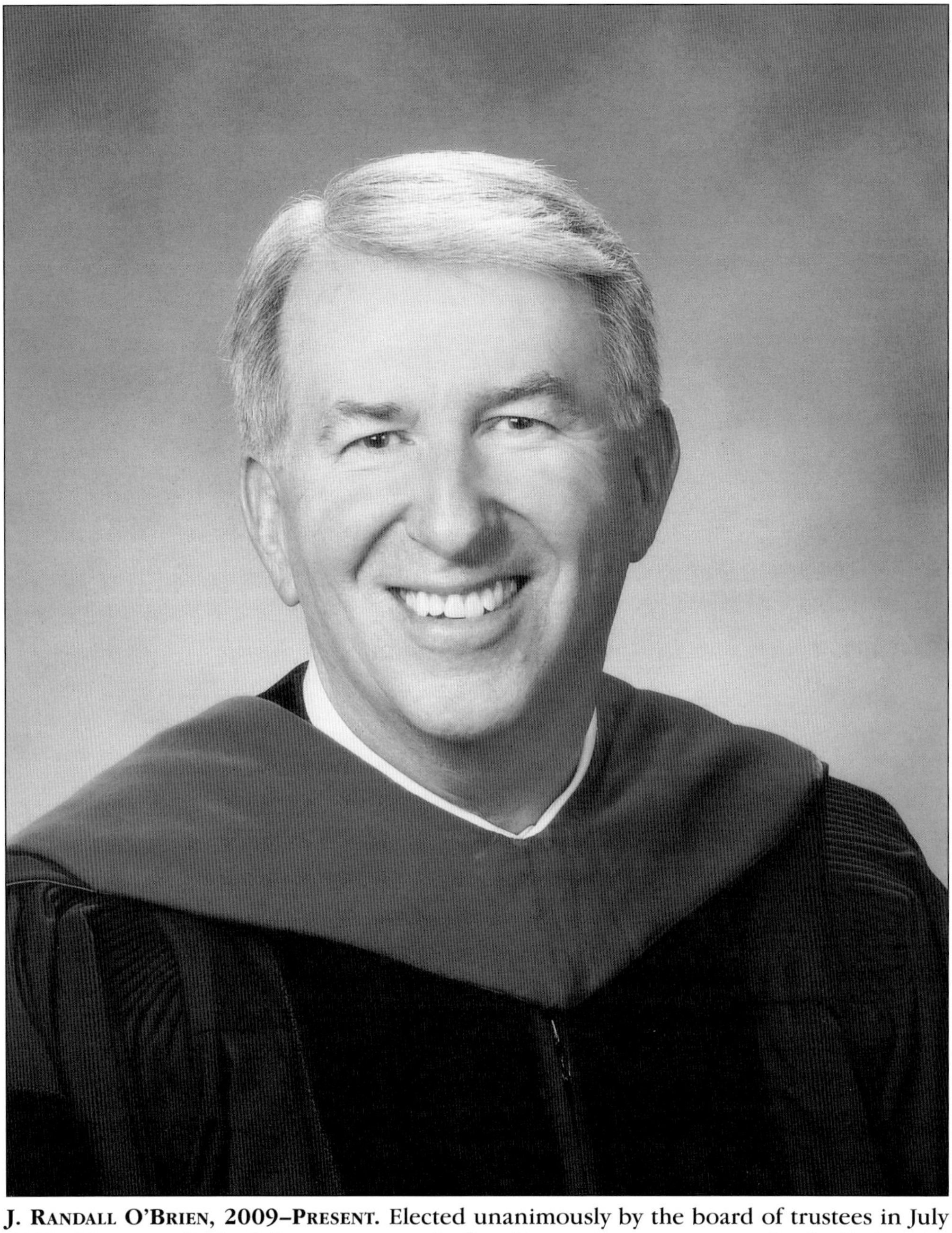

J. Randall O'Brien, 2009–Present. Elected unanimously by the board of trustees in July 2008, O'Brien split the fall semester concluding his service as provost at Baylor University and becoming familiar with Carson-Newman. He began fulltime service in January 2009 and set about positioning the college in the best circumstances for the future. Ted Russell Hall, housing the school of business, was completed in April. The school continued to receive national recognition as *Forbes* called it one of "America's Best Colleges." In 2012, C-N received the highest federal recognition possible to denote an institution's commitment to community service, being awarded the Presidential Award in the President's Higher Education Community Service Honor Roll. (Photo by Ricke Hester.)

Three

The Heart of Campus
Faculty and Staff

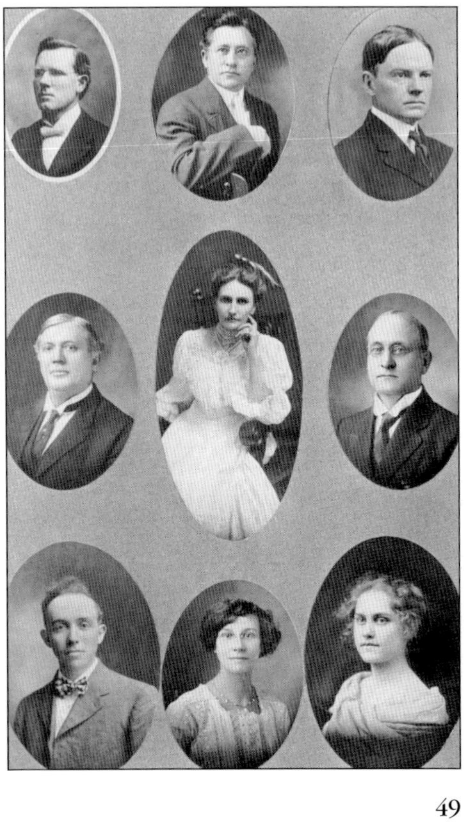

Carson & Newman Faculty, 1912. In 1912, the school produced its first annual entitled the *Swann*. Pictured are several of the faculty, including Tennessee Jenkins (center). Throughout the school's history, the faculty and staff have worked tirelessly fulfilling its mission "to help our students reach their full potential as educated citizens and worldwide servant leaders by integrating academic excellence and Christian commitment within a caring community."

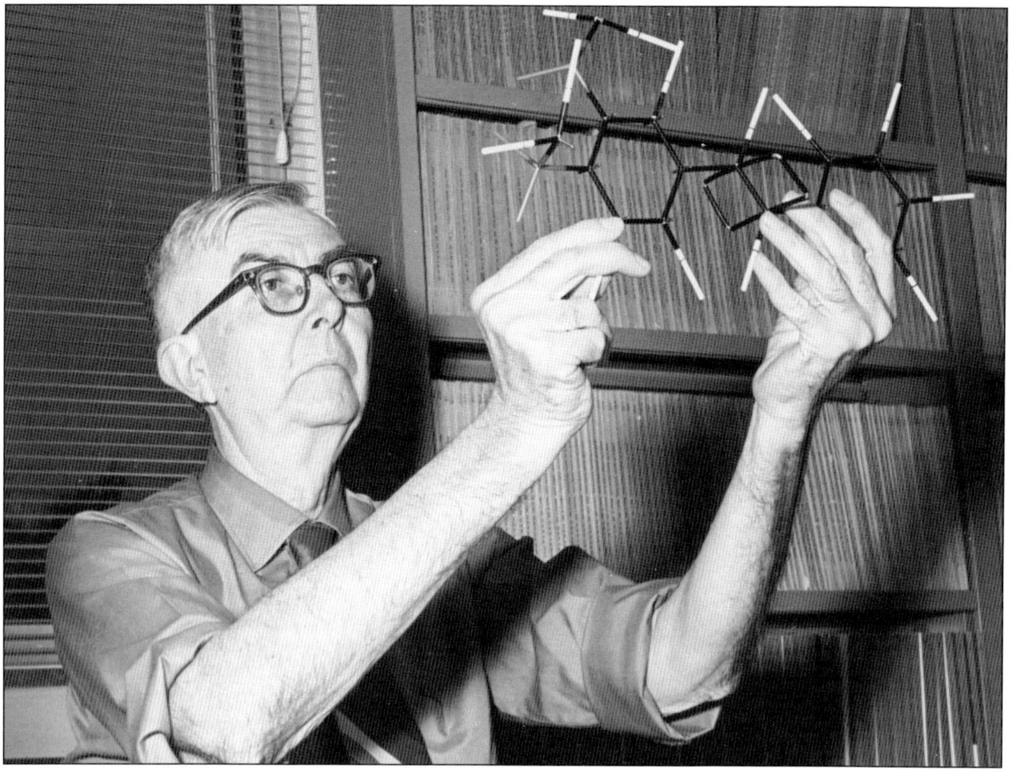

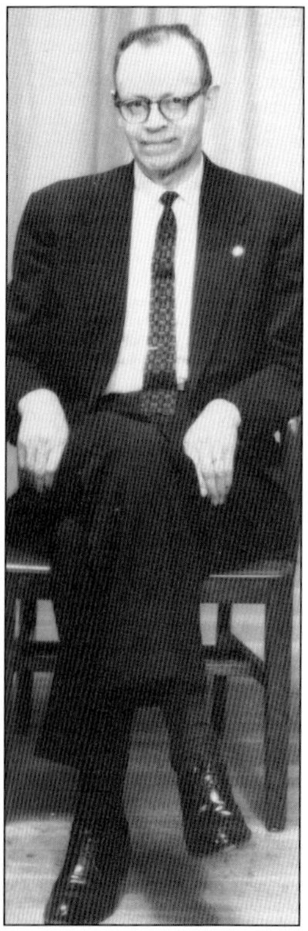

CARL TABB BAHNER. A professor of chemistry and coordinator of research, Bahner was hired in 1937 and retired in 1973. He continued teaching at Walters State Community College, and then went to Bluefield College. He returned to Carson-Newman in 1991. Internationally known for his research of compounds for cancer therapy, he coauthored nearly 100 articles. He and his wife were active with the Baptist Student Union and volunteer band, influencing countless students both inside and outside the classroom.

W.W. BASS. Dr. Bass joined the faculty in 1934 and taught English for 39 years. Serving as department chair beginning in 1956, he retired as professor emeritus. In 1938, he married home economics professor Madeline Walsh. Bass organized the Modern Portia Club for young ladies interested in reading and reviewing current fiction and biography. He was known for his love of poetry as well as for the hats he wore while walking on campus. He passed away in 1998.

W.H. "DAD" BETTIS. Assistant custodian (later assistant superintendent) of buildings and grounds, Bettis served 18 years as "professor of campusology" from 1920 to 1938. Known for his faithful service and ever willingness to befriend students, his passing in 1940 was a loss to the Carson-Newman family. (Courtesy of Johanna P. Dilworth.)

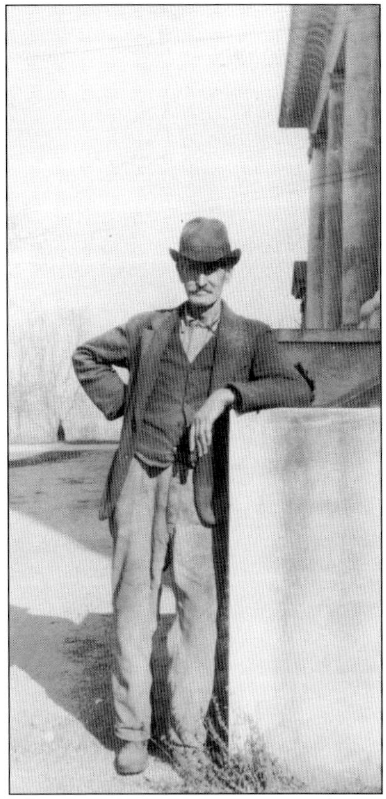

J. CRIPPS BRASHEAR. Brashear came to Carson-Newman in 1948 and became the chair of the history and political science department in 1957. A world traveler, he traveled over 800,000 miles. He retired in 1973 but continued teaching some classes at Walters State Community College. He died in December 1977.

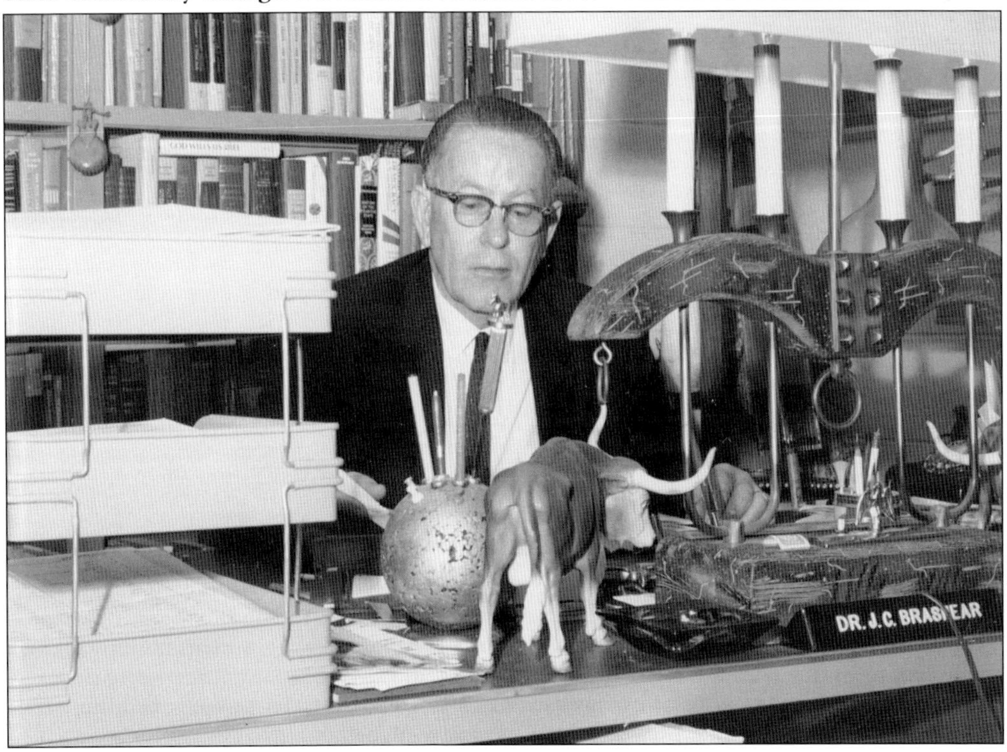

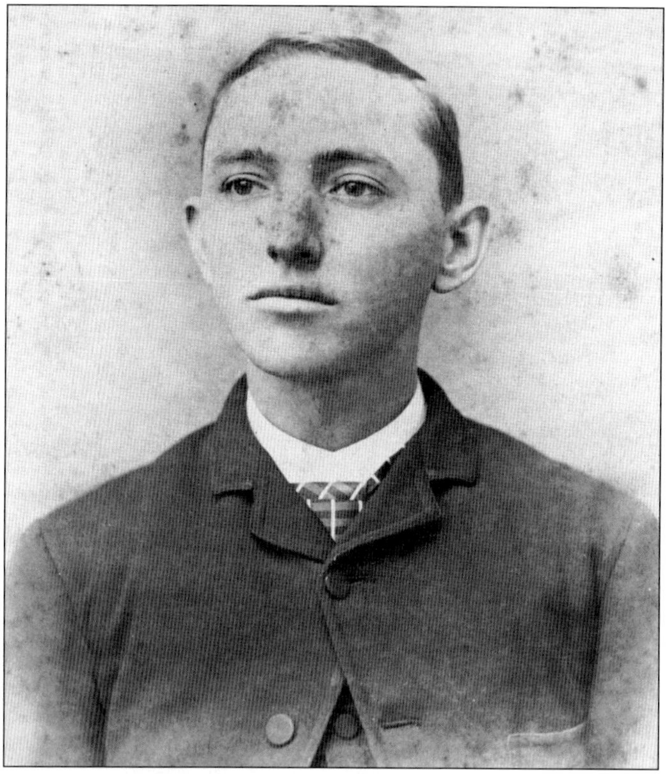

Edmund Cody Burnett. Burnett received his undergraduate degree from Carson College in 1888. After completing his formal education, Dr. Burnett taught Greek and modern languages from 1891 to 1894. In 1907, he became a staff member of Carnegie Institute of Historical Research in Washington, D.C., a position he held for 30 years. Among his many works was the eight-volume set the *Continental Congress*. He died in Washington in 1949. His family donated his library, papers, and letters to the Carson-Newman College library.

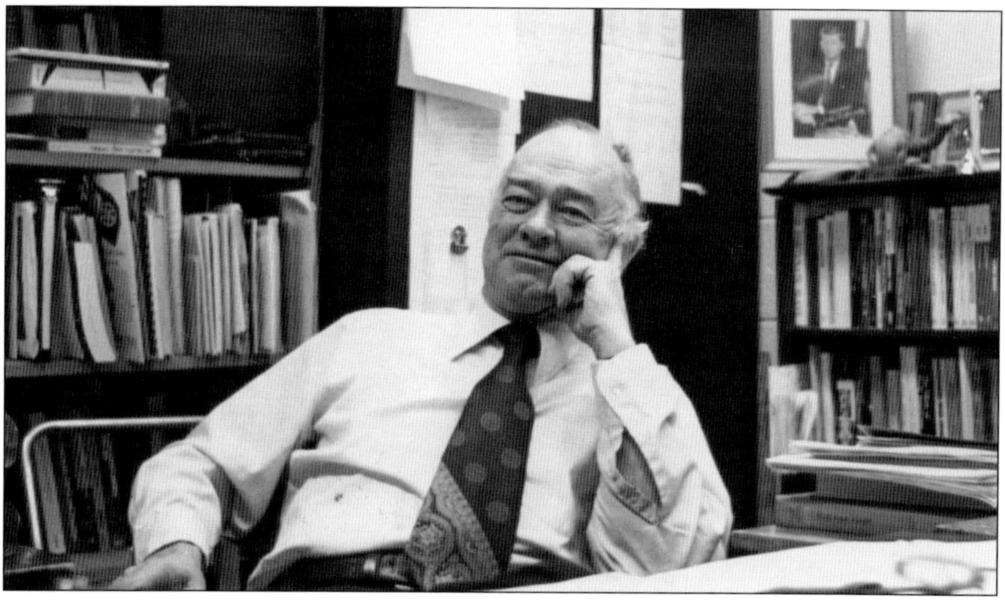

Robert M. Burts Sr. A 1969 Distinguished Faculty Award recipient, Burts was a professor of history for 32 years beginning in 1956. He served as chair of the history department and then the social sciences division. Burts was instrumental in setting up the student honors program and later served as the program's second chairman. For many years, he also served as chairman for the Lyceum (later known as the Concert Lecture Series) committee. Dr. Burts passed away in 2005.

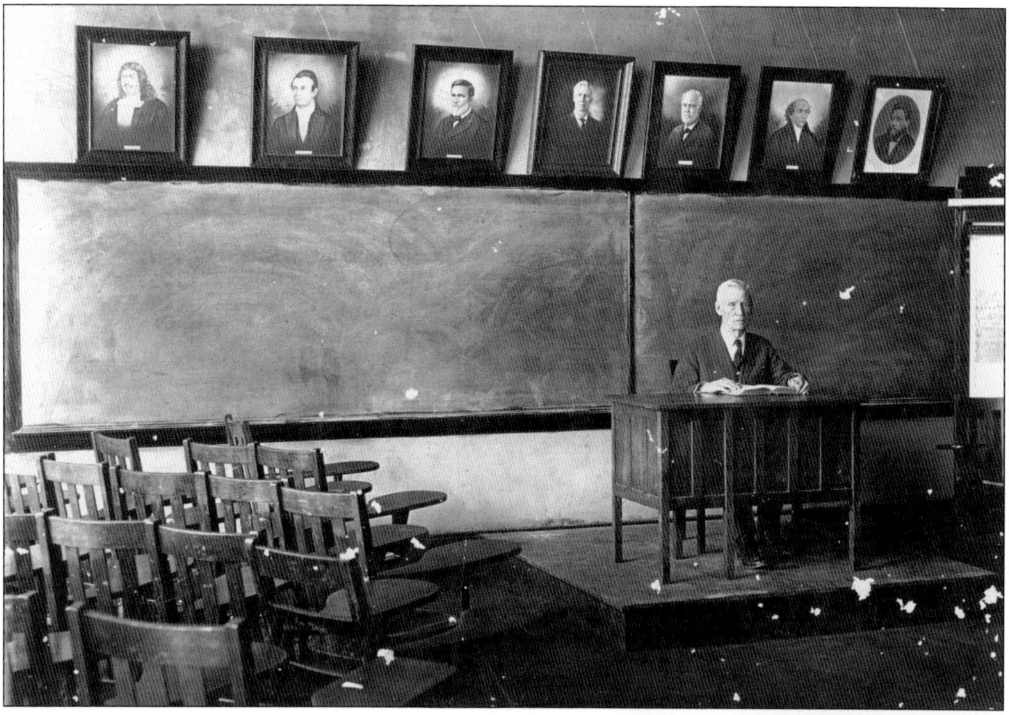

J.L. CAMPBELL. Before coming to Carson-Newman in 1920, John Lorne Campbell served as the secretary of the Foreign Missionary Society of Ontario and Quebec. He also pastored in New York City and Cambridge, Massachusetts. He became well-known as a lecturer, author, and Bible conference teacher. He served as head of the Bible department and was known for his commitment to scholarship. In 1922, Campbell worked to reorganize the disbanded Ministerial Association, which was later named for him.

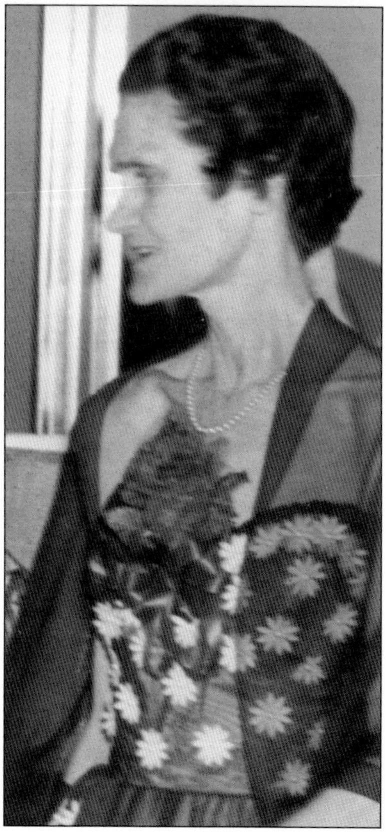

BERNICE CARTER. After teaching English and Latin in several secondary schools, Carter came to Carson-Newman in 1945 as instructor of English and assistant dean of women. In 1954, she gave up her teaching responsibilities and became dean of women for a growing student population. She retired in 1969 and lived in Jackson, Tennessee, until her passing in 1985.

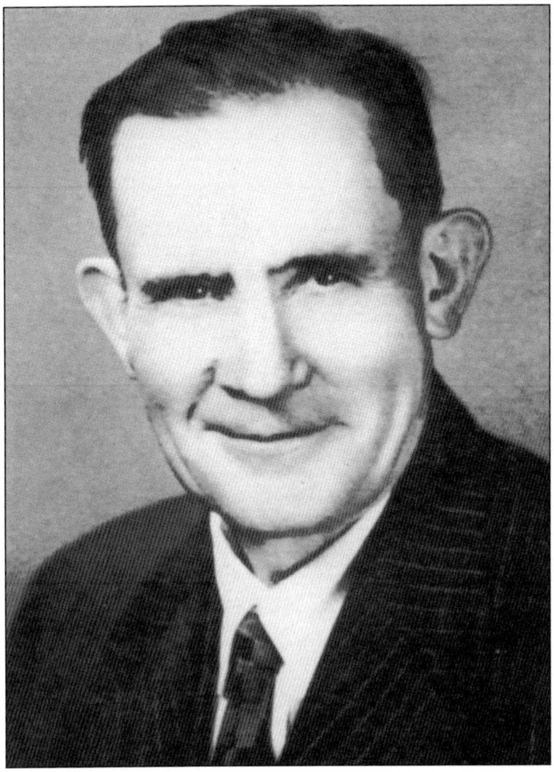

A.E. Cate. Arlie E. Cate graduated from Carson-Newman in 1916 and from Southern Baptist Seminary in 1924. Cate was a veteran of World War I and later served as a chaplain in the Army Reserves. He began his career at Carson-Newman in August 1924, teaching philosophy and education. He served as college dean from 1925 to 1947. From that time, he devoted all his energies to teaching and was head of the philosophy department until his death in 1955.

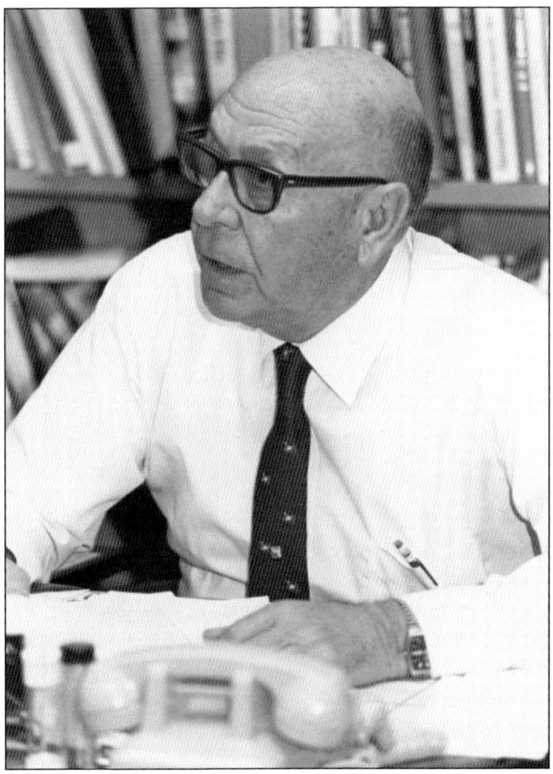

Joe Chapman. Joe and Frances Chapman were married on her graduation day in Sarah Swann dormitory. He later returned to his alma mater as a professor of biology in 1947, specializing in the field of botany. In 1952, he took over as head of the department. Chapman served as alumni secretary from 1957 to 1963 and was in charge of homecoming and editing the *Alumni Bulletin*. In 1973, he was honored with the Distinguished Faculty Award. Chapman passed away in 1993.

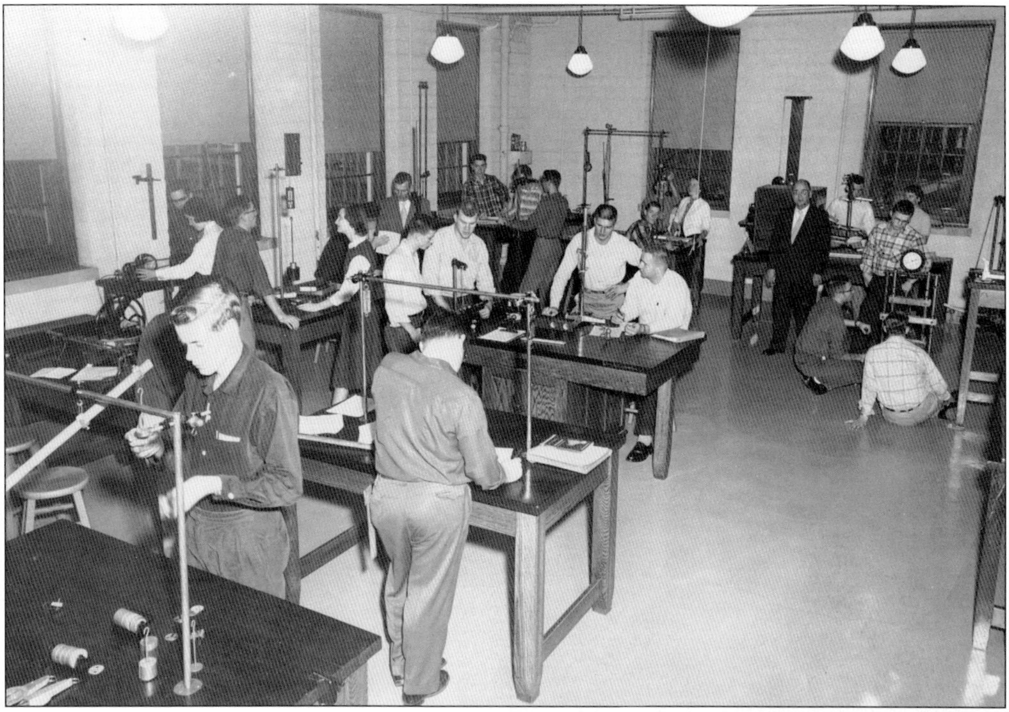

Alexander A. Chavis. Chavis was a professor of physics and astronomy from 1926 through 1957. He worked to develop the department and finally create a major within that field. He was also responsible for helping construct the observatory that used to stand on campus. Chavis served as manager of athletics and alumni secretary for 31 years, publishing two directories.

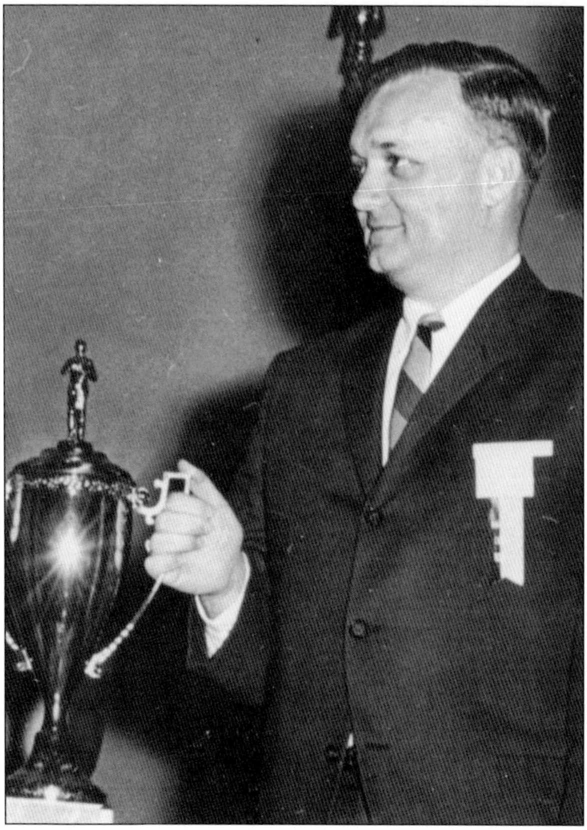

Royal Forrest Conklin. Conklin came to Carson-Newman in 1954 as a professor of English and speech and also served as intercollegiate debate coach. In 1965, he helped bring widespread recognition to the school when his team won the National Collegiate Debate Championship at West Point, New York. Conklin was an ordained minister who also spent two years in the Navy Corps before coming to Jefferson City. He passed in April 2011.

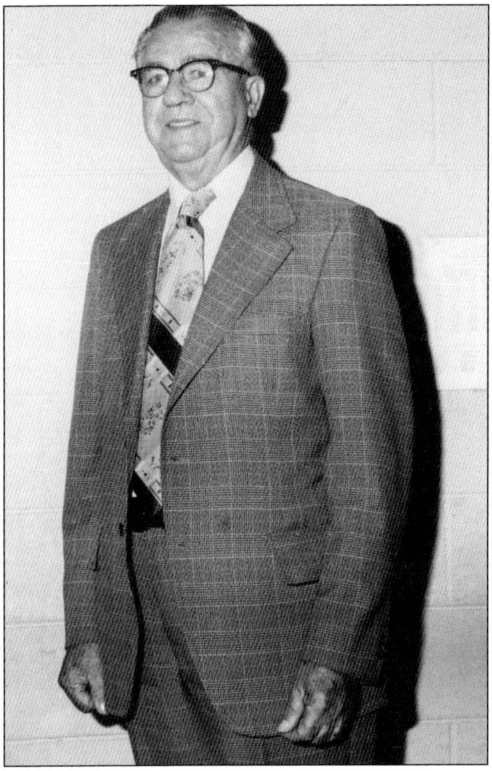

Edgar Marion Cook. A 1923 graduate, Cook returned in 1934 and took on the responsibilities of dean of men and professor of psychology and education. In 1939, he became head of that department and in 1957, he added the role of academic dean until his retirement in 1962. During his tenure, he was responsible for helping to develop initiatives such as freshmen orientation and various student-testing programs. He also authored ". . . *it Happened on a College Campus*," a brief history of Carson-Newman.

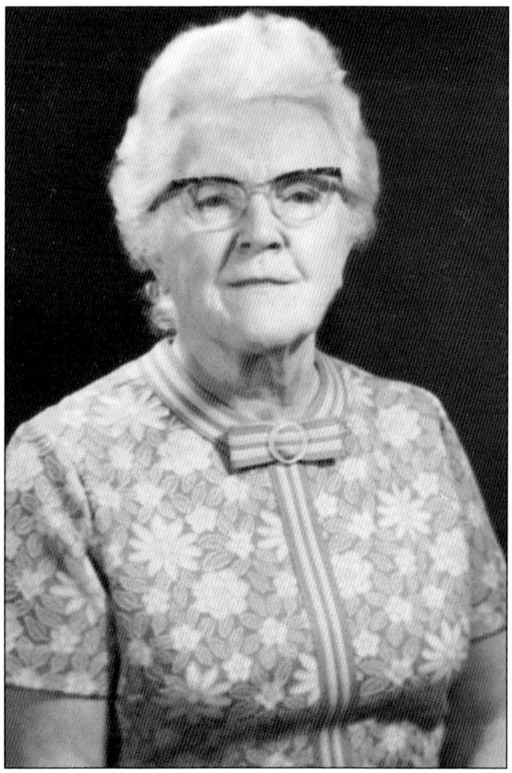

Ersa Davis. From 1923 until 1968, Miss Ersa was the foundation of the music department. Under her direction the department greatly developed and expanded. Her work also led to accreditation by the National Association of Schools of Music. A 1932 graduate, she was given the Distinguished Alumni Award in 1971 and an honorary doctorate of music degree in 1978. In 1963, the recital hall in the Chambliss Fine Arts Building was named after her.

J.F. Ellis. In 1926, Ellis came to the school after several years as an educator in public schools and several colleges. For 21 years, he taught history, political science, and geography. As a layman, he developed an understanding of Greek and Hebrew and an appreciation of sacred music. A devoted scholar, he proved to be an interesting and popular chapel speaker. His wife, Corina, served as a professor of home economics as well as dietician for one year.

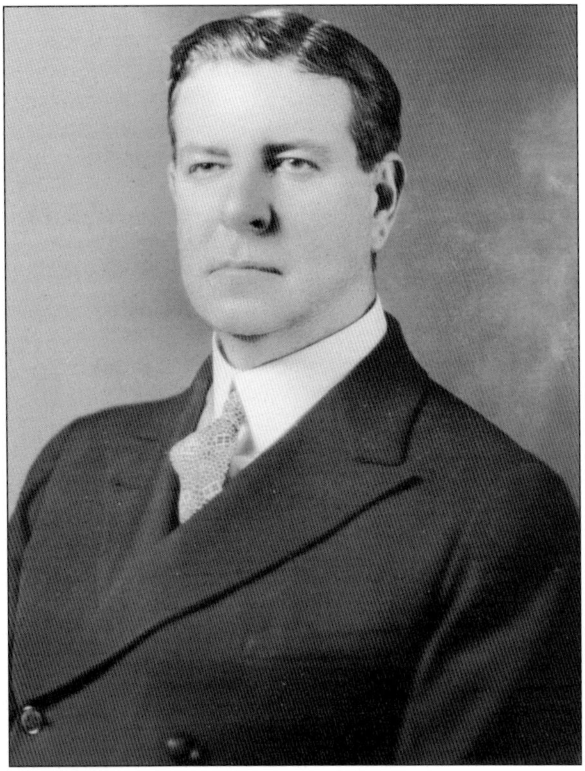

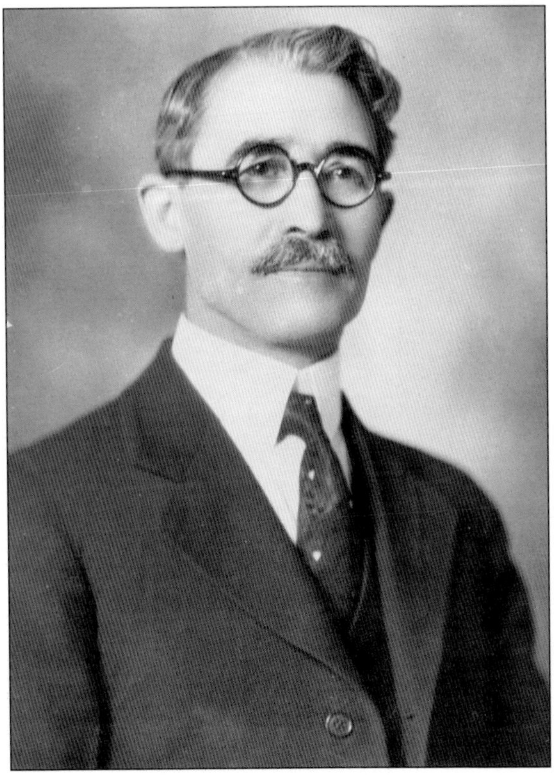

J.D. Everett. Another former educator and superintendent of public schools, Everett joined the faculty in 1919 as a professor of education. He also served as acting dean from 1924 to 1925. When the Baptist Student Union was organized in 1927, Everett was named its counselor. In 1936, the Carson-Newman chapter of the Future Teachers of America was named after him. Leila Everett joined her husband on the faculty teaching mathematics, Latin, and Spanish after having also taught in the preparatory department.

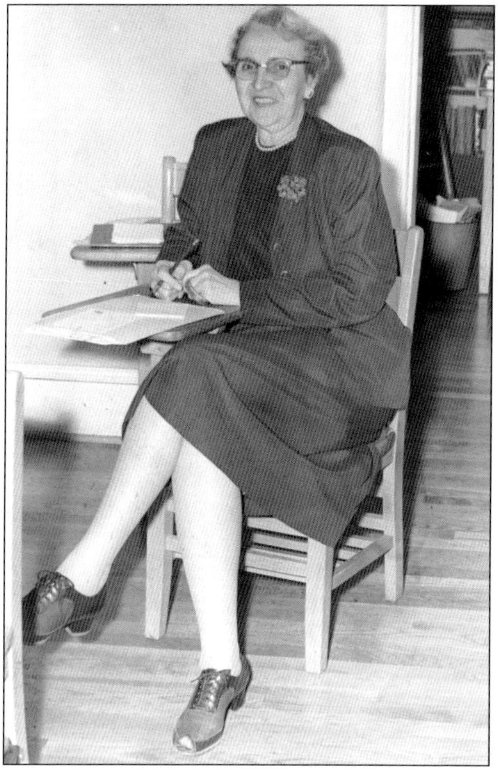

Janie Swann Huggins. After graduating from Carson-Newman, Huggins spent many years teaching high school. She then returned to her alma mater in 1940 to teach English and French, specializing in 18th century literature. During World War II, she served as registrar and then returned to teaching English. She also revived the May Day celebration, assisted with the centennial pageant, and sponsored many student groups. In 1976, she was awarded the Distinguished Alumni Award. Retiring in 1969, she went on to teach at Lincoln Memorial University for three more years. (Photograph by Roy Dyer.)

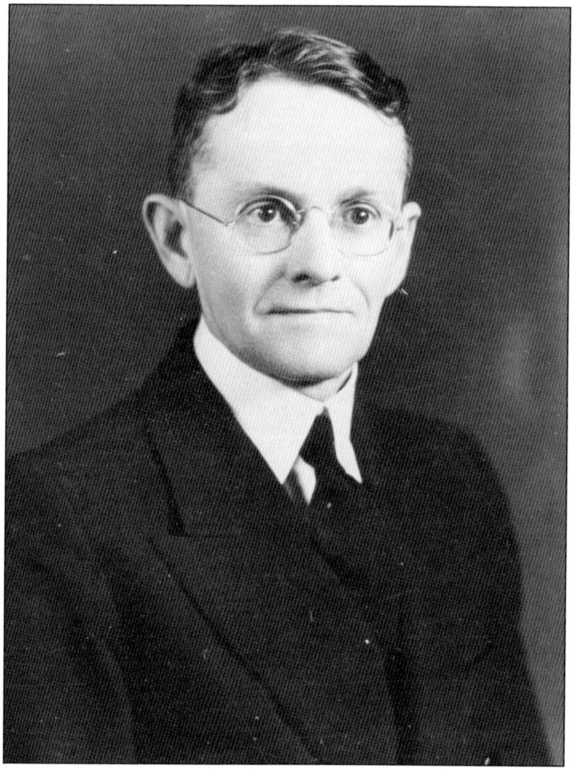

T.C. Hutton. Dr. Hutton was known as a dedicated scholar and a Christian gentleman. He began teaching as professor of classical languages in 1919 and also served the school in a dual role as its first registrar. He continued this practice until 1930. His passion was Latin and Greek and he saw the classics as powerful agents to shape young minds. He died unexpectedly in 1947.

Mae Iddins. One of the longest serving faculty members, Iddins was a professor of physical education from 1928 through 1970. She coached the girls' basketball team until the school discontinued female intercollegiate competition. She organized an intramural program for women, which allowed them to compete for letters. She also organized and established the physical education major for men and women. During World War II, she taught mathematics in the school's Navy V-12 program. Iddins was given the Distinguished Alumni Award in 1972. A scholarship award was established in her name for seniors. (Photograph by Cargilles' Art Gallery.)

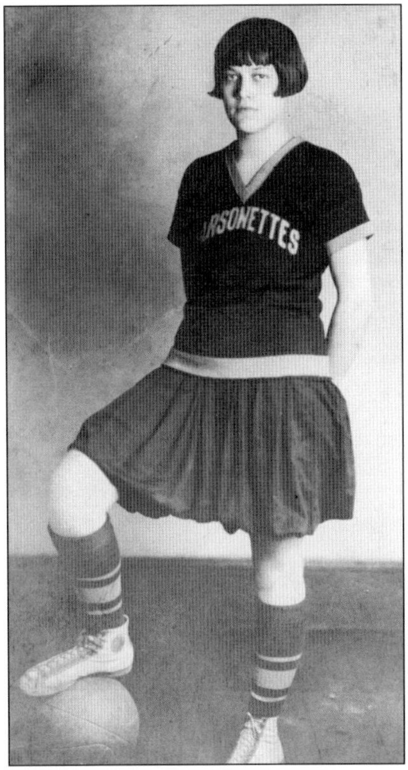

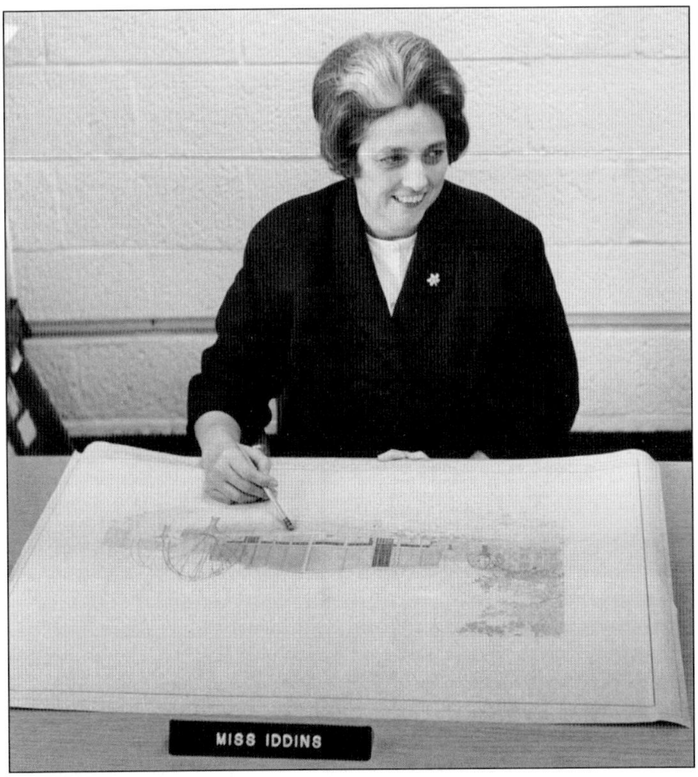

Mildred Iddins. The sister of Mae Iddins, Mildred served as librarian from 1944 until 1981. Before coming back to her alma mater, she was a high school librarian and also served during World War II in the Army Special Services library in Fort Oglethorpe, Georgia. She oversaw two library relocations and was responsible for its extensive growth and development during her tenure. Always mindful of the importance of preserving historical materials, she collected what would become the foundation for the archives. In 1987, she was honored by having the special collections named after her.

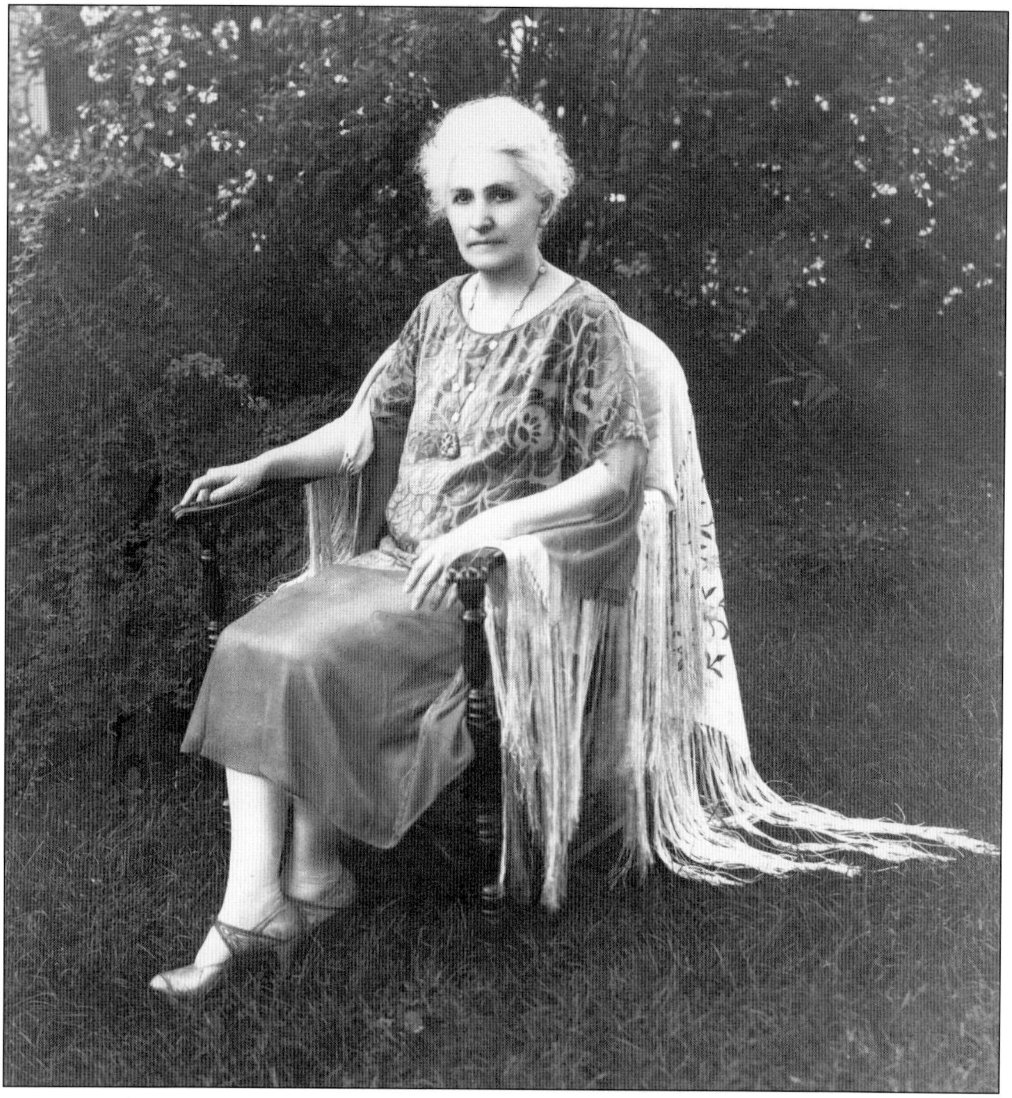

TENNESSEE JENKINS. Jenkins graduated in 1893 and then began a 48-year teaching career. She primarily taught history, but early on she also taught French and physical education. In 1907, she became head of the history department and remained so until her retirement in 1944. She was the first president of the Hypatian Literary Society and is credited with suggesting the moniker Fighting Eagles. One of the institution's most beloved professors, "Miss Tenny" was called the "Sweetheart of Carson-Newman." The house she lived in on Russell Street where the music building now stands was moved around the corner to West College Street and now serves as the offices for the English Language Institute.

J.D. Ives. A professor of biology, Ives came to Carson-Newman in 1923. He was a very popular teacher, an active church member, and scoutmaster of Boy Scout Troop 76 for 20 years. He retired in 1952 after 31 years of service. In 1961, he was awarded an honorary doctorate of science degree. (Courtesy of Johanna P. Dilworth.)

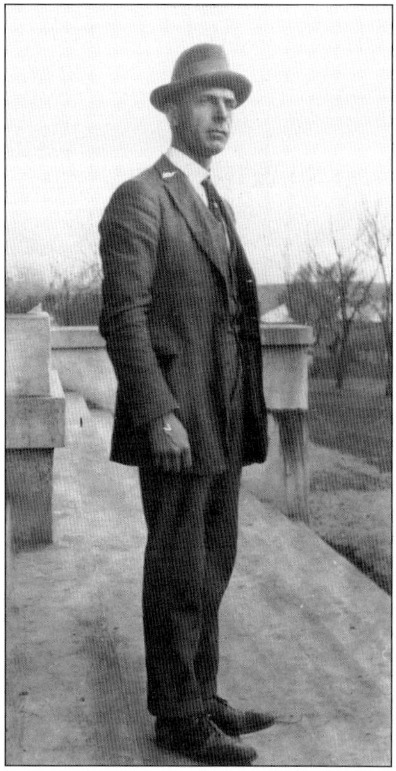

Charles H. Jones. During his tenure, Jones became an institution. From 1946 to 1982, he taught voice, music theory, and piano. He also directed the highly regarded A Cappella Choir. Much loved by his students, he was fondly known as "Fessor." In 1977, he was awarded the Algernon Sydney Sullivan Award for community service and in 1981 he received the Distinguished Faculty Award. Fessor passed away on December 25, 2007.

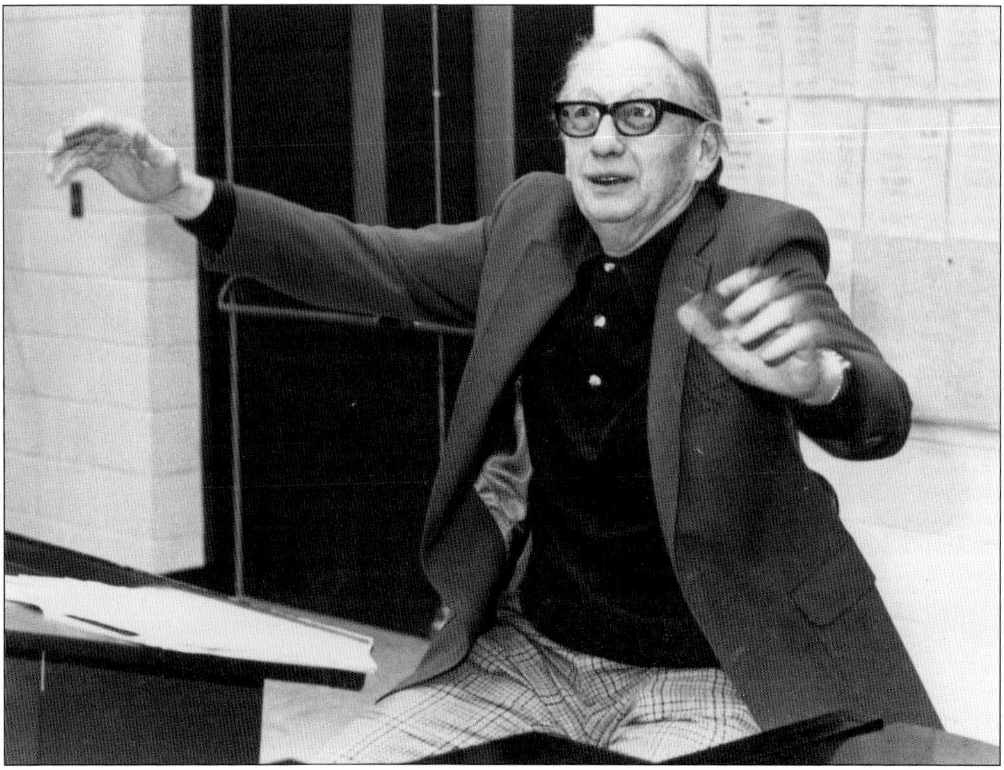

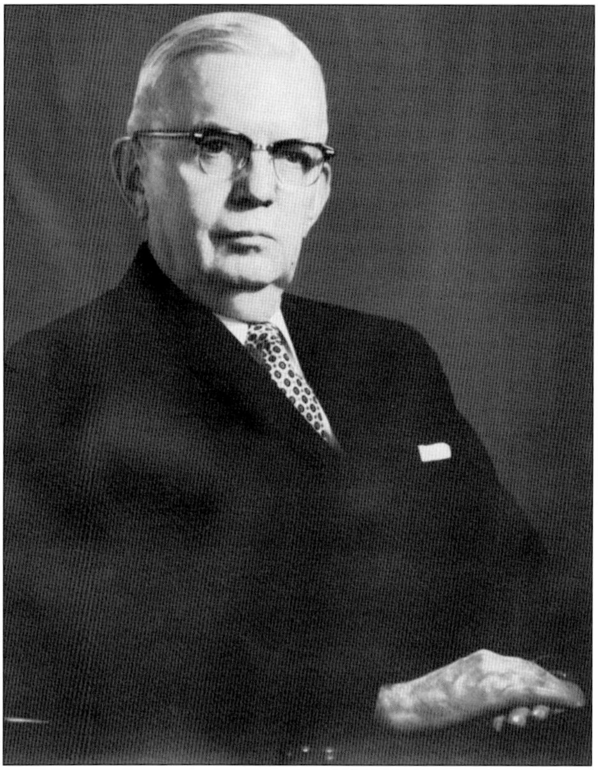

Russell Bradley Jones. Jones graduated from Southern Baptist Theological Seminary in 1920 and pastored churches in Tennessee, Maryland, and Georgia. From 1932 to 1936, he was president of the Manila Evangelistic Institute in the Philippines. In 1949, Jones was elected first vice president of the Tennessee Baptist Convention and served as its president in 1950. The following year he came to Carson-Newman, and until 1960, he was head of the Bible and religious education department. His specialties were Bible, preaching, missions, and religions and cults. Jones served as contributing editor of the *Baptist and Reflector* and authored 14 books. His service is remembered each fall when the Russell Bradley Jones Lecture is given in his honor.

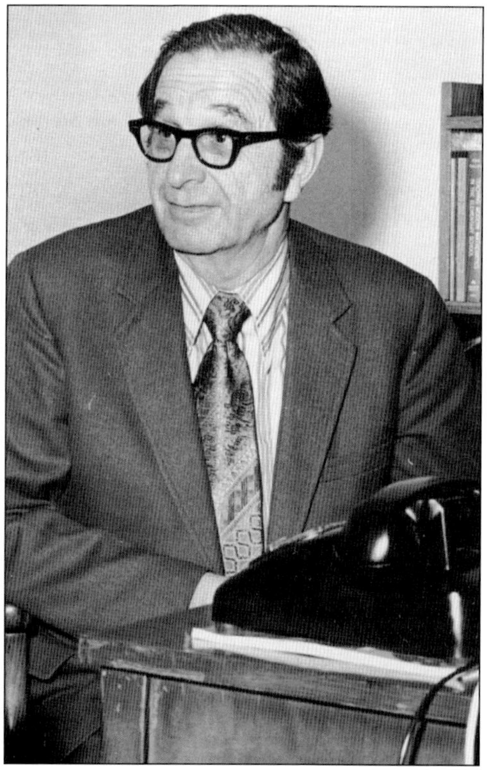

Ray Koonce. Ray F. Koonce came to Carson-Newman in 1956 as a professor of psychology and retired in 1978. He served as director of guidance and placement and as psychology division chairman. He authored two books and numerous articles. He was inducted into the college's Psychology Hall of Fame in 1989. Virginia Koonce joined the psychology faculty in 1959 and served until 1977. After their retirements the Koonces were both awarded emeritus status. Virginia died in 2001, followed by her husband a year later.

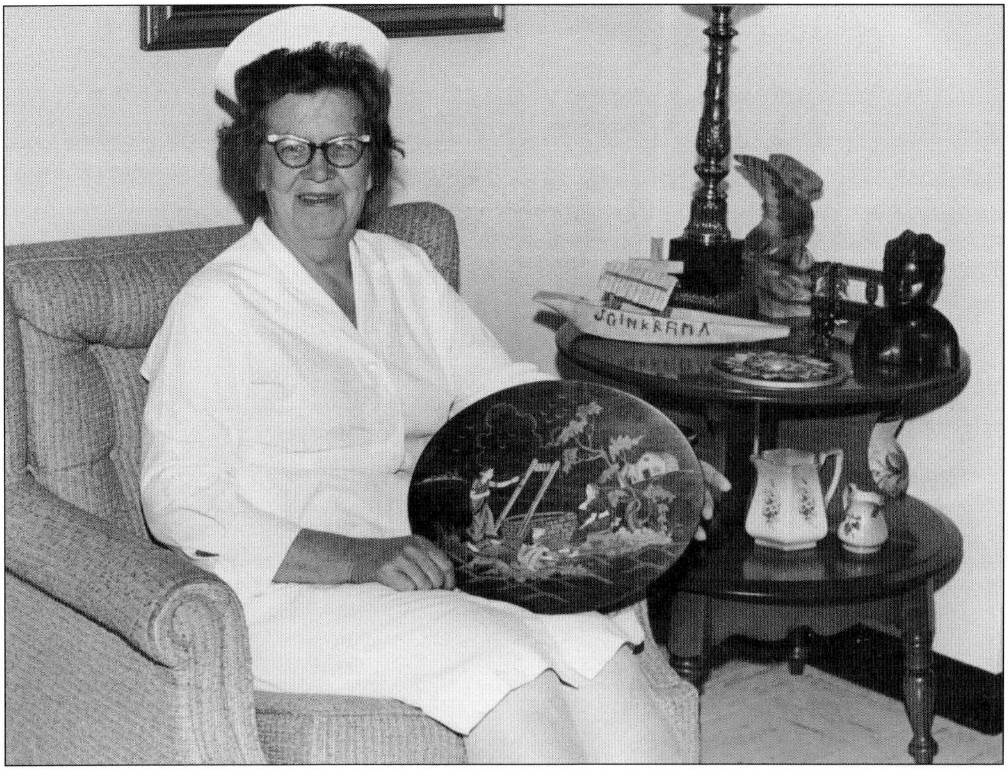

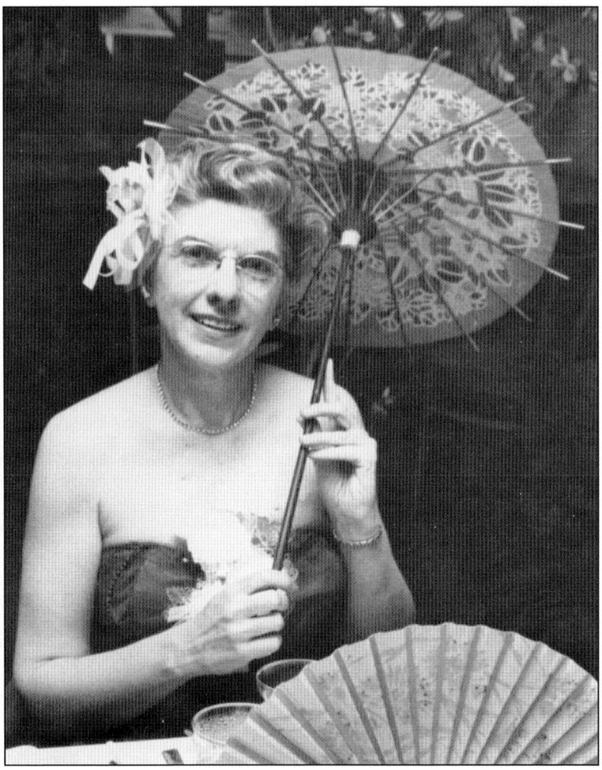

KATHLEEN MANLEY. A graduate of Carson-Newman, Kathleen served as the college's nurse from 1952 to 1971. She also served as instructor of health and director of student health services. A missionary to Nigeria for nearly 20 years, she returned home after a bout with yellow fever. In 1962, the newly built infirmary was named in her honor. She was also the recipient of the Distinguished Alumni Award in 1974.

PEARL MCHAN. Pearl, also known as Miss Mc, was dietitian and a professor of home economics for 25 years. While at Carson-Newman, she was also advisor to the International Students Club and Votinanthenes Club. She retired in 1976 and returned to her home in Winston-Salem, North Carolina. She is remembered for her delicious deserts. She died in 1996. (Photograph by Roy Dyer.)

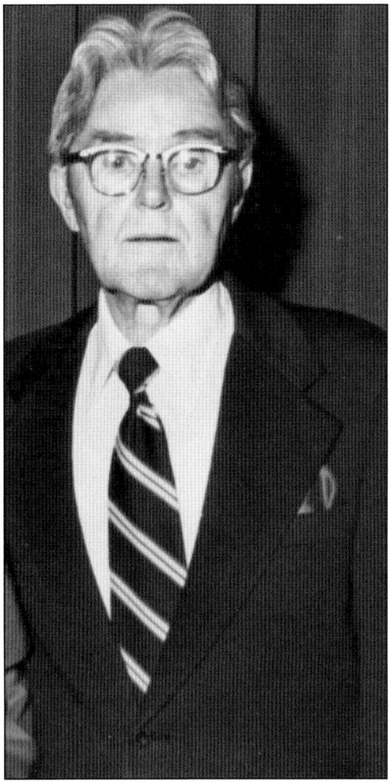

Herbert Jackson Miles. An ordained Baptist minister, Miles came to Carson-Newman in 1953 as a professor of sociology. In 1954, he became head of the philosophy and sociology department, succeeding Arlie Cate. He was widely known for his writings on marriage and family. Miles retired in 1972 and continued to write. He died in 1994.

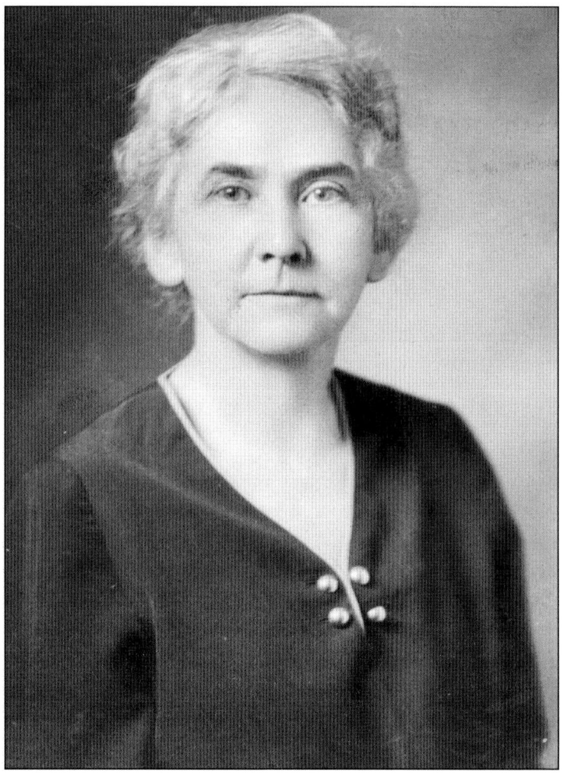

Winifred Moore. From 1928 to 1944, "Miss Winnie" taught modern languages. She came to Carson-Newman with extensive teaching experience at Judson College, Tennessee College, and Westhampton College. While receiving her master's degree in French from Columbia University, she taught German and French in New Jersey high schools. A great traveler, she also studied in Germany and France.

Albert Myers. Professor emeritus of chemistry, Myers graduated from Carson-Newman, as did both his parents and seven siblings. His family came to Jefferson City in 1928 when his father became treasurer of the school. After several teaching positions he returned and from 1954 to 1963, he taught chemistry. After four years at Houston Baptist College, he returned as chair of the chemistry department until retiring in 1981. He could often be seen riding his unique three-wheeled bicycle to and from campus. In 1985, Myers received the Algernon Sydney Sullivan award for community service and the Distinguished Alumni Award in 1988.

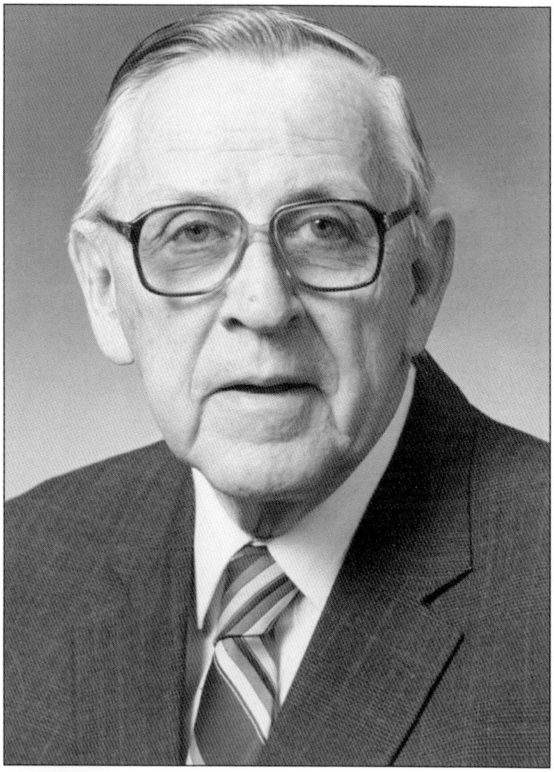

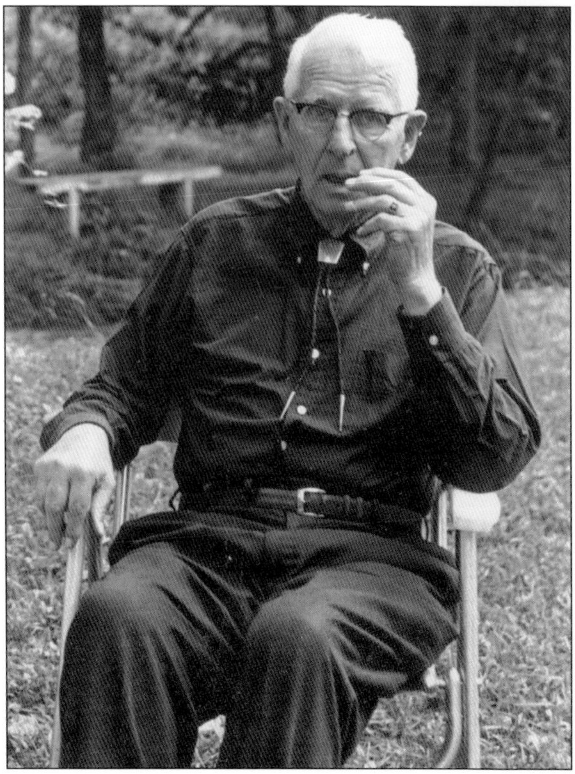

Roy Myers. After serving as a teacher, principal, and superintendent, as well as supervisor of certification for the state Department of Education, Myers was hired as treasurer and business manager in 1928. He would serve in that capacity until 1956. Through his able managing, Myers helped guide the school through the Depression years and World War II.

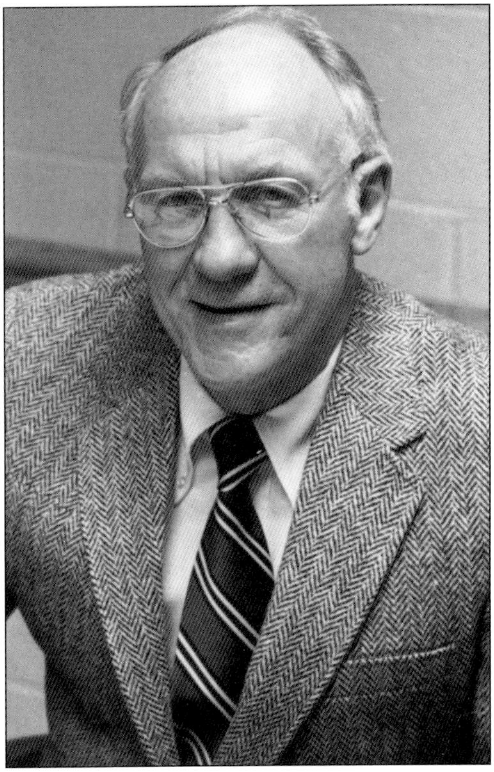

Gerald Naylor. Dr. Naylor joined the faculty in 1961 as a professor of biology. He was a World War II veteran, having served as a B-24 pilot. A graduate of Auburn University, he was a member of the football team. He received his doctorate in agronomy from North Carolina State University. He pastored churches in North Carolina and was a pastoral care counselor at Bowman Gray School of Medicine in Winston-Salem. While at Carson-Newman, he initiated the Summer Science Training Program for gifted high school students. Naylor retired in 1986 and passed away in 1996.

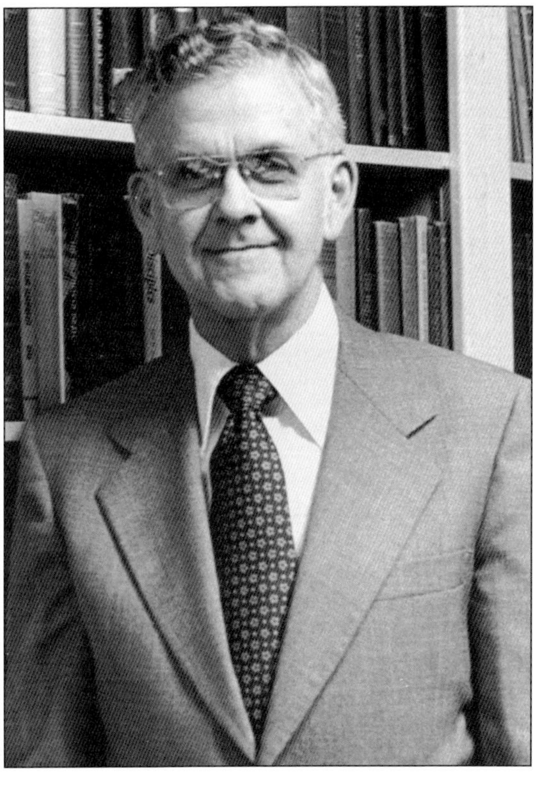

William Purdue. Dr. William J. Purdue, pastor of First Baptist Church, Kingsport, was named director of Carson-Newman's newly formed Bible school in 1979. He retired from this position in 1987. In 1988, he was presented the Algernon Sydney Sullivan Award for his dedication to Christian service and leadership.

PHILLIPPI QUISENBERRY CARLSON. Phillippi, also known as "Aunt Pie," became head resident for the Henderson Home for Young Ladies in 1966. For over two years, she served as a nurse in the Navy Medical Corps during World War II. She was known as an excellent cook, with chili being one of her specialty dishes. Later, she served as assistant head resident and executive housekeeper in New Men's Residence Hall. Carlson died in 2000.

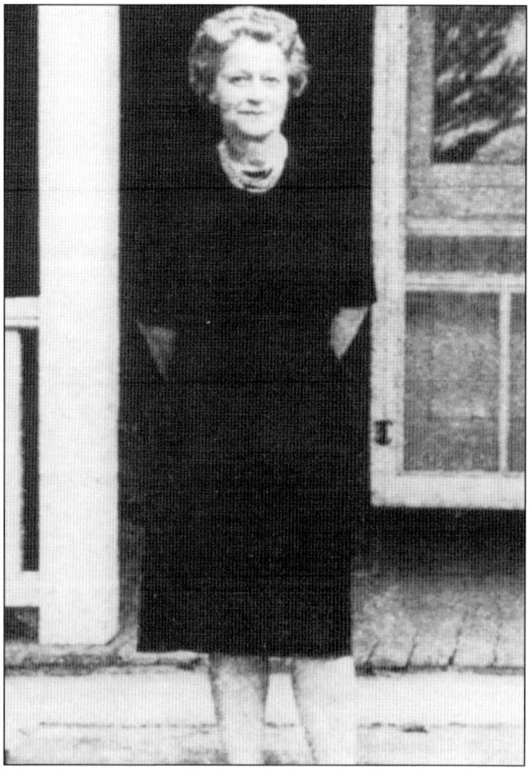

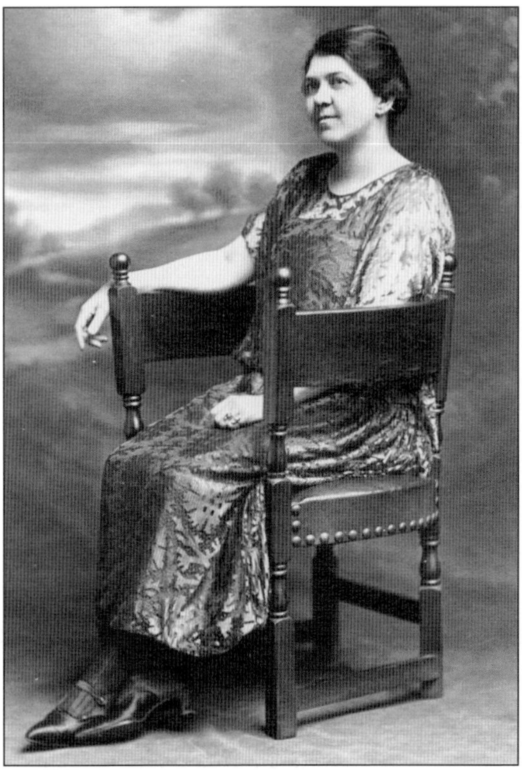

NORA ELECTRA MAPLES RANKIN. After graduating in 1896, she went on to further study at the Conservatory of Music in Cincinnati, Ohio. She returned in 1898 as director of music and teacher of piano at Carson and Newman College. After leaving for some time, she returned in 1919. She also taught harmony, theory, and music history until her retirement in 1925. (Photograph by McCoy of Knoxville.)

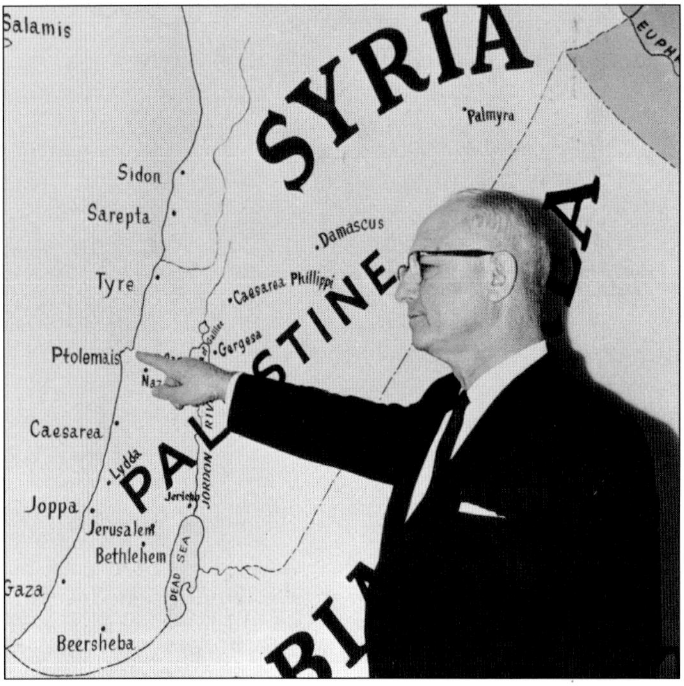

W. Edwin Richardson. Dr. Richardson came to Carson-Newman in 1960 as a professor and chair of the Bible department. A Baptist minister who served many churches, he was also a former president of two colleges, Cumberland University and Bethel College. Dr. Richardson retired in 1968 and passed away in 1971.

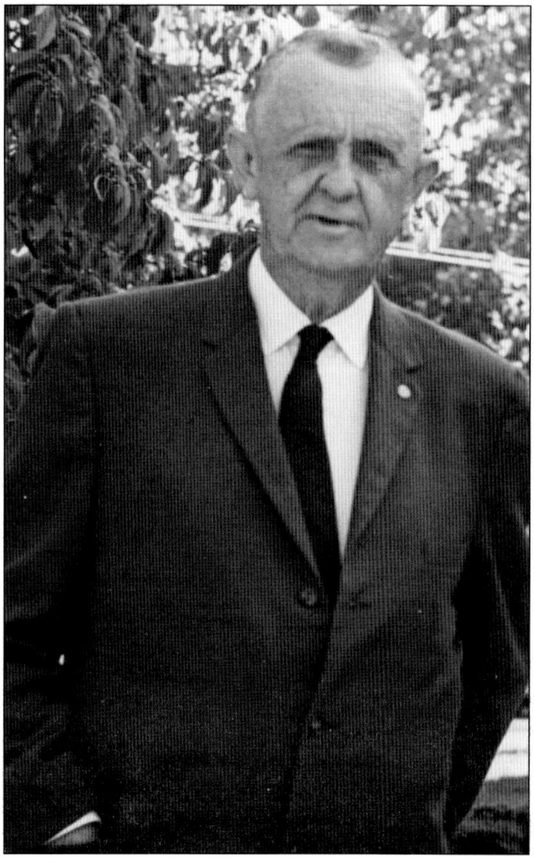

O.L. Rives. From 1947 to 1967, Rives was a professor of Bible and religious education. He had previously served as a supply teacher from 1928 to 1930. In between, he held three pastorates and served as a US Army chaplain, a position he held in both world wars. Active in Baptist life, he wrote Sunday school lessons for the *Baptist and Reflector* for many years and served on the Tennessee Baptist Convention's executive committee. (Photograph by Reece Tallent.)

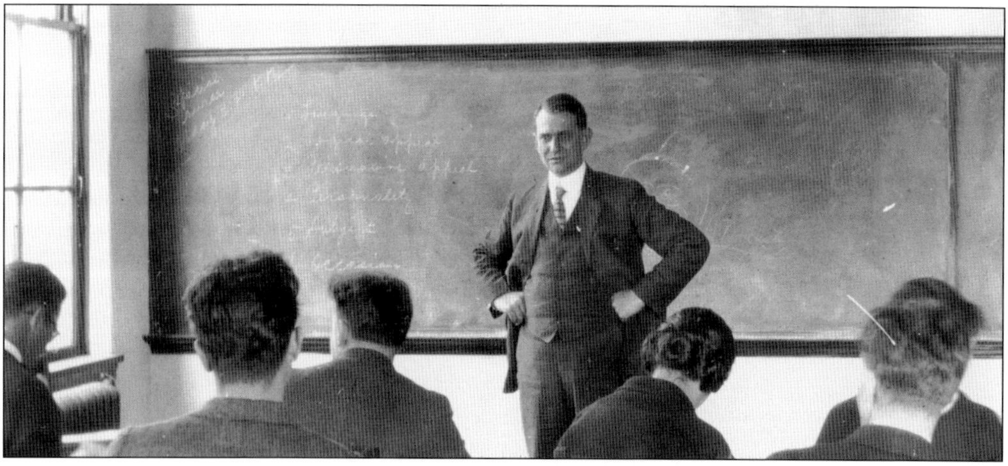

Elmer W. Sydnor. Dr. Sydnor began teaching English at Carson-Newman in 1918. He became department chair in 1934 and also took on the duties of coaching forensics, leading the team to numerous successful seasons and regional recognition. He was also responsible for establishing a student government program on campus. It began with an association for men in 1939 and one for women three years later. Later, he worked to help institute an association for commuters. The three were combined into a cooperative council, a forerunner of the present-day Student Government Association. Sydnor retired in 1955. (Courtesy of Johanna P. Dilworth.)

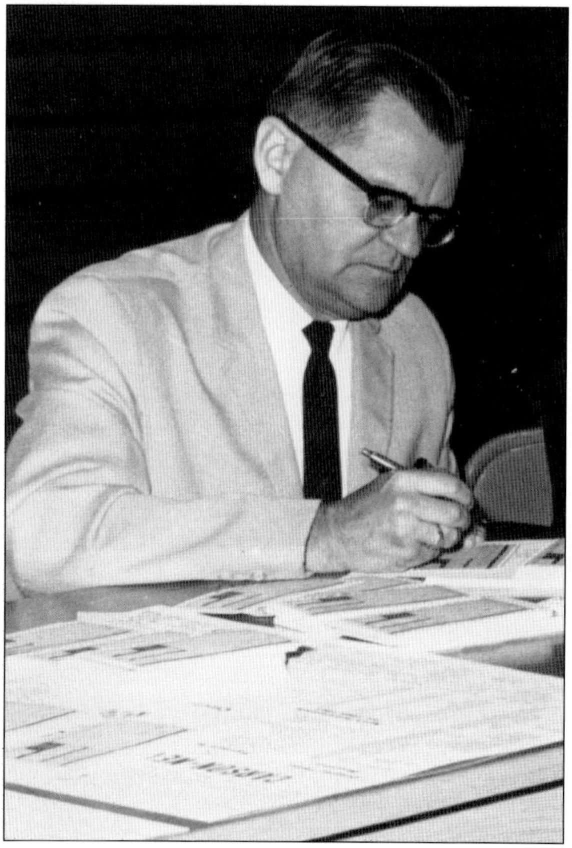

L. Dan Taylor. Before coming to Carson-Newman in 1946 as a professor of Greek and religion, Taylor pastored and taught high school. In 1955, a scholarship fund for ministerial students was established. He taught for 31 years and also served as faculty sponsor for the Definite Service Band, a student organization focused on missions.

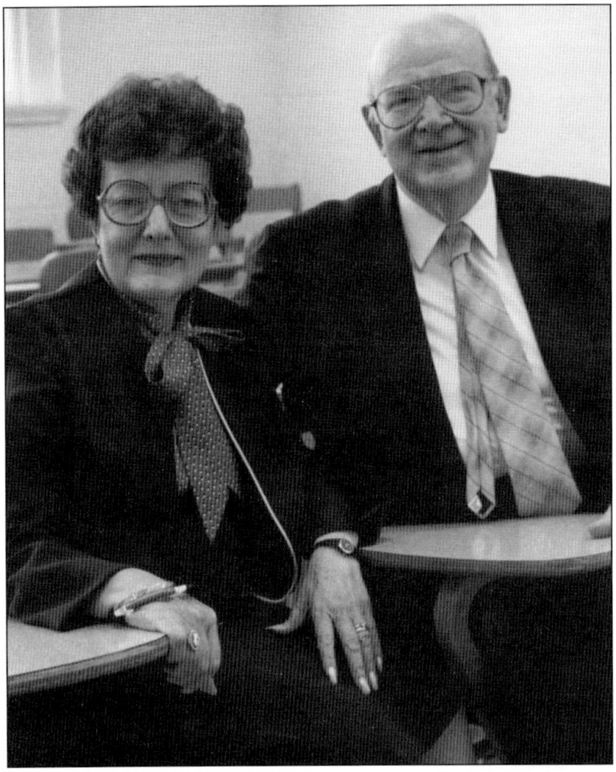

Robert and Ruth Turner. One of the memorable couples in Carson-Newman's history, the Turners taught for a combined 68 years. He returned to his alma mater in 1955 and taught English, speech, folklore, and journalism. Ruth also taught in the English department for 31 years, beginning in 1959. They were committed to the Elderhostel program hosted by the school in the summers. A former Lane Bryant Award winner for community service, he received the 1976 Distinguished Faculty Award. In 2006, the alumni association established the R.R. Turner Spirit of the College Award in his honor, to be awarded to the current faculty or staff member whose commitment and service exemplify the spirit of Carson-Newman. Dr. Turner passed away in 2004, followed by Ruth in 2005.

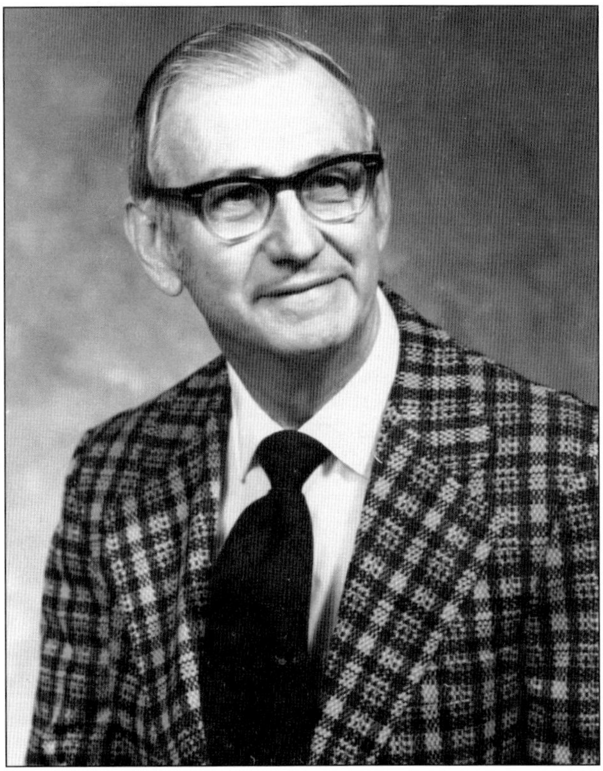

Clarence H. Watson. Watson was another minister who joined the faculty in 1953 after pastoring in Kentucky, Texas, and Alabama, and serving as associate state Sunday school secretary for the Florida Baptist Convention. For eight years, he held the title of director of off-campus education for Christian service. Watson then taught in the religion department for 25 years. He retired in 1986 and taught part-time for two more years.

Four

Making Memories
College Life

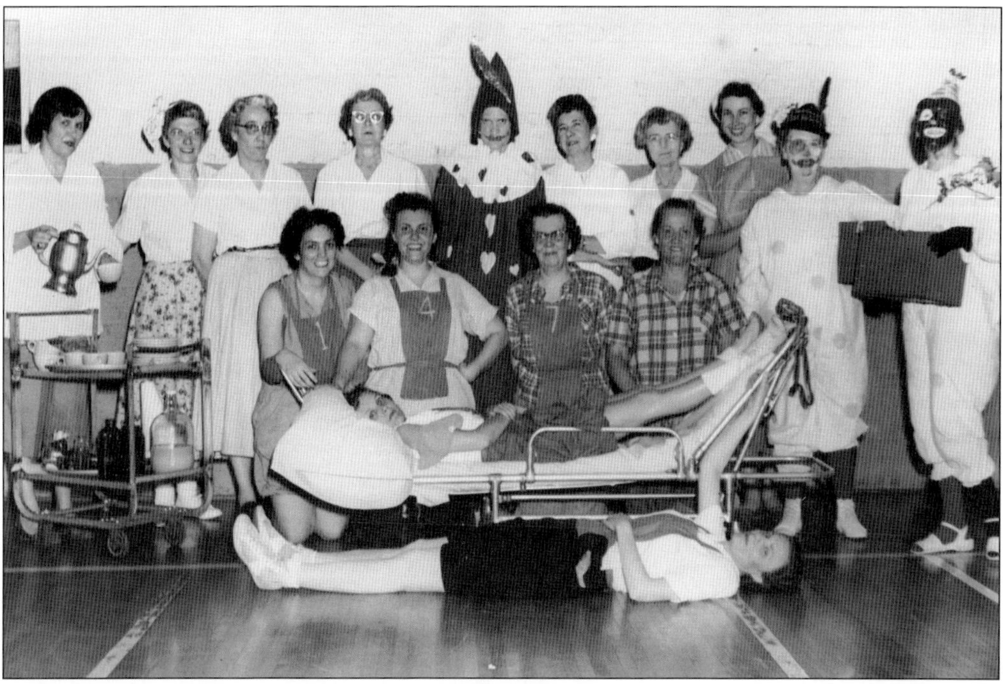

Faculty/Student Basketball Game. Showing off their lighter side, the 1960s faculty team consisted of, from left to right, (first row) Mildred Iddins, Mabel Smith, Kathleen Manley, and Mae Iddins; (second row) Ruth Miller, Pearl McHan, Nina Rubin, Janie Huggins, Bernice Carter, Agnes Hull, Aileen Johnson, and Freddie Clark. The two clowns at right and two patients in front are unidentified. (Photograph by Roy Dyer.)

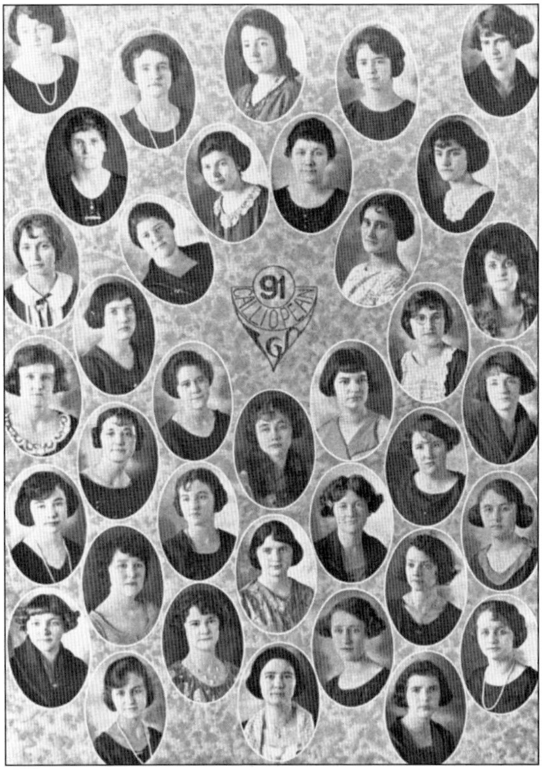

CALLIOPEAN LITERARY SOCIETY. Shortly after the two colleges were united in 1889, Prof. J.T. Henderson called all the female students together and suggested establishing literary societies. Tennessee Jenkins and Ida Lawrence were named leaders of the Hypatians and Calliopeans, respectively. They each chose girls alternately until all girls were chosen. With the completion of Sarah Swann Residence Hall, they both relocated their society halls. The Calliopeans were chartered on October 9, 1901. Their motto was "Remember Lot's Wife" and they were the sister organization to the Columbians.

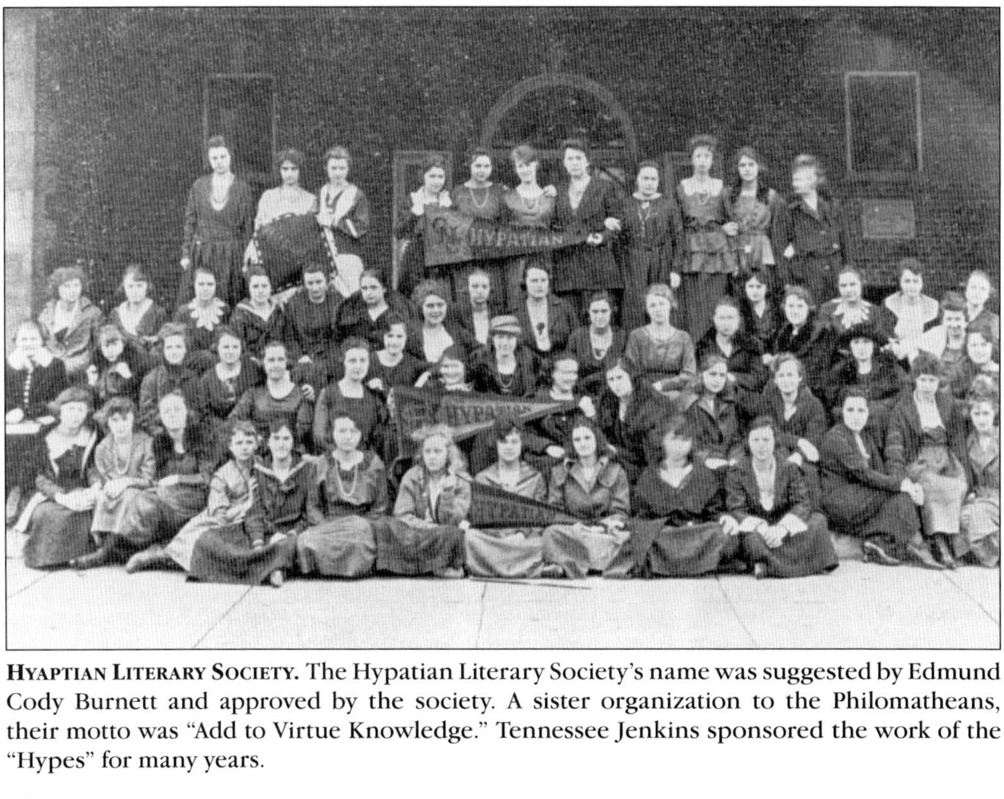

HYAPTIAN LITERARY SOCIETY. The Hypatian Literary Society's name was suggested by Edmund Cody Burnett and approved by the society. A sister organization to the Philomatheans, their motto was "Add to Virtue Knowledge." Tennessee Jenkins sponsored the work of the "Hypes" for many years.

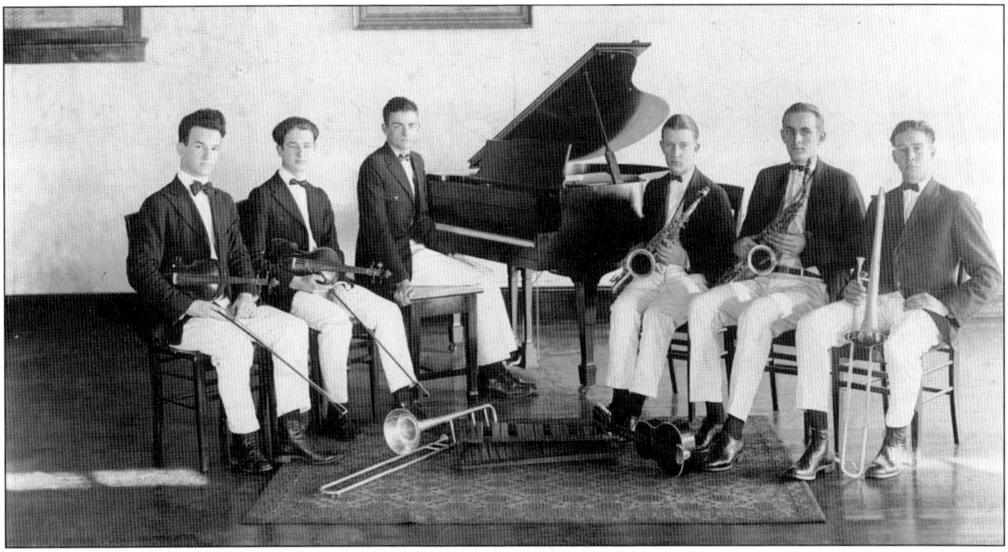

COLUMBIAN LITERARY SOCIETY. One of the two oldest student organizations, and brother society to the Calliopeans, the Columbians were founded in 1851 but not officially chartered until 1858. "Wisdom, Truth, and Eloquence" was their motto. Originally meeting each Friday night, they engaged in debates and other literary exercises "for the purpose of mutual improvement in the arts and sciences, and general literature." (Photograph by Cargilles' Studio.)

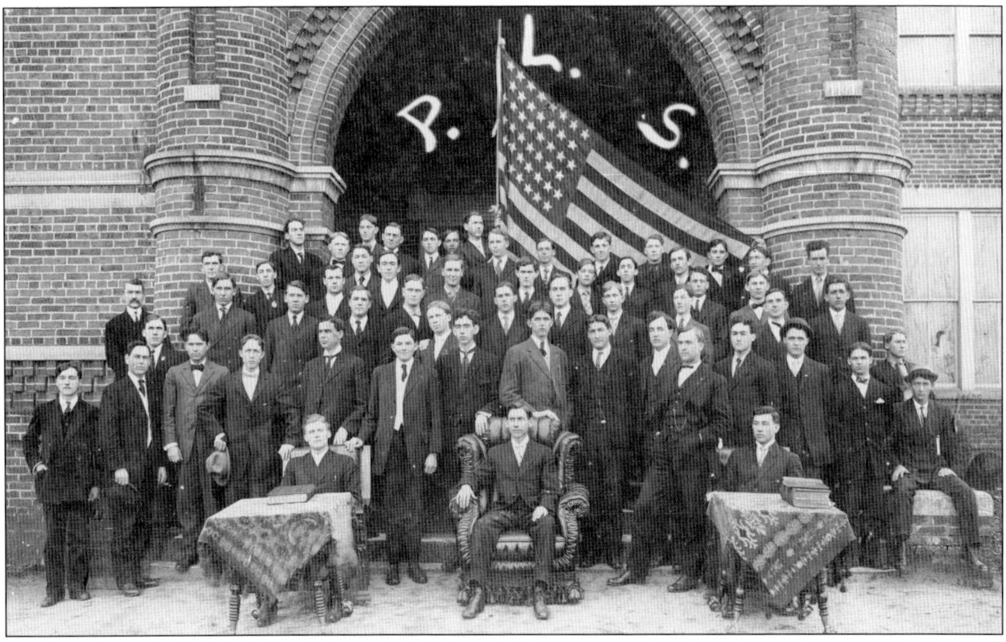

PHILOMATHEAN LITERARY SOCIETY, 1905. The second of the two oldest student organizations, the Philomathean Literary Society was formed in the fall of 1851 and was chartered during the 1857–1858 session of the Tennessee legislature. Maintaining a strong rivalry with the Columbians and close ties with the Hypatians, the Philos conducted debates and other forensic activities "for the purpose of useful knowledge and the general diffusion of the sciences." Their motto was "Love of Learning, Honor, and Power."

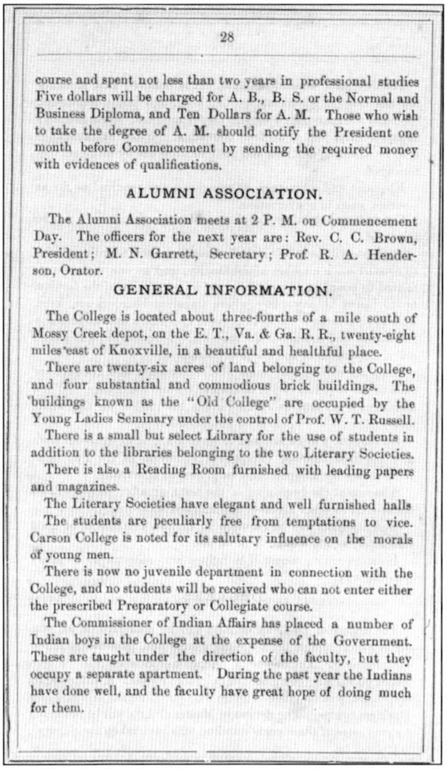

28

course and spent not less than two years in professional studies Five dollars will be charged for A. B., B. S. or the Normal and Business Diploma, and Ten Dollars for A. M. Those who wish to take the degree of A. M. should notify the President one month before Commencement by sending the required money with evidences of qualifications.

ALUMNI ASSOCIATION.

The Alumni Association meets at 2 P. M. on Commencement Day. The officers for the next year are: Rev. C. C. Brown, President; M. N. Garrett, Secretary; Prof. R. A. Henderson, Orator.

GENERAL INFORMATION.

The College is located about three-fourths of a mile south of Mossy Creek depot, on the E. T., Va. & Ga. R. R., twenty-eight miles east of Knoxville, in a beautiful and healthful place.

There are twenty-six acres of land belonging to the College, and four substantial and commodious brick buildings. The buildings known as the "Old College" are occupied by the Young Ladies Seminary under the control of Prof. W. T. Russell.

There is a small but select Library for the use of students in addition to the libraries belonging to the two Literary Societies.

There is also a Reading Room furnished with leading papers and magazines.

The Literary Societies have elegant and well furnished halls

The students are peculiarly free from temptations to vice. Carson College is noted for its salutary influence on the morals of young men.

There is now no juvenile department in connection with the College, and no students will be received who can not enter either the prescribed Preparatory or Collegiate course.

The Commissioner of Indian Affairs has placed a number of Indian boys in the College at the expense of the Government. These are taught under the direction of the faculty, but they occupy a separate apartment. During the past year the Indians have done well, and the faculty have great hope of doing much for them.

THE CHEROKEE INITIATIVE. The 1883–1884 college bulletin described a new program that the institution engaged in under Pres. S.W. Tindell. Contracting with the Office of Indian Affairs, Carson College admitted 20 Cherokee Indians, four of whom lived with the president. The enterprise was not successful, however, as the next year's catalog simply noted: "The Indian Department has been suspended."

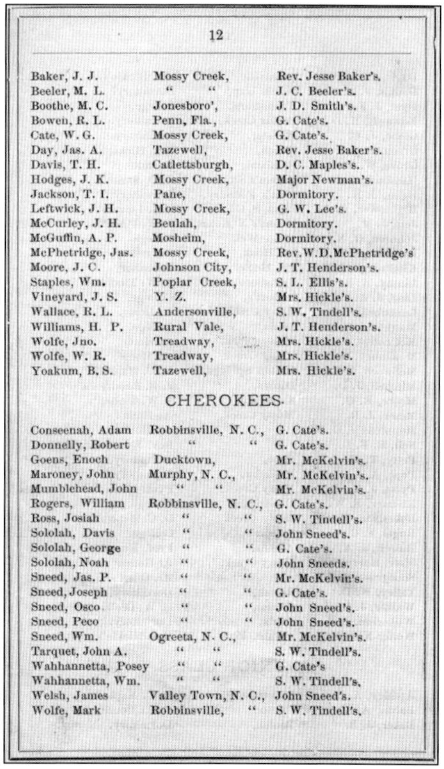

12

Baker, J. J.	Mossy Creek,	Rev. Jesse Baker's.
Beeler, M. L.	" "	J. C. Beeler's.
Boothe, M. C.	Jonesboro',	J. D. Smith's.
Bowen, R. L.	Penn, Fla.,	G. Cate's.
Cate, W. G.	Mossy Creek,	G. Cate's.
Day, Jas. A.	Tazewell,	Rev. Jesse Baker's.
Davis, T. H.	Catlettsburgh,	D. C. Maples's.
Hodges, J. K.	Mossy Creek,	Major Newman's.
Jackson, T. I.	Pane,	Dormitory.
Leftwick, J. H.	Mossy Creek,	G. W. Lee's.
McCurley, J. H.	Beulah,	Dormitory.
McGuffin, A. P.	Mosheim,	Dormitory.
McPhetridge, Jas.	Mossy Creek,	Rev.W.D.McPhetridge's
Moore, J. C.	Johnson City,	J. T. Henderson's.
Staples, Wm.	Poplar Creek,	S. L. Ellis's.
Vineyard, J. S.	Y. Z.	Mrs. Hickle's.
Wallace, R. L.	Andersonville,	S. W. Tindell's.
Williams, H. P.	Rural Vale,	J. T. Henderson's.
Wolfe, Jno.	Treadway,	Mrs. Hickle's.
Wolfe, W. R.	Treadway,	Mrs. Hickle's.
Yoakum, B. S.	Tazewell,	Mrs. Hickle's.

CHEROKEES.

Conseenah, Adam	Robbinsville, N. C.,	G. Cate's.
Donnelly, Robert	" "	G. Cate's.
Goens, Enoch	Ducktown,	Mr. McKelvin's.
Maroney, John	Murphy, N. C.,	Mr. McKelvin's.
Mumblehead, John	" "	Mr. McKelvin's.
Rogers, William	Robbinsville, N. C.,	G. Cate's.
Ross, Josiah	" "	S. W. Tindell's.
Sololah, Davis	" "	John Sneed's.
Sololah, George	" "	G. Cate's.
Sololah, Noah	" "	John Sneeds.
Sneed, Jas. P.	" "	Mr. McKelvin's.
Sneed, Joseph	" "	G. Cate's.
Sneed, Osco	" "	John Sneed's.
Sneed, Peco	" "	John Sneed's.
Sneed, Wm.	Ogreeta, N. C.,	Mr. McKelvin's.
Tarquet, John A.	" "	S. W. Tindell's.
Wahhannetta, Posey	" "	G. Cate's
Wahhannetta, Wm.	" "	S. W. Tindell's.
Welsh, James	Valley Town, N. C.,	John Sneed's.
Wolfe, Mark	Robbinsville, "	S. W. Tindell's.

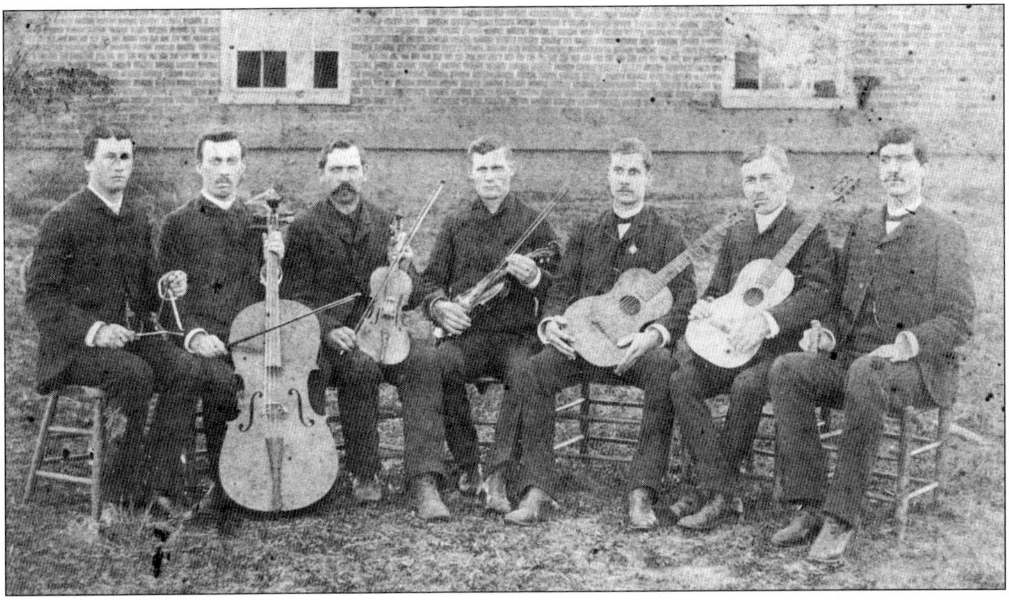

Music Class, 1887. By the early 1880s, both Carson College and Newman College offered music classes. When the colleges joined, the program continued to grow, but was classified as a special department outside of the liberal arts curriculum offering its own certificate. After the turn of the century, musical graduate, bachelor of music, and master of music degrees were offered.

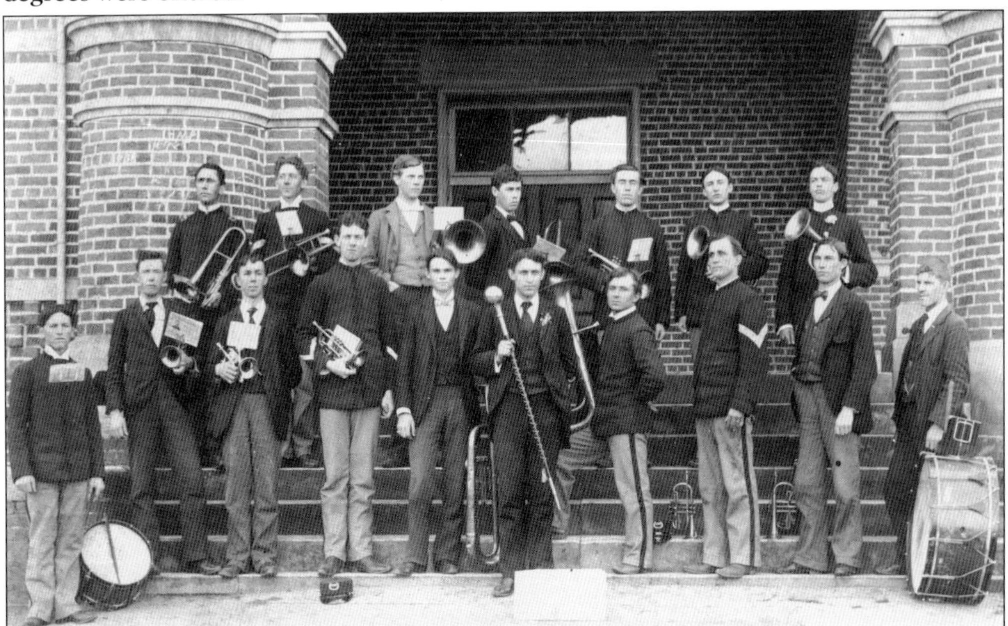

Band, 1897. The first band was organized in 1897. According to the 1896–1897 catalog, "14 young men of the institution recently organized a brass band. Under the leadership and instruction of C.L. French they have made rapid progress, and the band is now one of the chief attractions of the college. Six of the instruments are the property of the school, which makes the band permanent."

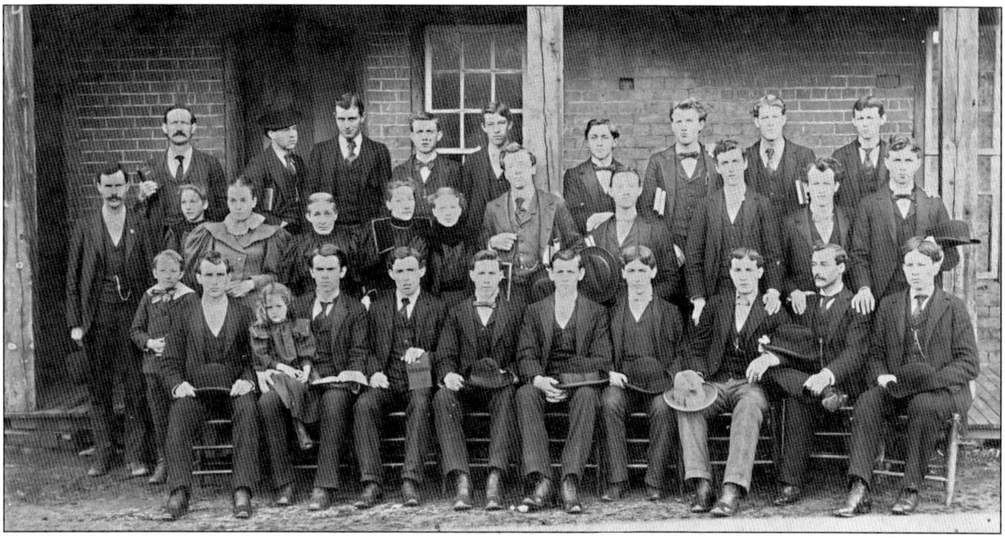

Boarders at Mrs. Hale's, 1897. Before dormitory space was provided for all students, many found rooms at Mrs. Hale's home. Another home that provided rooms for students was that of Mrs. M.E. Evans, better known as "Ma." For over 25 years, she also operated the Tea Room from her home located on the corner of Branner and South College Streets. She served breakfast and dinner to students and faculty alike and was a favorite of many of the athletes. She closed the Tea Room in 1946 due to illness. In 1953, Coach Sam B. "Frosty" Holt wrote a letter to his former players asking them to donate money to financially assist "Ma" Evans. (Courtesy of Cora Louise Carson.)

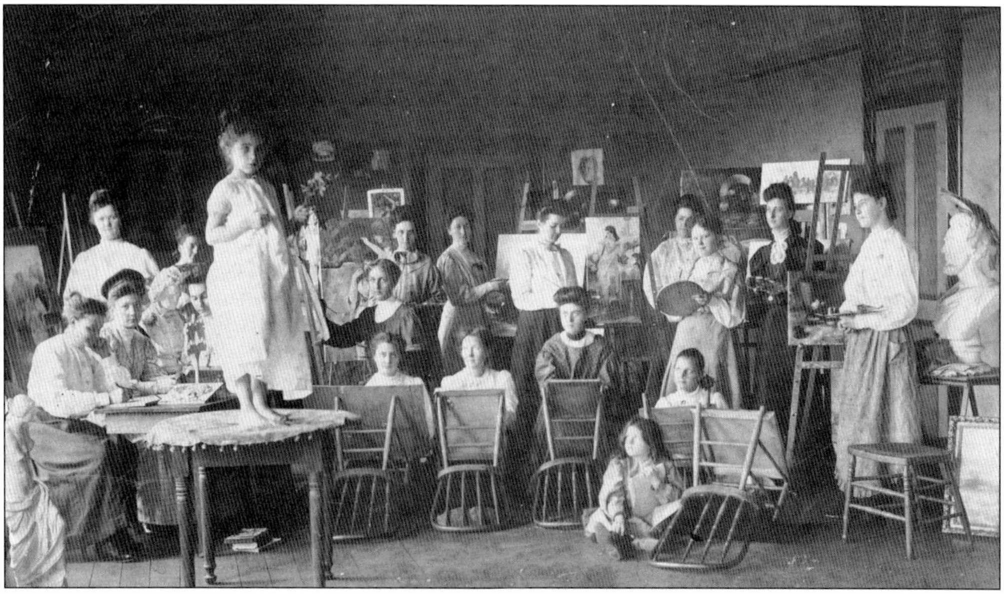

Art Class, c. 1907. Art classes were offered from at least the mid-1890s and played a significant part in the growing liberal arts curriculum. During the early 1900s, Blanche Lee Ellis, an 1887 graduate, was instrumental in heading the development of the art department. Carson-Newman holds the distinction of being the first Baptist liberal arts institution to attain national accreditation, being an institutional member of the National Association of Schools of Art and Design (NASAD) since 1992.

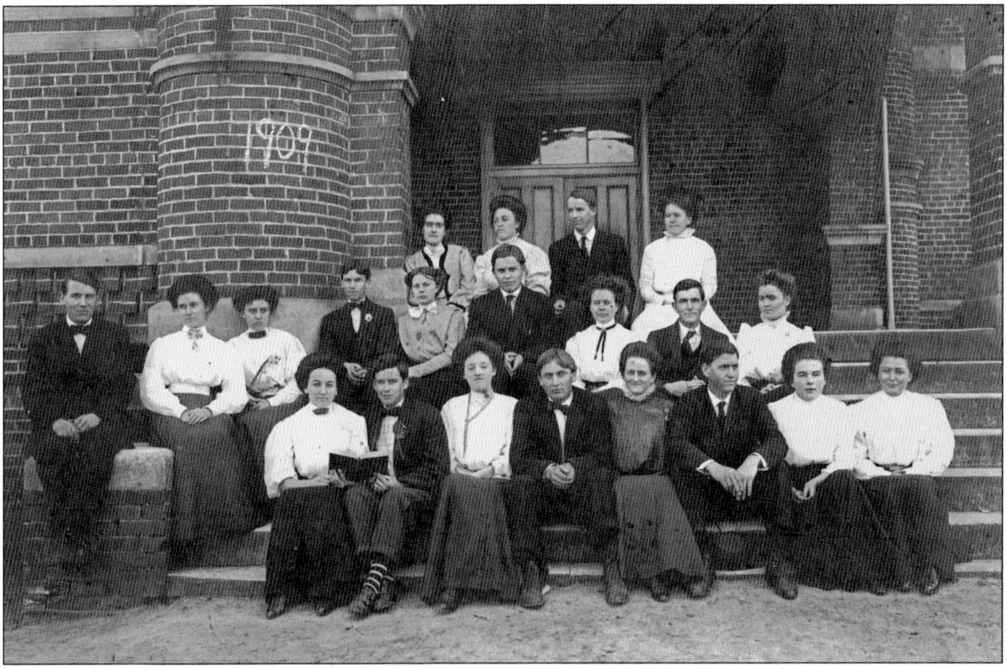

HAWKINS COUNTRY CLUB, 1909, AND STUDENT CLUB, 1905. Many unusual and creative groups have existed on campus over the years. Sitting on the stairs of the original administration building above are the members of one such group, the Hawkins Country Club. Among the members was Roy Myers (top row) who would go on to serve as treasurer from 1928 to 1956. Below, these unidentified students formed a club whose name is lost, but humor was obviously one criterion for membership.

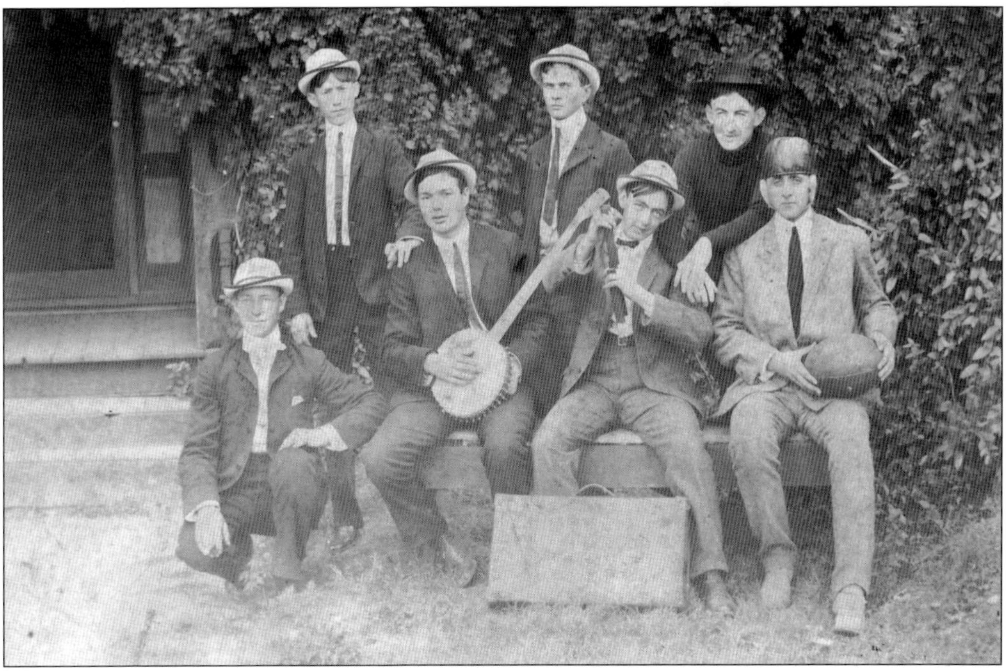

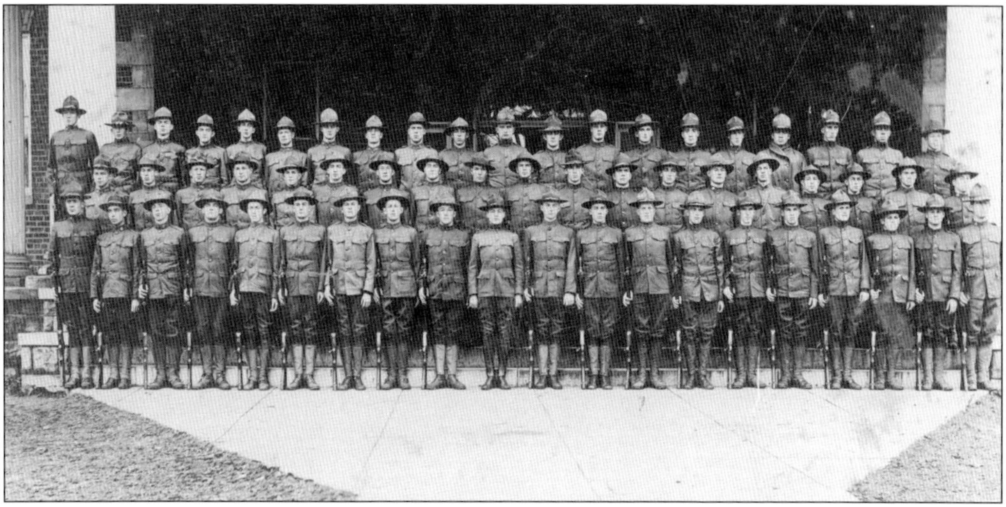

World War I, 1918. Under the leadership of President Burnett and President Gentry, Carson-Newman weathered the trying days of World War I. Enrollment dropped as students left for military service, but thanks to the implementation of a Student Army Training Corps, the college remained afloat.

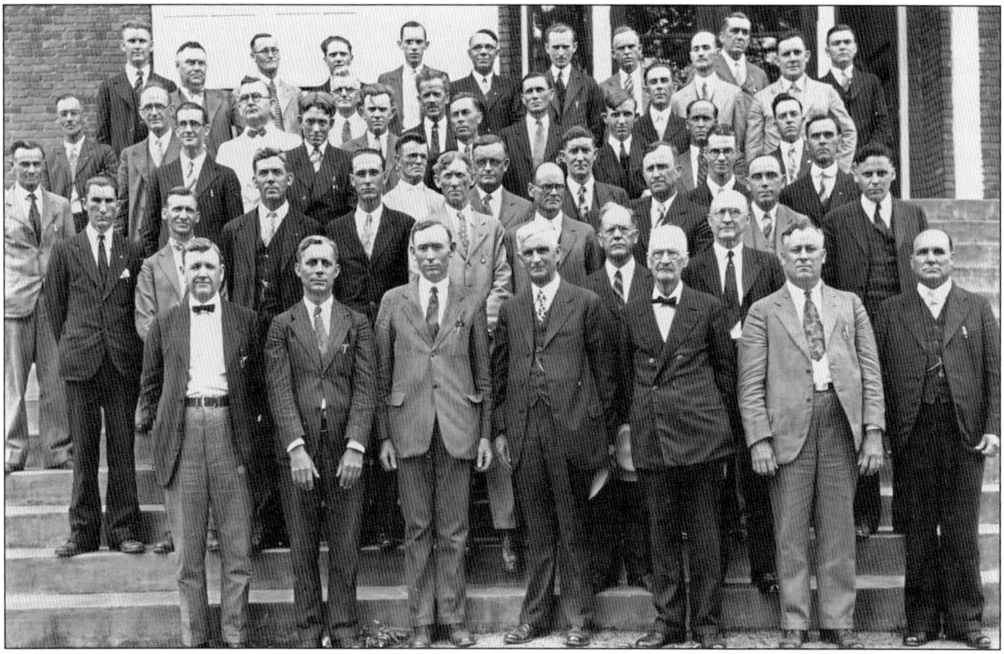

Preachers' School. The first East Tennessee Baptist Preachers' School held at Carson-Newman was a joint effort with the Tennessee Baptist Convention's Education Department. Organized by Pres. J.T. Warren and Dr. A.F. Mahan, it ran four weeks. The school became an annual affair with many pastors coming each year for one week to gain knowledge and fellowship. Schools were also held in other parts of the state. The first women's class was started in 1942 and the school was suspended in 1999. Presently, a half-day church leadership conference summit is sponsored by the Office of Church Relations each spring. In the fall, a half-day Pastors' Conference with emphasis on winter Bible study is held while a Ministering to Ministers Retreat is offered in January and July of each year.

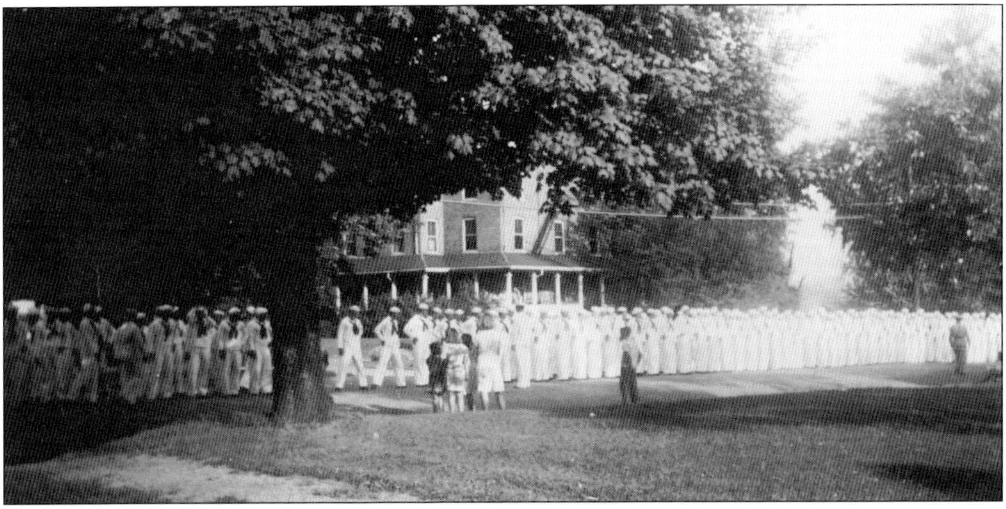

Navy V-12 Program and Mark of Commendation. During World War II, the school contracted with the Navy for a pre-officer training Navy V-12 unit (above). The program lasted from July 1, 1943, until June 30, 1945. During this period, several hundred Navy men trained while living in Sarah Swann Residence Hall and Blanc-Davis Hall. They published a biweekly newsletter called the *Periscope* and had their own orchestra and choir. They also participated in Carson-Newman's intramurals and intercollegiate athletics. A three-semester academic year was set up, which reverted back to a two-semester program with the termination of the program. President Warren and Jack Dyer, signalman on the destroyer-tender *Piedmont* and Warren's son-in-law, posed with the mark of commendation plaque issued by the Navy for the institution's effective cooperation (below). (Above, courtesy of Barbara Dyer; below, courtesy of Jack Dyer.)

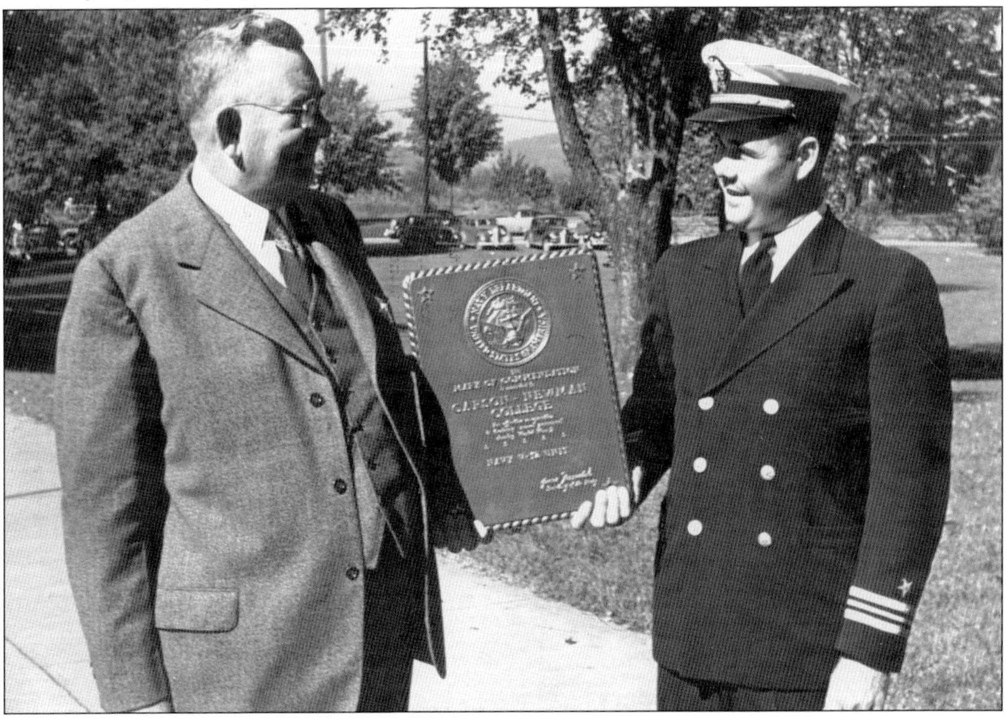

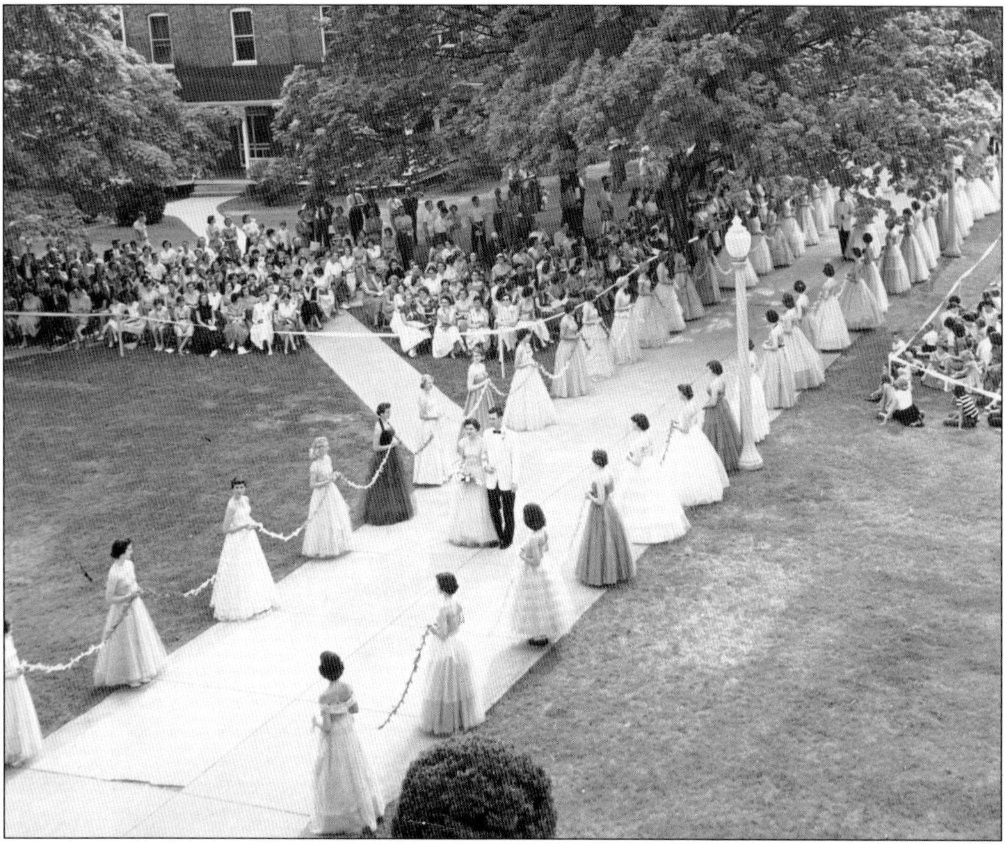

MAY DAY, 1943, AND THE MAYPOLE. For many years, the May Day celebration was an annual event at Carson-Newman, seen in the above photograph. Consisting of pageants, dramatic presentations, skits, the presentation of the "Royal Court," musical performances, tributes, and of course, the May Pole winding (below), this annual festival provided an unforgettable day for students and staff alike.

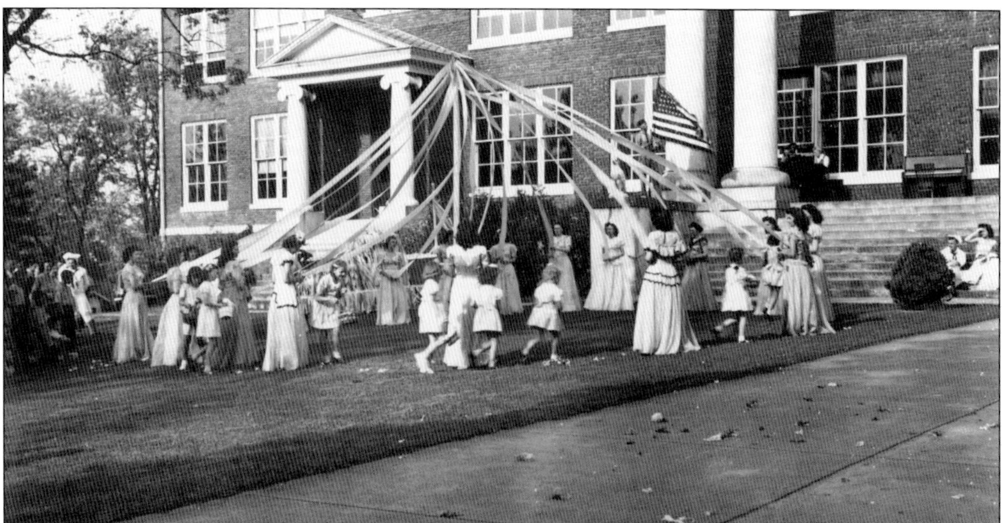

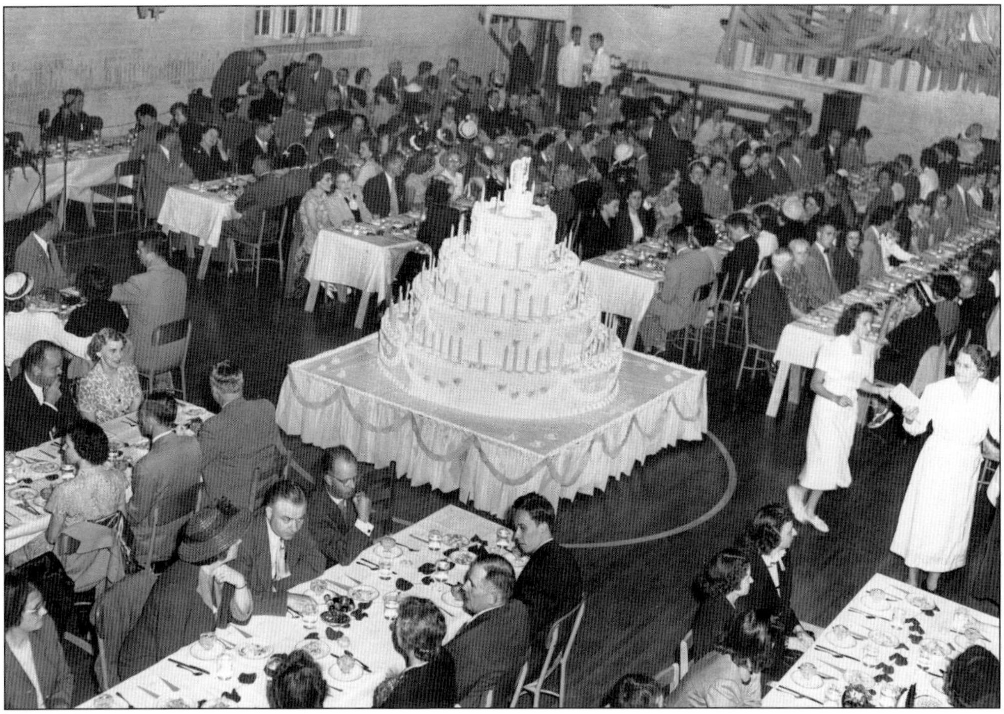

Centennial Celebration. Receptions, recitals, readings, and a reenactment of the wedding of Carson and Newman Colleges were all the start of a busy week celebrating the school's 100th anniversary May 21–25, 1951. A centennial pageant depicting the glorious history of the school was presented to a crowd of thousands. The grand finale featured R.R. Bryan standing in a picture frame passing the torch to current president Harley Fite. The centennial cake was the central piece in the decoration scheme of Butler-Blanc Gymnasium during the centennial alumni dinner. The cake was six feet in diameter and required 200 pounds of icing to cover it. Galbraith Bakery of Morristown decorated it.

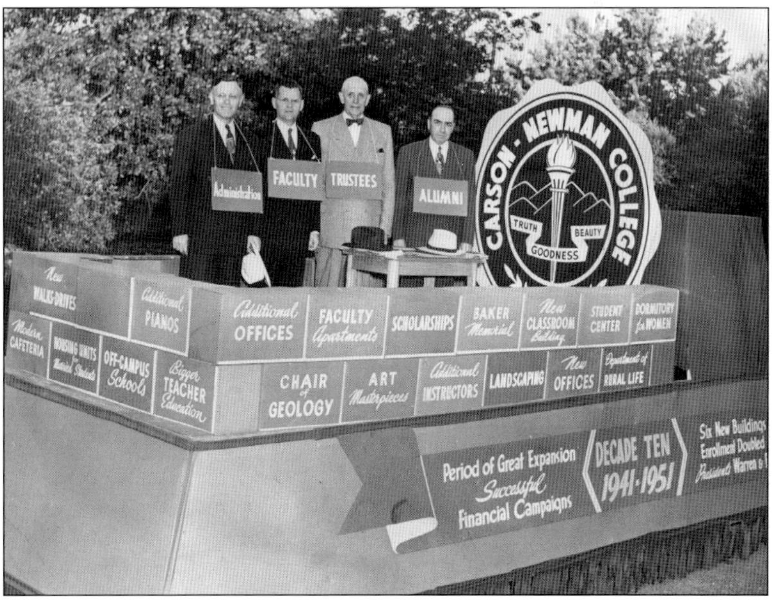

Centennial Floats. A parade featuring 10 floats depicting the 10 decades of Carson-Newman followed the pageant. The floats creatively captured the school's religious, academic, social, and economic history. Prof. Alexander Chavis and Dr. Acuff served as cochairmen of the float committees.

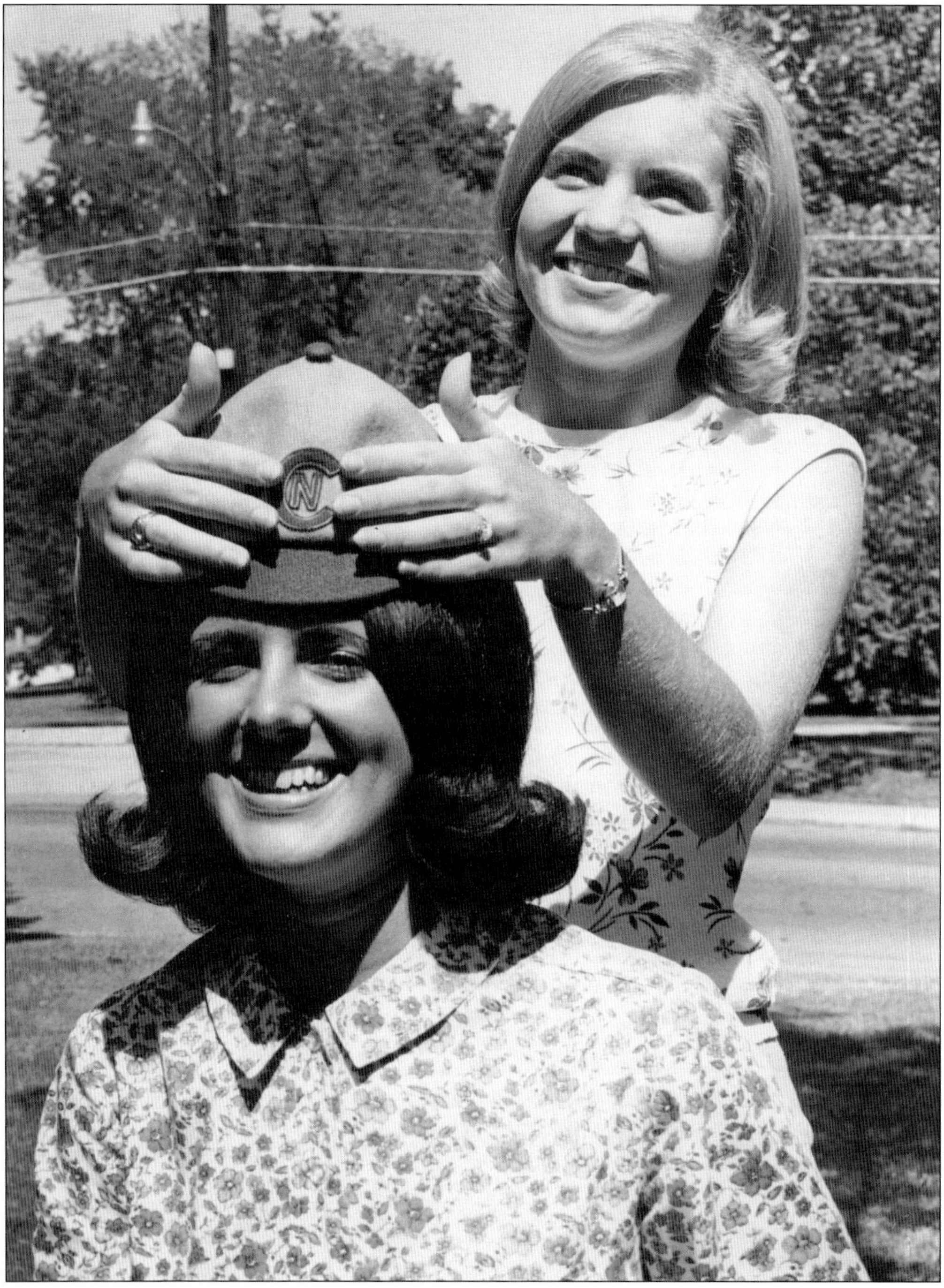

Freshmen Beanies. In 1947, a committee of upperclassmen was formed to plan a program especially for new freshmen. The week before homecoming, also known as Rat Week, was filled with recreational activities designed to acquaint new students with the spirit and tradition of the college. During their first semester, freshmen were required to wear caps (beanies) on campus every day except Sunday. In the late 1970s, the beanies were discontinued and more activities to encourage campus involvement were initiated.

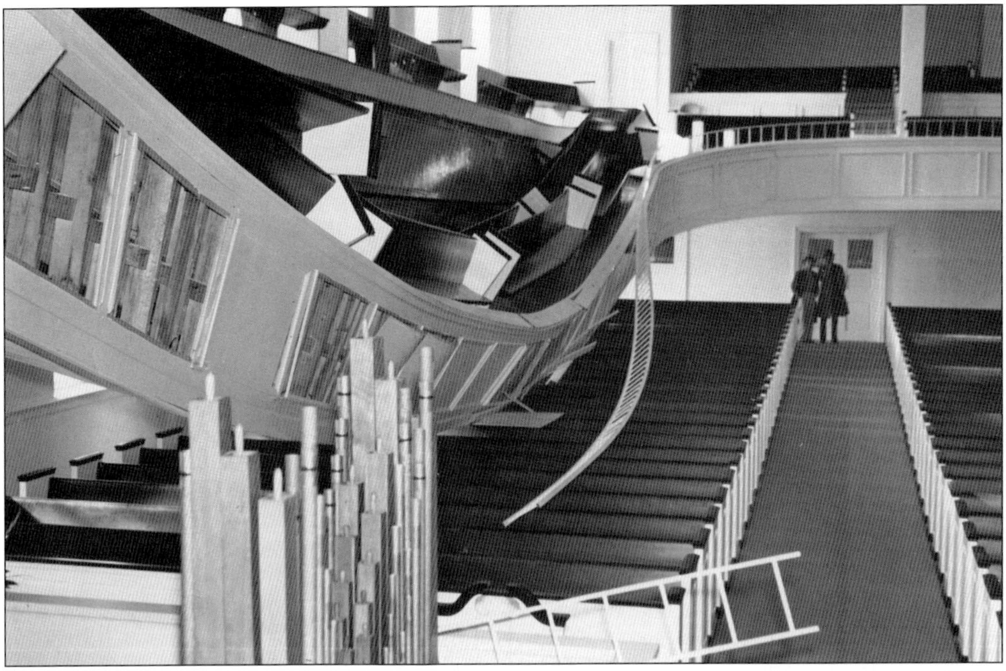

First Baptist Church Balcony Collapse. On December 17, 1962, during a chapel performance of the "Hallelujah Chorus" from Handel's *Messiah*, the south balcony of First Baptist Church in Jefferson City sagged and fell to the pews below. Approximately 150 students were in the section when a weld in one of the supporting beams broke and 43 students sought treatment for shock and a variety of non-serious injuries. The new church building had been completed only three months before. (Photograph by Chet Brogan.)

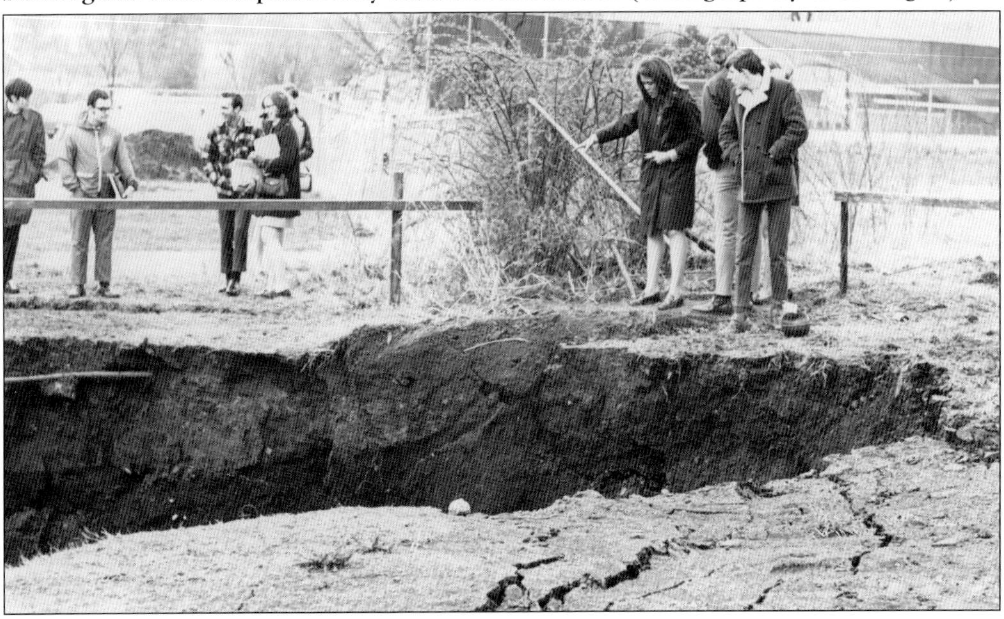

Sinkhole. Sinkholes have been a common occurrence in this area, often associated with the extensive mining done over the years. In March 1980, a large sinkhole fell in near the Carson-Newman baseball field. No one was injured and the fill-in began right away.

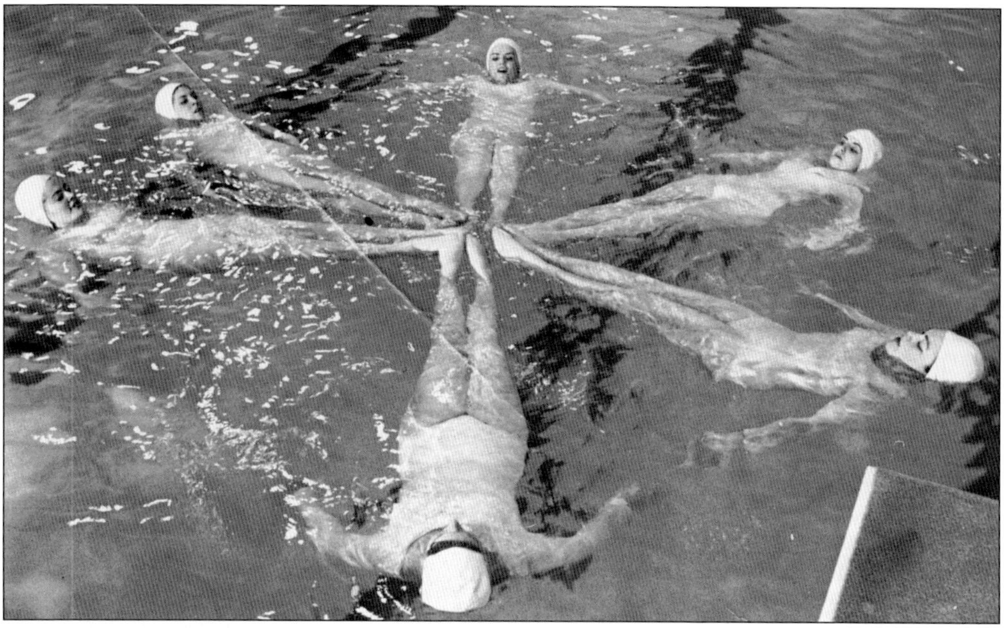

Synchronized Swimming and Aqua Fantasy, 1960s. Each year during the 1950s and early 1960s, Frances Roden and her synchronized swim class (above) worked all semester to put on a water show for the campus and town. Each show had a different theme, such as Aqua Fantasy or Calendar of the Year. Shown below is Aqua Fantasy. (Above, courtesy of Mildred L. Iddins Special Collections' College Archives; below, photograph by Merlyn Hyers.)

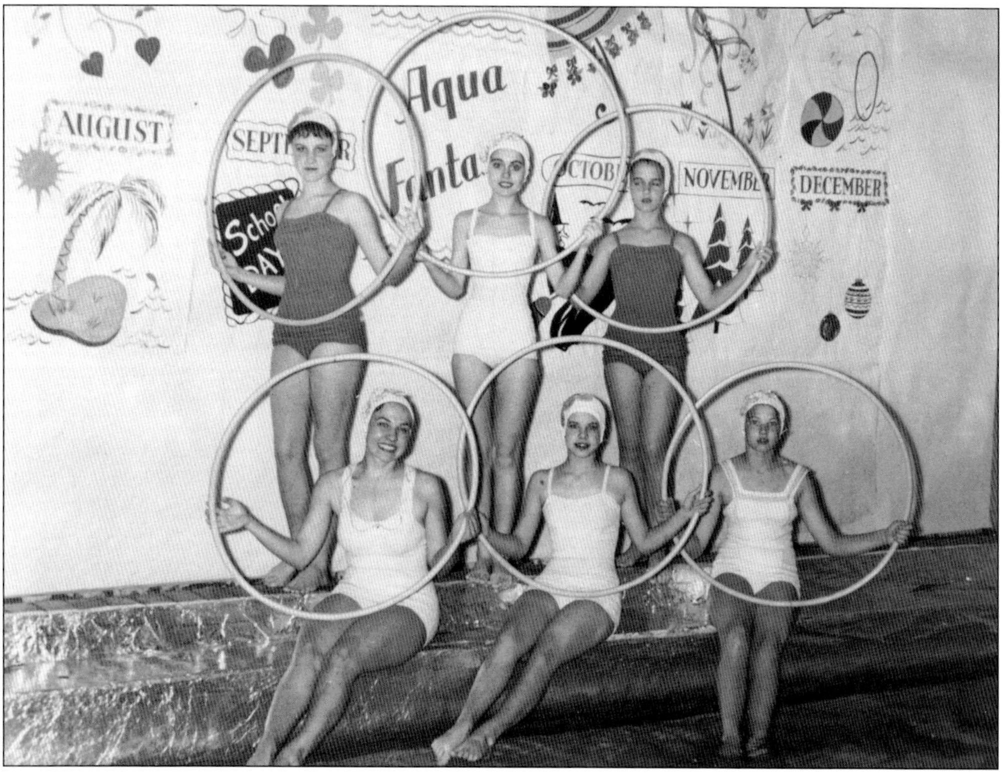

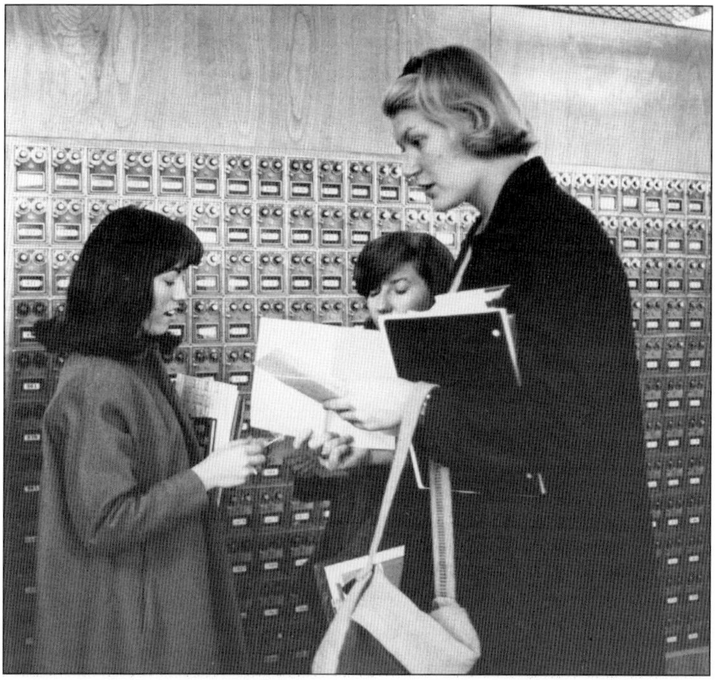

Baker Building Post Office. From 1951 until 1993, when the new Maddox Student Activities Building was built, the campus post office was located in the Baker Building. Also housed there was the bookstore and canteen, making Baker a central location for social activities.

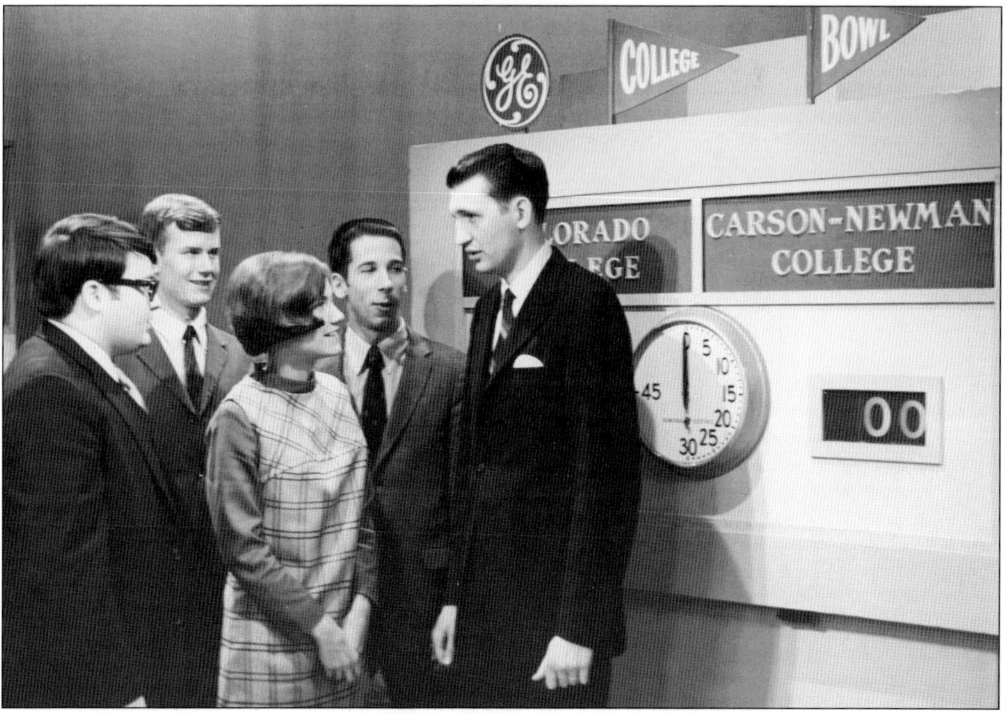

College Bowl. During the 1968–1969 season, Ron Meisburg, Valecia Ingle, David Bodenhamer, Malcolm Cauthen, and alternate Linda Livesay represented Carson-Newman at the nationally televised General Electric College Bowl. Coached by Danny Champion, the team traveled to New York where they were unfortunately defeated by Colorado College by the score of 205 to 135. (Photograph by Conrad Waldinger.)

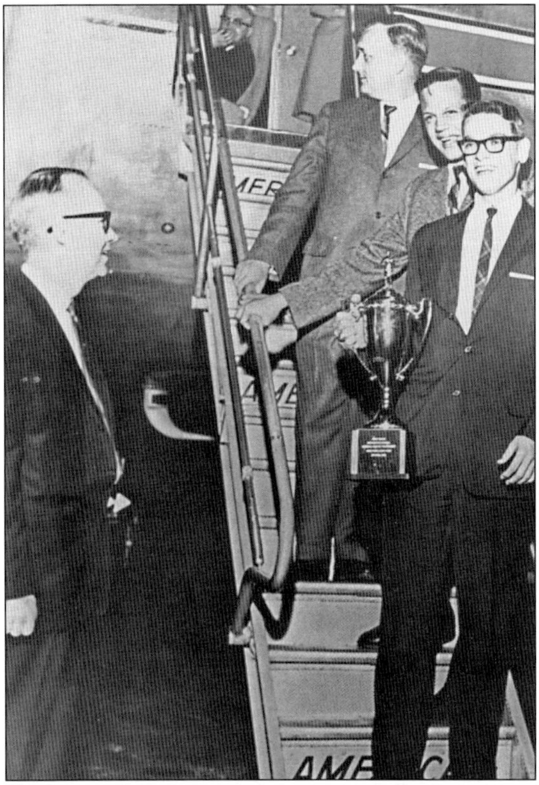

National Debate Tournament Champions, 1965. The 1964–1965 debate team coached by Forrest Conklin won the National Debate Tournament at West Point, New York, defeating the University of Miami. Seniors Barnett Pierce and John Wittig comprised the winning team.

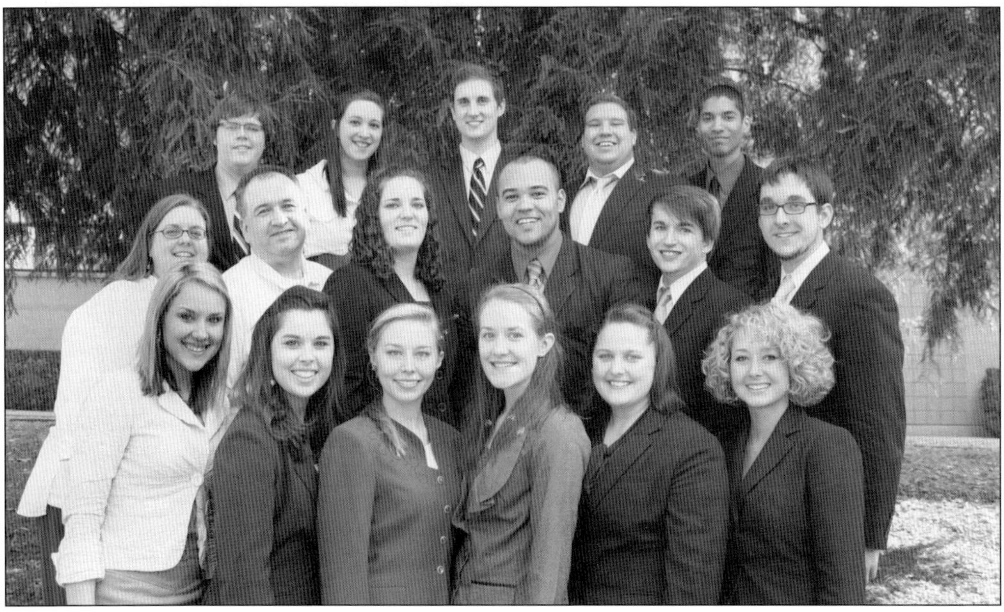

Forensic Team, 2011. In the spring of 2011, the Carson-Newman forensics team successfully defended its individual events title at the National Christian College Forensics Invitational championship held at Azusa Pacific University outside of Los Angeles. This victory marked the third consecutive win at this national tournament. The current teams coached by Chip Hall have won five consecutive state titles through 2011. (Courtesy of Chip Hall.)

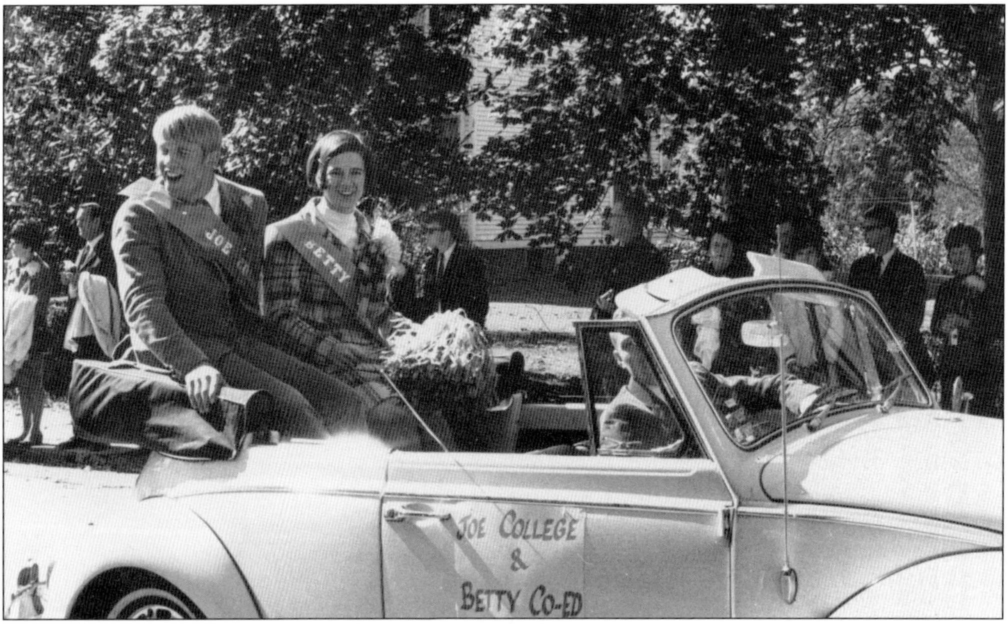

Joe College and Betty Co-Ed and Homecoming Parade. Homecoming has always been one of the most popular events in the college's history. Parades, floats, the homecoming court, Joe College and Betty Coed (above), football, and class reunions are all a part of homecoming activities designed to make alumni feel welcome as they renew old acquaintances, meet former professors, and see improvements in the campus. Seen below is the homecoming parade. (Above, courtesy of Mildred L. Iddins Special Collections' College Archives; below, photograph by Charles Key.)

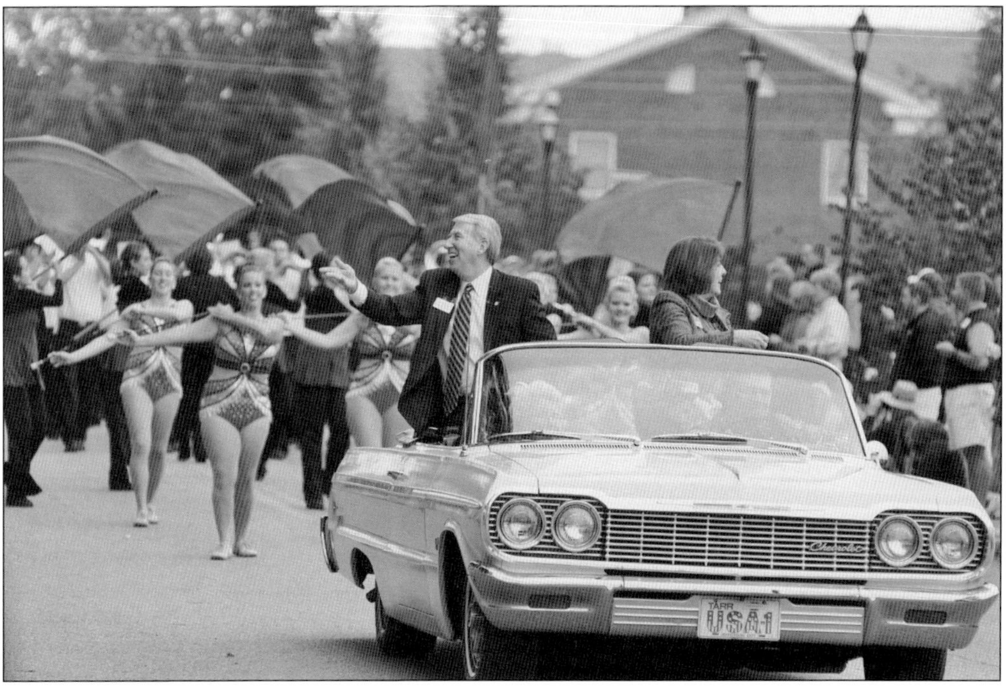

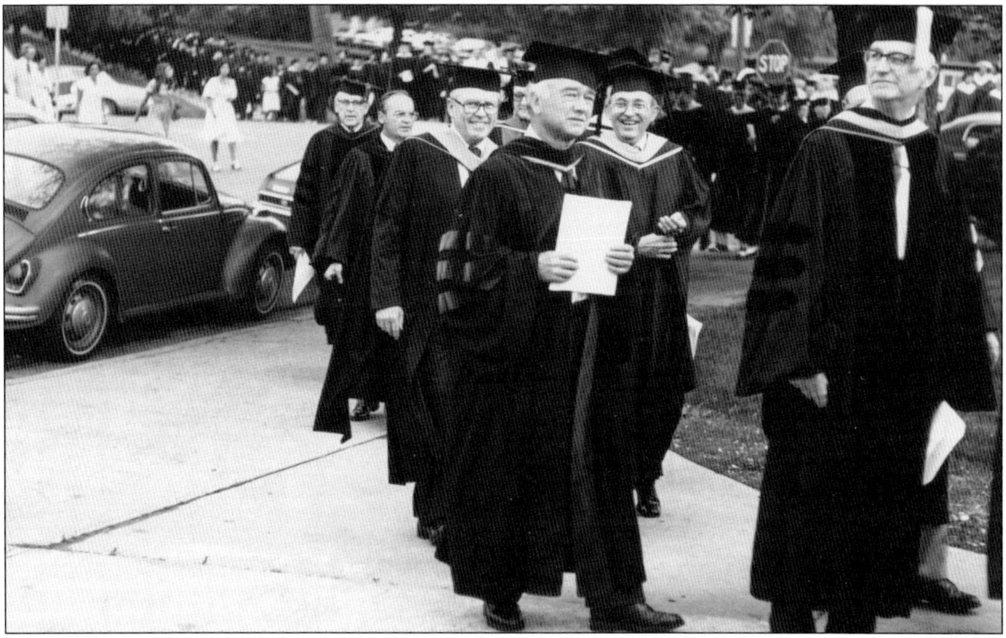

Faculty Processional and Commencement. The spring of 2012 witnessed the 158th commencement ceremony. Held at Burke-Tarr Stadium, commencement is one of the highlights of the academic year. Traditionally, the recipient of the annual Distinguished Faculty Award leads the faculty procession carrying the ceremonial mace, a symbol of the continuing search for excellence. The faculty processional can be seen above and the commencement is seen below. (Above, courtesy of Mildred L. Iddins Special Collections' College Archives; below, photograph by Charles Key.)

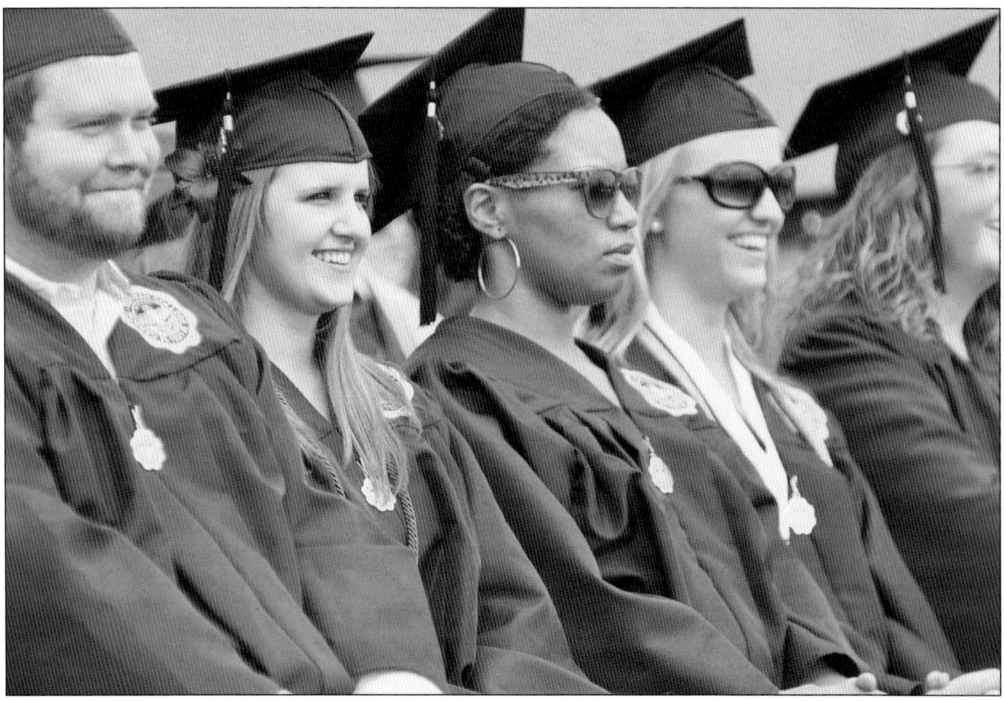

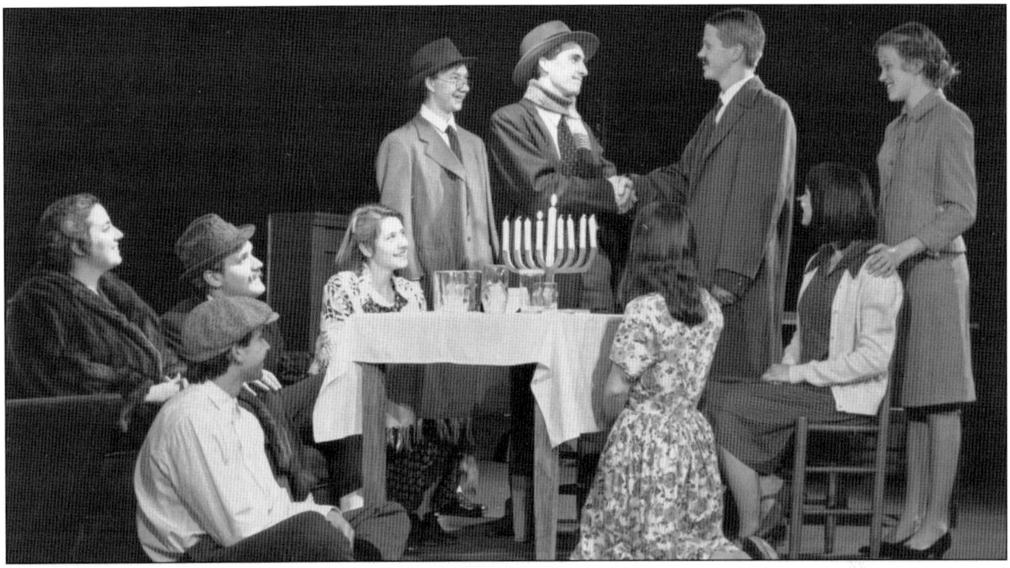

DRAMA. Led by such greats as W. Powell Hale, Prof. Harvey Hatcher, and Dr. John Lee Welton, the drama department at Carson-Newman has thrived for over 100 years. Such plays as *A Midsummer Night's Dream*, *The Glass Menagerie*, *The Diary of Anne Frank* (above), *The Miracle Worker*, and countless others have given students the opportunity to learn the workings of theatre. In 1974, when Henderson burned and with it Gentry Auditorium, "Papa" Welton and his students, who had already begun rehearsals for *The Remarkable Mr. Pennypacker*, scurried around and found a place to hold the play, naming it Phoenix Theatre. (Courtesy of John Lee Welton.)

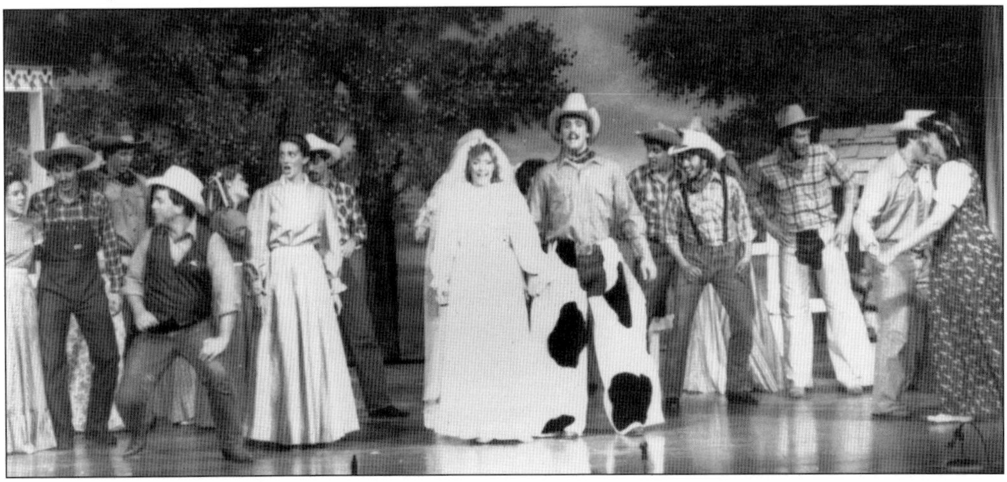

LYRIC THEATRE, *OKLAHOMA*. Organized in 1964, Lyric Theatre is a collaborative production between the theatre program and school of music. An integral part of homecoming, the production is auditioned the first week of school, sets are built and painted, songs are learned, and costumes are gathered in preparation for four performances. Shows are chosen based on educational and artistic merit and consistency in fulfilling the school's mission. Recent productions include *The Secret Garden*, *West Side Story*, *Into the Woods*, *Thoroughly Modern Millie*, *She Loves Me*, and *Fiddler on the Roof*. Students work in all areas for a specific production, receiving hands-on training as actors, technicians, members of the artistic staff, running crew, and management and receive credit in art, music, or theatre.

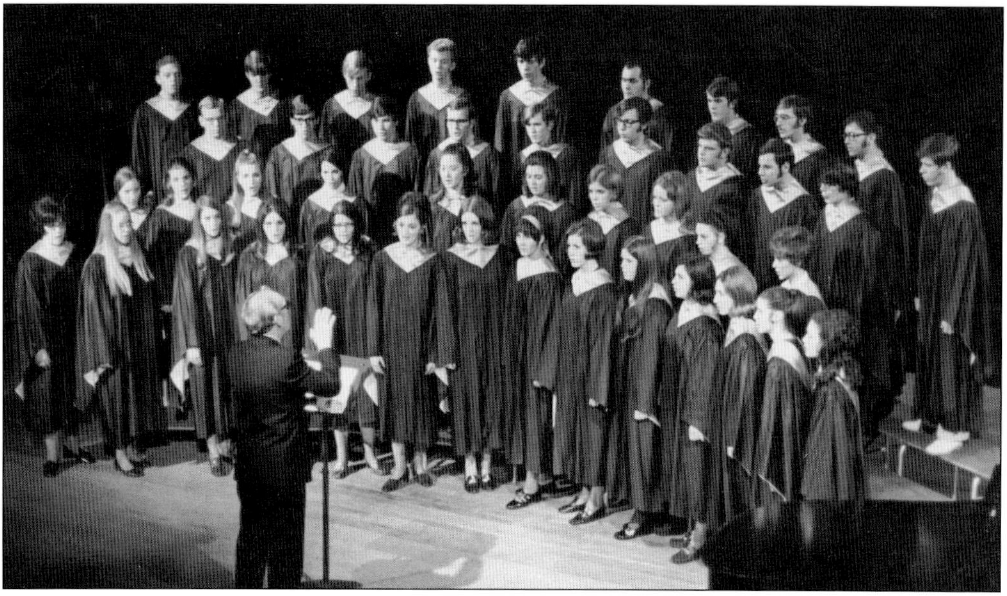

A Cappella Choir, 1970–1971. A Cappella Choir was formed in 1932 under the direction of Luther Carter. The group was originally called the Glee Club. Under the direction of Prof. Charles "Fessor" Jones, 650 concerts were held in Baptist churches, 40 programs in high schools, 2 appearances at the invitation of the American Choral Director's Association, 2 appearances at the Southern Baptist Convention, 10 at the Tennessee Baptist Convention, and 10 appearances with the Knoxville Symphony Orchestra. *The Lord Bless You and Keep You* has been the choir's benediction since 1939. (Courtesy of Eric Thorson.)

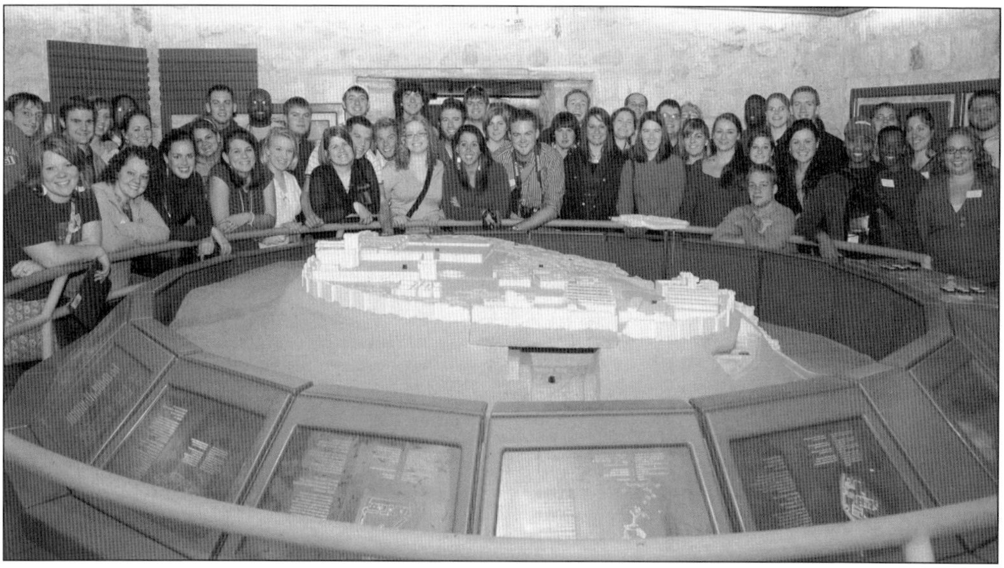

Holy Land Tour. Carson-Newman's A Cappella Choir made a goodwill concert trip to the Holy Land in December 2007. The 12-day Prepare the Way tour included performances in Amman, Jordan, as well as Nazareth and Jerusalem. The highlight of the tour was a concert with the Edward Said Palestinian Youth Orchestra in Bethlehem's Manger Square on Christmas Eve. Members of the choir are shown with a three dimensional model of the ancient fortress at Tel Megiddo (Armageddon). (Photograph by Mark Brown.)

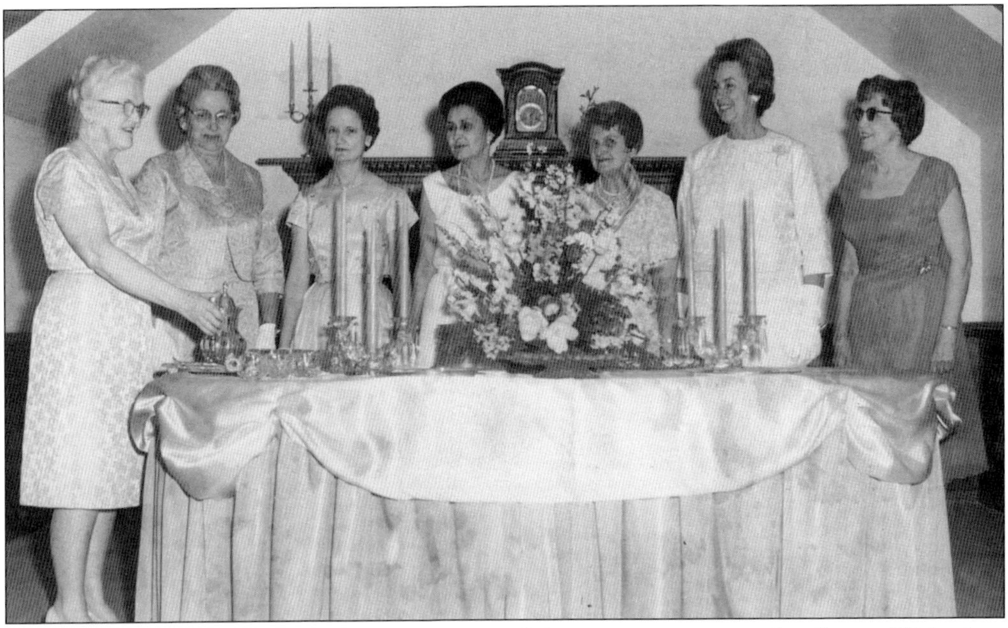

FACULTY WOMEN'S CLUB. In 1920, the women of the Carson-Newman family established an organization to improve communication and provide greater opportunities to get to know one another. Officers for 1966 were Ersa Davis, Esther Fite, Henrietta Jenkins, Lois Sloan, Beatrice Rives, Freddie Clark, and Charmye Copeland. Each spring, the group invited ladies of the community to Sarah Swann Residence Hall for tea. The last tea was held in 1978.

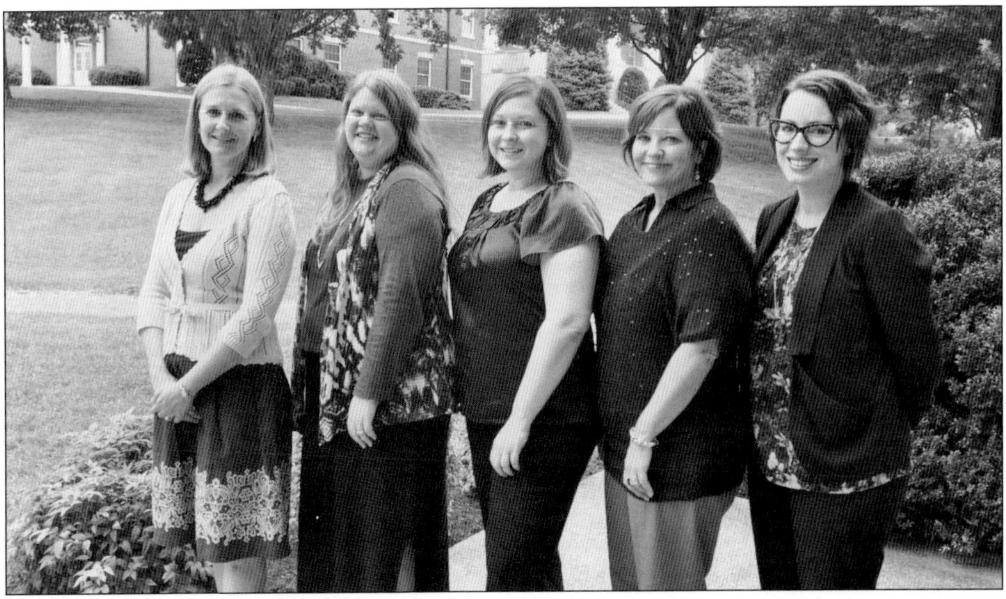

FACULTY WOMEN'S CLUB OFFICERS, 2011. The Faculty Women's Club continues today as a social and service organization. Scholarships are awarded each year to female students in honor of former Carson-Newman first lady Esther Fite. The Faculty Women's Club of 2011–2012 officers are, from left to right, Christine Jones (president), Amy Reed (vice president), Kelli Williams (historian), Tanya Ramsey (secretary), and April Dye (publicity). Not pictured is Carolyn Hacker, treasurer. (Photograph by Mark Brown.)

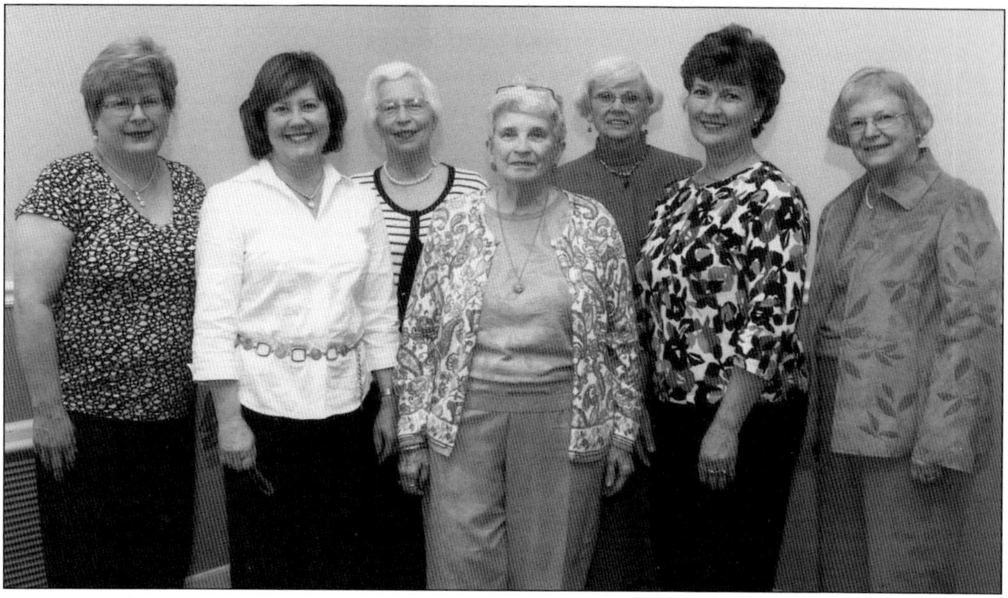

Les Amies. Les Amies was organized in 1979 with the purpose of acquainting members with the school's faculty and students. Women of the surrounding area are invited to join in order to strengthen interest in the institution and to spread information about its work and needs. A Les Amies scholarship fund was also established. The officers of 2010 are, from left to right, Elizabeth Hollingsworth, Dr. Kina Mallard, Kathy Dobyns, Nancy Love, Mary Darby, Diane Grantham, and Beverly McClellan. (Courtesy of the *Standard-Banner.*)

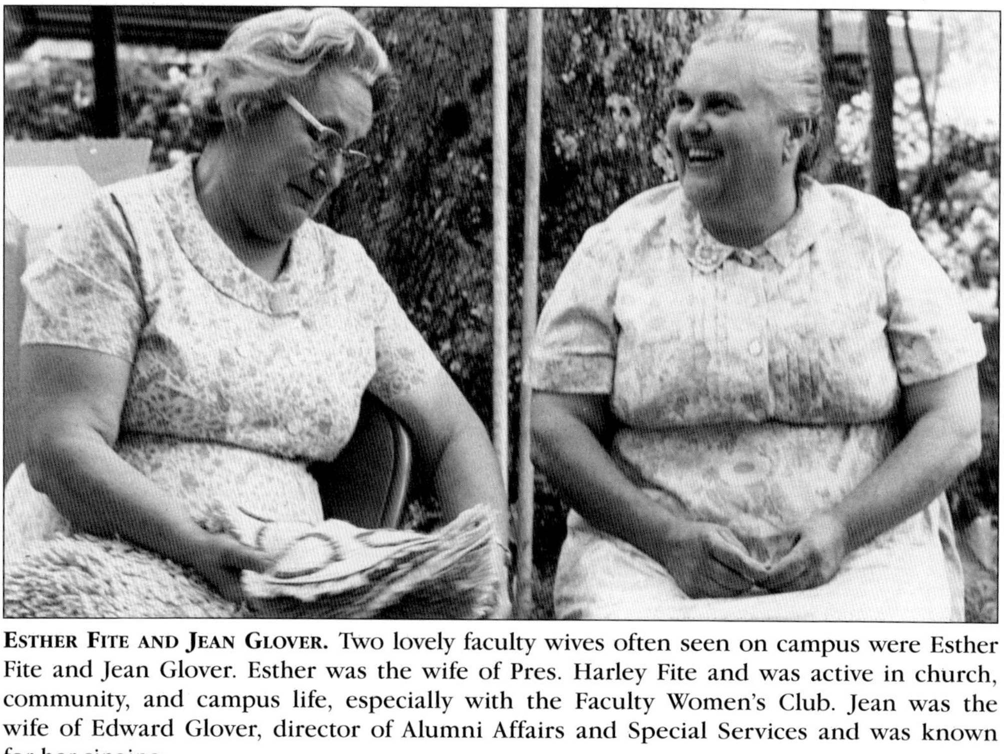

Esther Fite and Jean Glover. Two lovely faculty wives often seen on campus were Esther Fite and Jean Glover. Esther was the wife of Pres. Harley Fite and was active in church, community, and campus life, especially with the Faculty Women's Club. Jean was the wife of Edward Glover, director of Alumni Affairs and Special Services and was known for her singing.

Five

THE FORGE OF COMPETITION
ATHLETICS

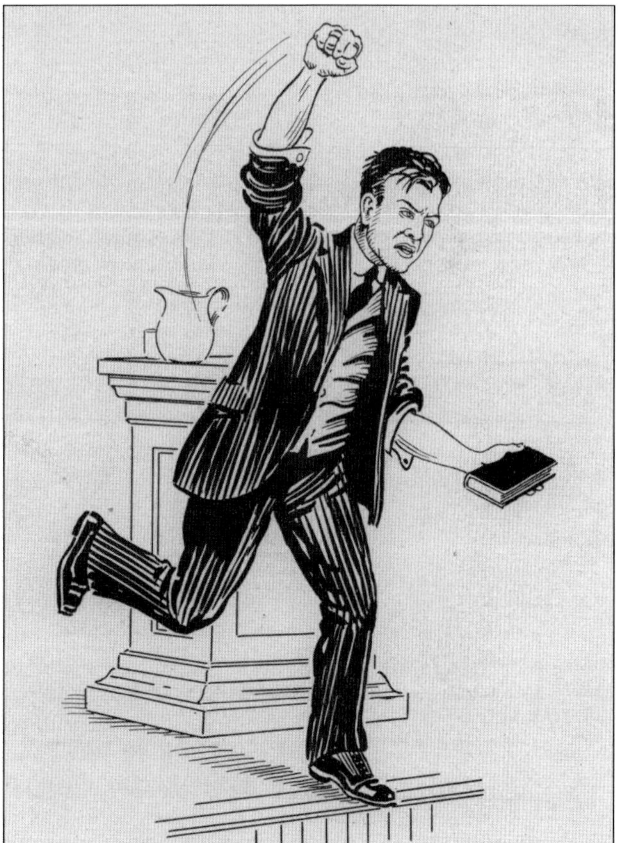

THE FIGHTING PARSON. In 1921, Carson-Newman's male sports teams took on the name the Fighting Parsons. In 1931, longtime history professor Tennessee Jenkins offered a $10 gold piece in a contest to rename the teams. The winning entry was the Fighting Eagles, later abbreviated to the Eagles.

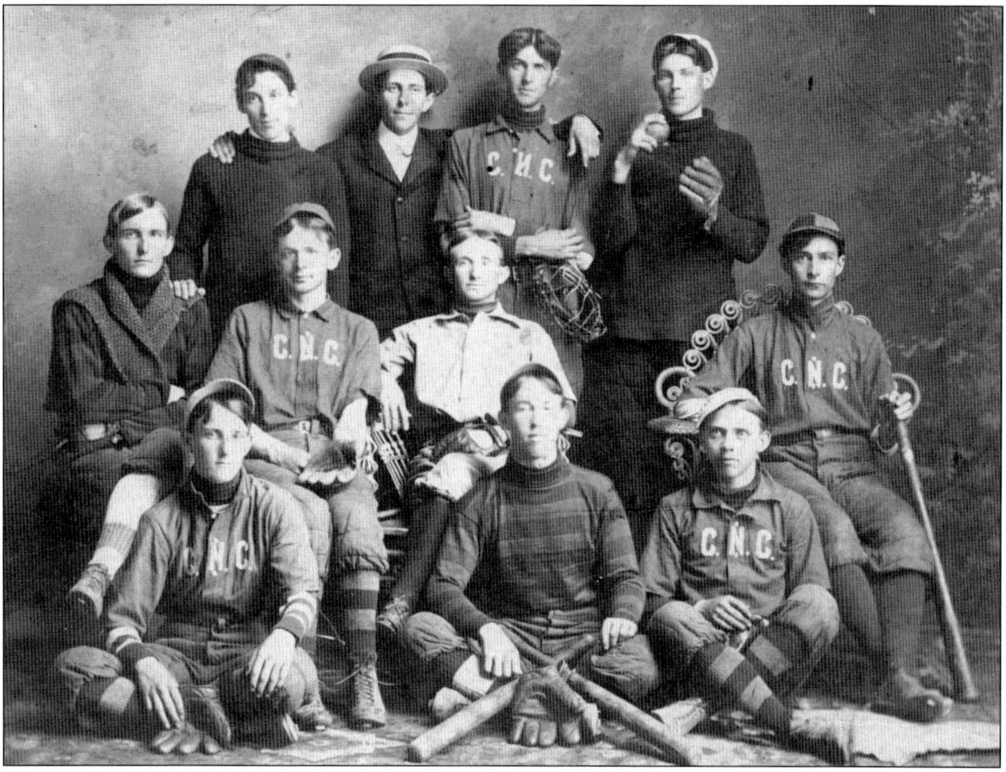

Baseball, 1905. The school's first intercollegiate athletic event took place with Carson and Newman defeating the University of Tennessee 4–3 in a baseball game in 1895. Ten years later, the catalog stated that, "during the last session much interest was taken by students and faculty in the manly exercises" while a "committee of the faculty will supervise the athletics, looking after the arrangement of games with outside teams and the like. None but bona fide students, actually studying in our college will play on our teams." (Photograph by S.A. Boy.)

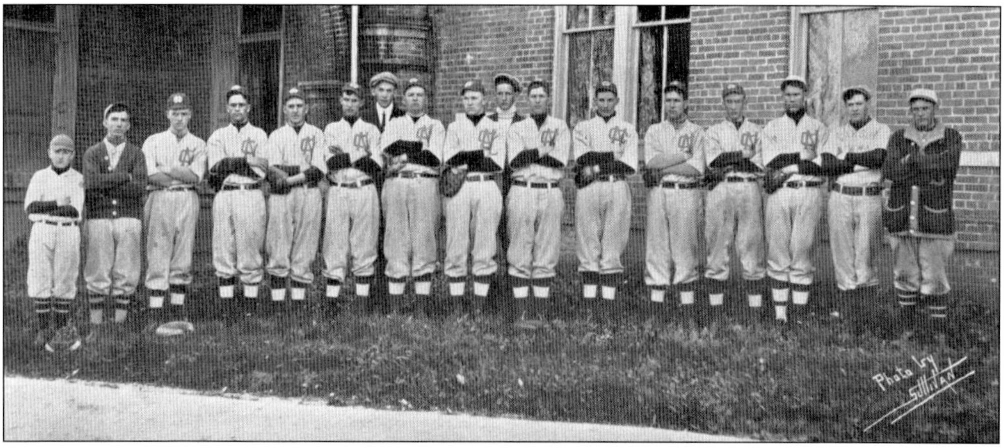

Baseball, 1913. In 1912, Carson-Newman joined the newly formed East Tennessee Athletic Association along with five other schools. Under the leadership of Prof. W.L. Gentry, the association oversaw football, baseball, basketball, and track competitions, including student eligibility. Schools competed for a championship pennant in each sport.

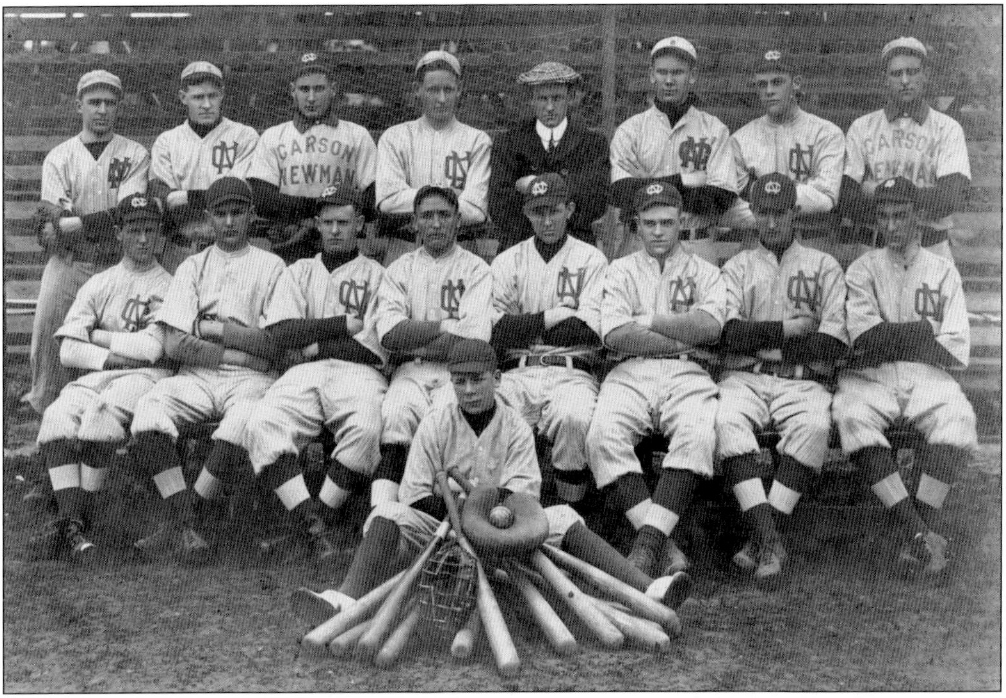

Baseball, 1914. Although records are incomplete, under the leadership of manager Bert W. Wills, the baseball squad put together a 7–1–1 record through the first nine games of the season. Opponents included Washington College, Cumberland University, Lincoln Memorial University, and Tusculum College. Junior John Kilpatrick was team captain and later went on to serve as director of athletics for Carson-Newman.

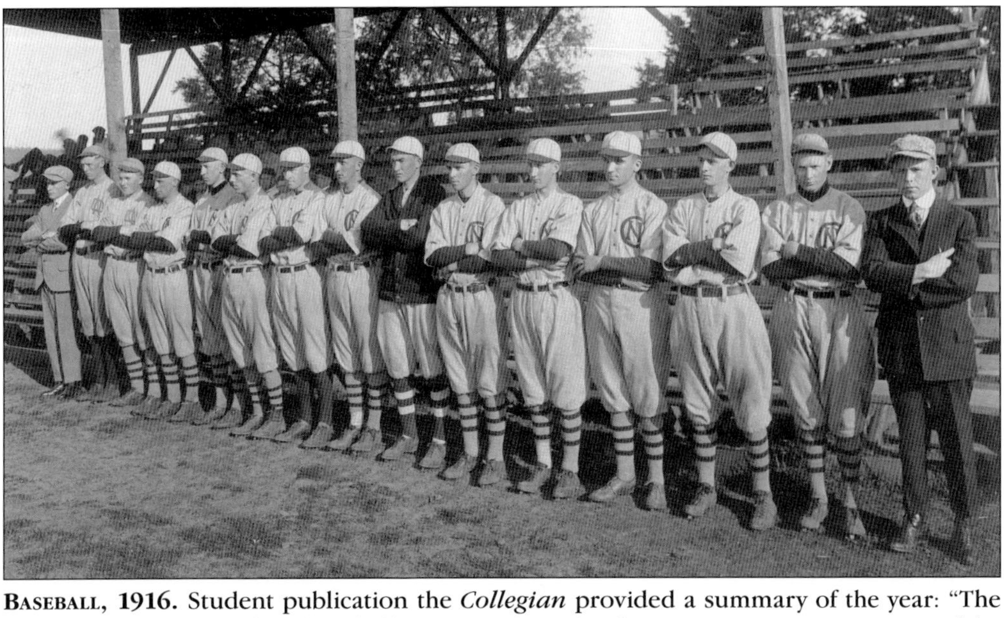

Baseball, 1916. Student publication the *Collegian* provided a summary of the year: "The least that can be said of our baseball season is that it has been a success in every sense of the word. The team as a whole is made up of a wide-awake bunch ready to 'take on' any team composed of bona fide students."

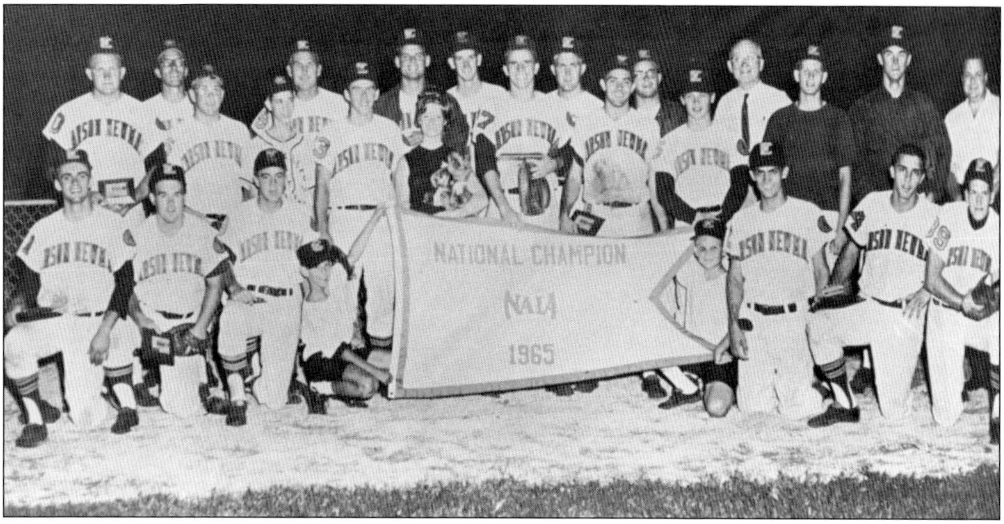

NAIA BASEBALL CHAMPIONS, 1965, AND ALL-TOURNAMENT SELECTIONS. Coached by Bobby Wilson, this Eagles team fielded what would eventually be six All-Americans, including future major leaguer Clyde Wright. Winning the Volunteer State Athletic Conference Championship, Tournament Championship, District Championship, and the National Championship, they finished with a stellar 36–3 record. The above photograph shows the NAIA Baseball Champions in 1965; the All-Tournament Selections are seen below.

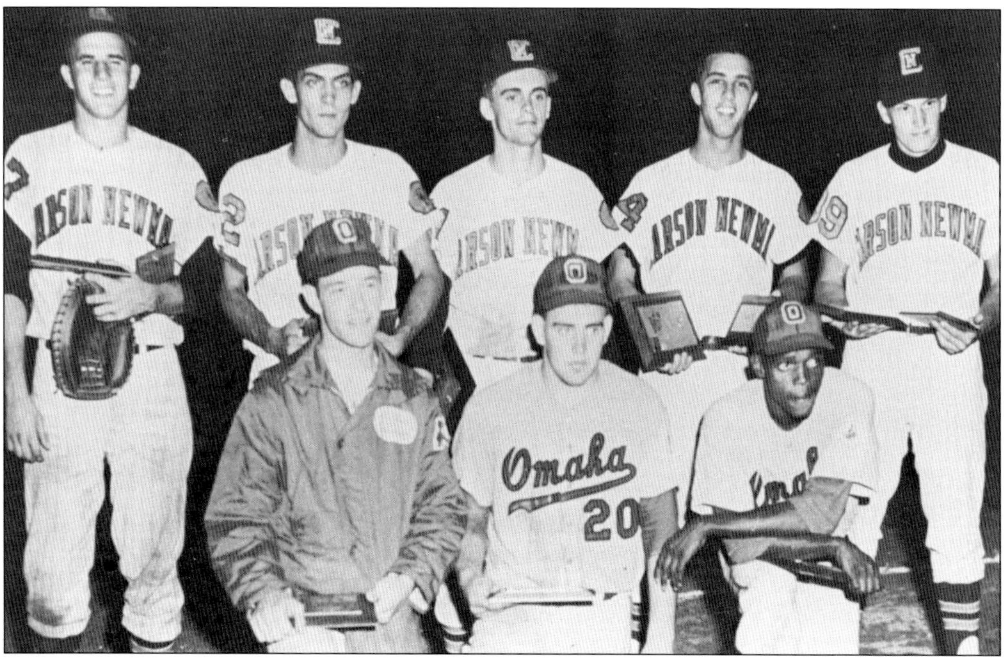

Bobby Wilson. Wilson was born on January 11, 1924, and played football and baseball for the University of Mississippi. He was drafted by the Cincinnati Reds and the Philadelphia Eagles. He chose baseball and had a three-year minor league career with Cincinnati. He then spent 12 years coaching high school football and baseball. "Frosty" Holt hired him as assistant coach; after he became ill, Wilson was named head baseball coach. Under his direction, the Eagles won 10 conference titles and in 1965, they won the NAIA National Championship. He was inducted in the NAIA Baseball Hall of Fame in 1986 and also claimed spots in the Ole Miss and Carson-Newman athletic halls of fame. During homecoming 2011, the Bobby Wilson Indoor Training Facility was dedicated in his honor.

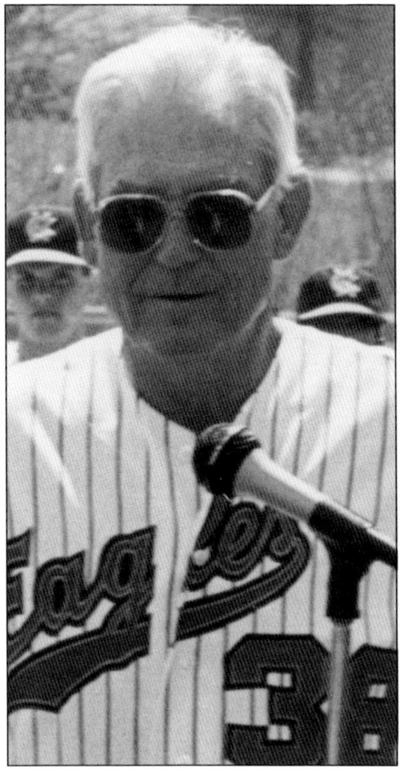

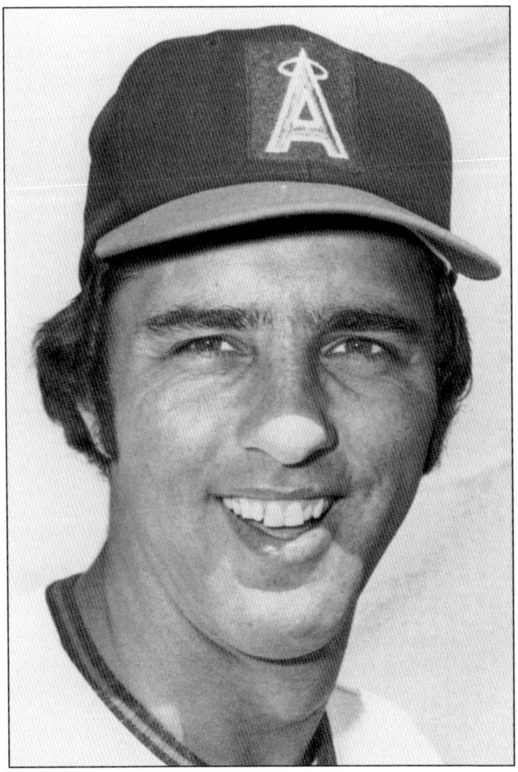

Clyde Wright. Born on February 20, 1943, in Jefferson City, Tennessee, Wright played baseball from the time he was a young boy. He graduated from Jefferson High School in 1961 and Carson-Newman in 1965, where he won the NAIA National Baseball Championship his senior year. He was drafted by the Los Angeles Angels where he played for eight years. He pitched the first no-hitter ever thrown at Anaheim Stadium and won over 100 major league games. He spent one year with Milwaukee and another with Texas and later played three years in Japan. (Courtesy of Angels Baseball.)

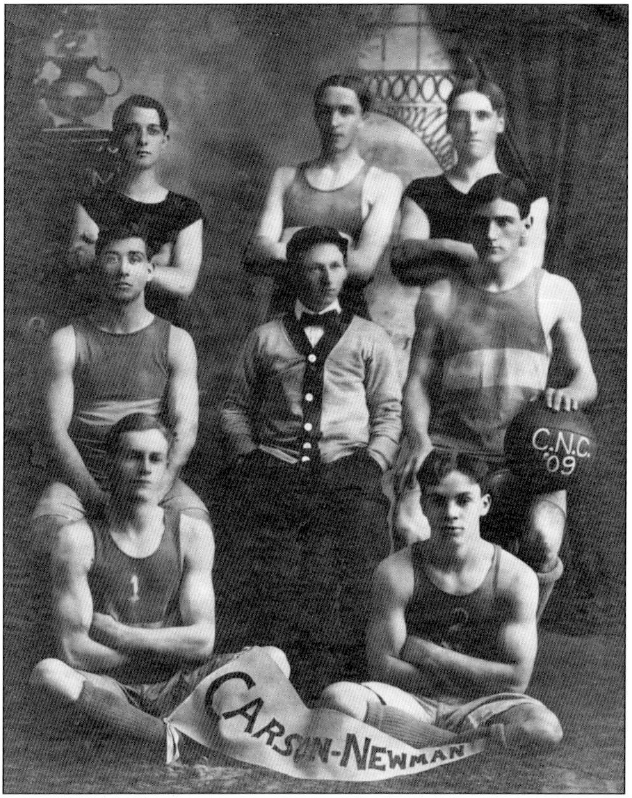

BASKETBALL, 1909. Basketball was introduced to the campus in 1908. Originally played on outdoor courts, the team moved indoors sometime during Pres. J.M. Burnett's administration from 1912 to 1917. Games were originally played on the stage of the auditorium in the original administration building. (Courtesy of Robert and Gay Clark Warren.)

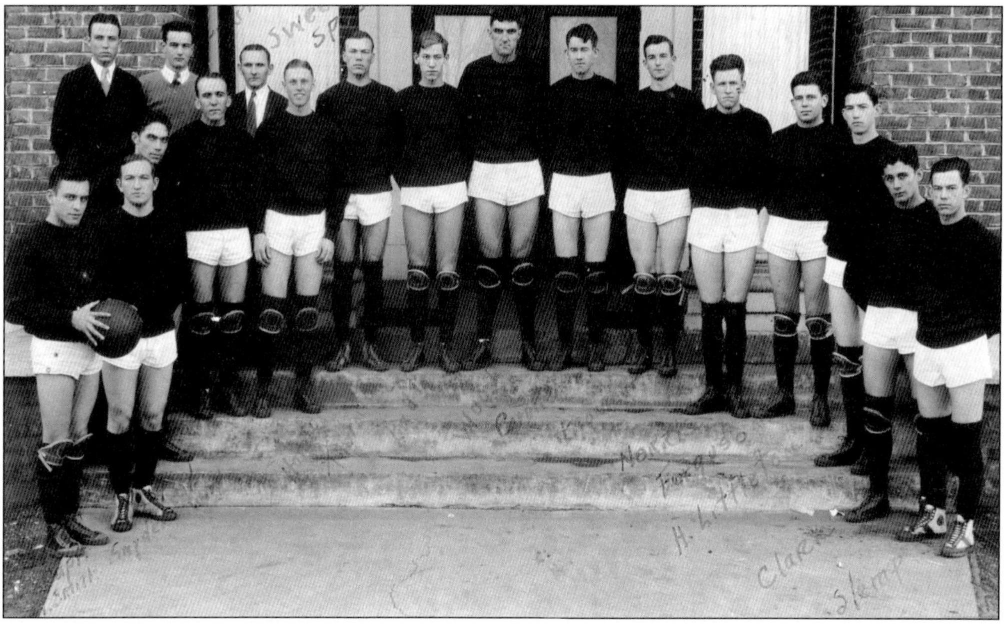

BASKETBALL, 1931. Sam "Frosty" Holt did double-duty coaching both football and basketball. According to the *Orange & Blue*, "As a result of this thoughtful direction, Coach Holt turned out a basketball team that licked everything in the conference, and went on to the finals in the tournament."

The Parsonnettes. While the men's athletic teams took on the Fighting Parsons moniker in 1921, the women were known as the Parsonettes. (Courtesy of Henry Chiles.)

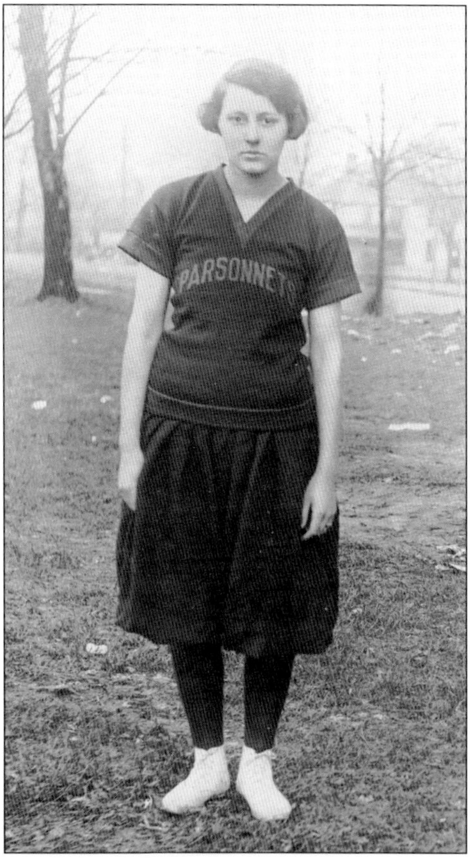

Women's Basketball, 1924. By the 1920s, women's athletic competitions were taking place. The 1924 team finished 4–11 with wins over Maryville, Tennessee Polytechnic Institute, and Cumberland. Future coach and physical education professor Mae Iddins (third from left) was the starting center.

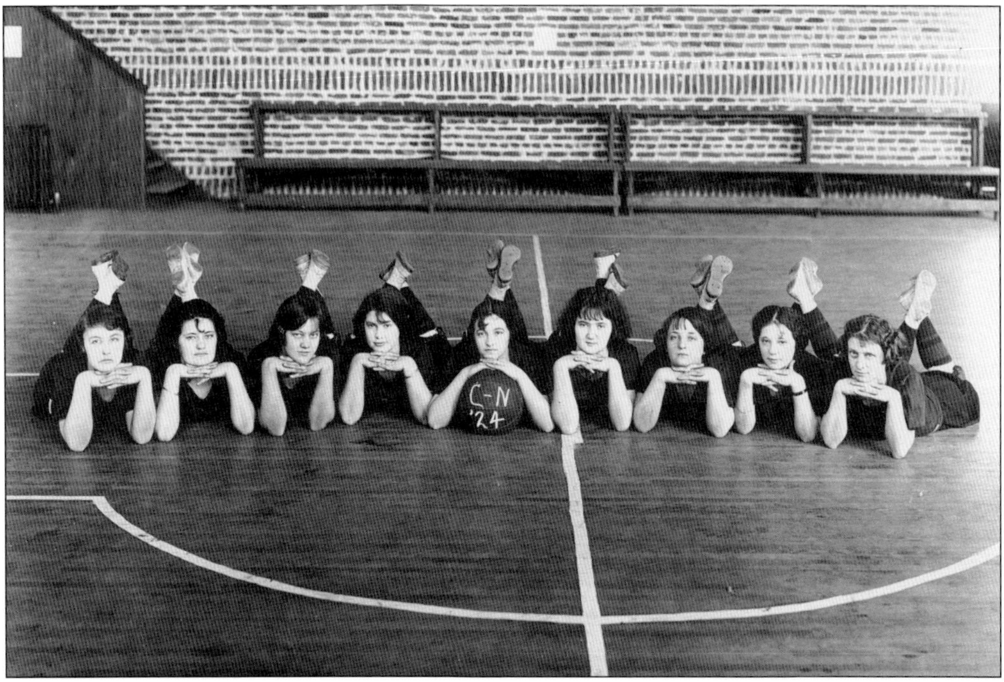

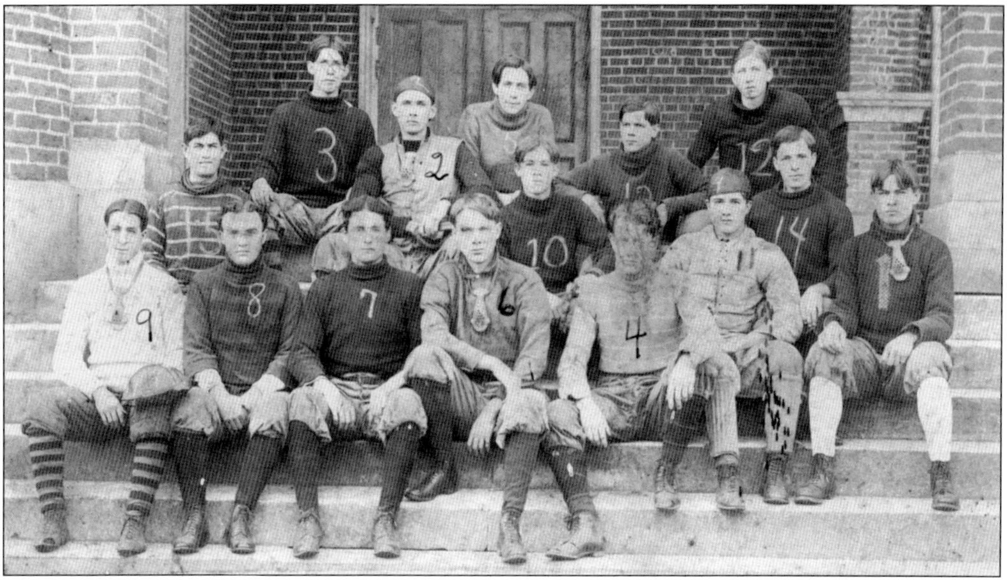

FOOTBALL, 1904. Organized football began at Carson-Newman around 1895 with the help of Luther M. Beeler, a graduate who had gone on to study at Yale, and student James S. Floyd. After a few seasons, interest in the program dropped until 1903 when a new team was organized and became a member of the East Tennessee Football Association. The association's bulletin announced "it affords an excellent keepsake as showing the brawny men who struggled on the field for their college during the year 1903 but it will serve to furnish, to a large degree, an idea of the composite of the teams of 1904 who will struggle again for supremacy." (Courtesy of Leona Wisenbaker.)

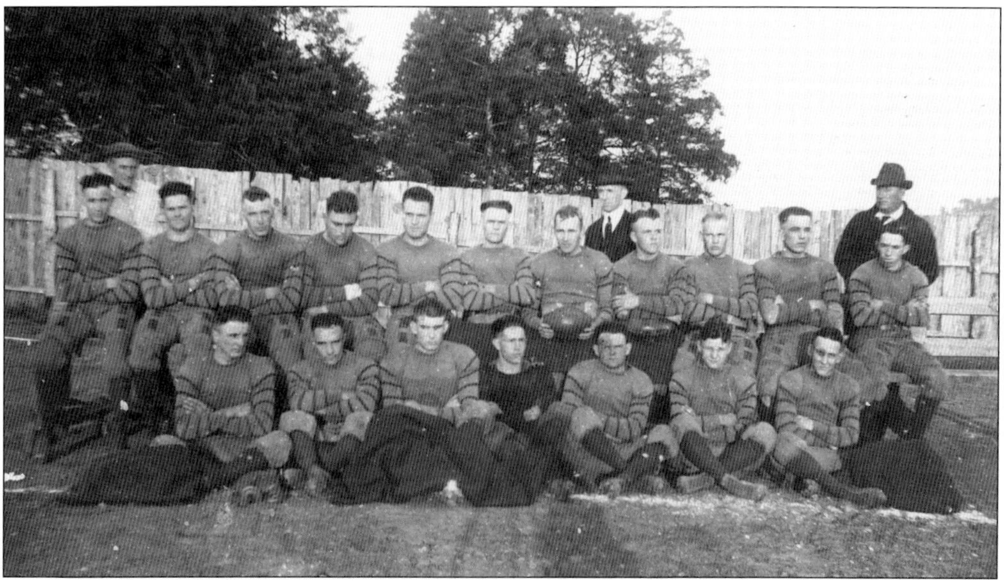

FOOTBALL, 1920s. The 1920s were the first full decade of organized football at Carson-Newman. Led by Sam "Frosty" Holt, Lake Russell, and ministerial student Ira Dance (the inspiration for the Fighting Parson), the team finished with a 33–34–7 record. Coaches included John Kilpatrick (1915–1920), Dr. R.M. McCown (1921), Tom Moran (1922–1924), Russell (1925–1928), and Holt (1929–1949).

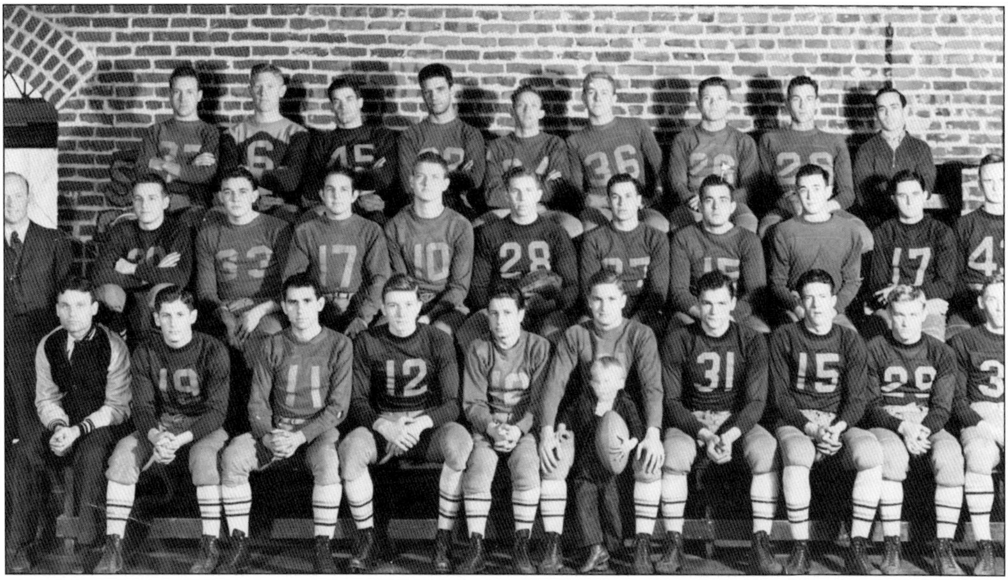

Football, 1936. Coached by Sam "Frosty" Holt and assistant Fred Noe, the 1936 team was undefeated, with a 10–0 record. They outscored opponents 219–27 and were led by Wendell "Yankee" Henderson (top row, fourth from left), who scored 81 points on 11 touchdowns and 15 extra points. (Courtesy of Milton Nixon.)

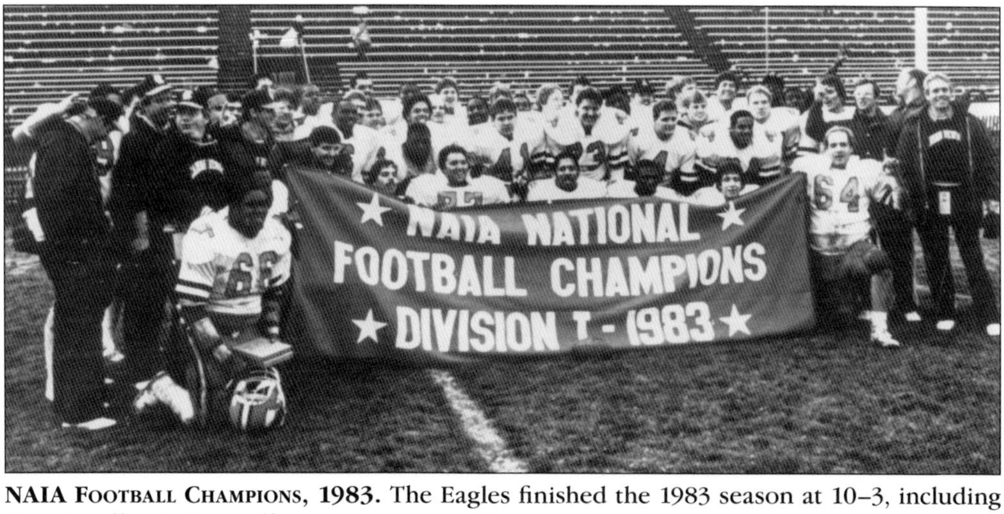

NAIA Football Champions, 1983. The Eagles finished the 1983 season at 10–3, including the playoffs. Shaking off an opening-game loss to Furman by 52–7, the Eagles went on to defeat Shepherd and Saginaw Valley State in the playoffs. They met the Mesa Mavericks in the championship game in Grand Junction, Colorado, where they brought home the school's first NAIA championship with a 36–28 win.

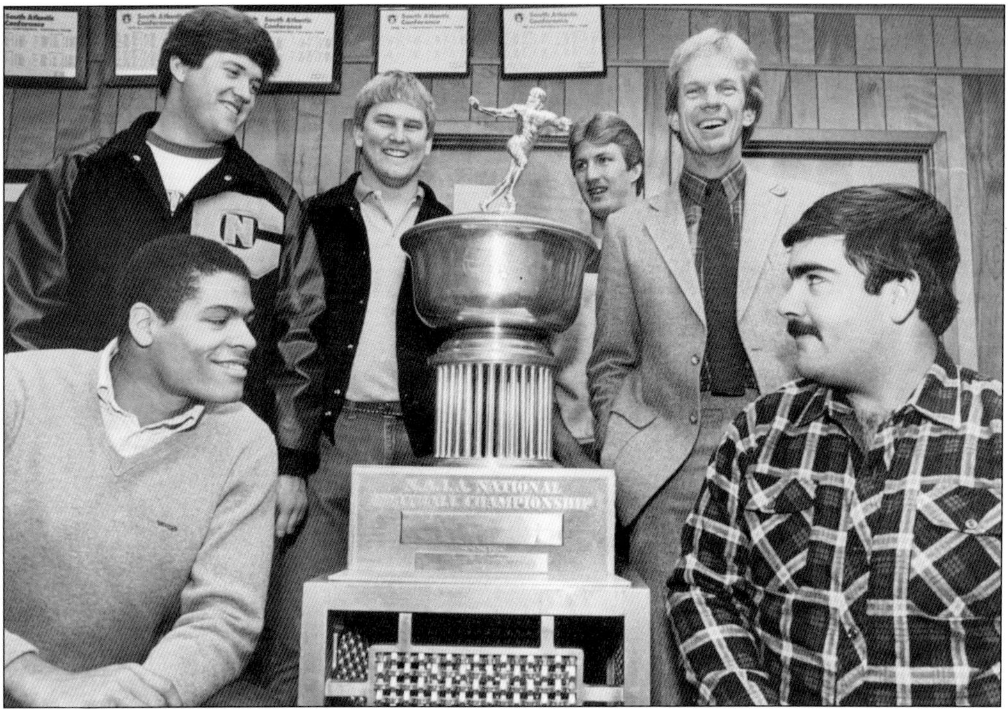

NAIA CHAMPIONS COACH KEN SPARKS, 1983. In only his third season as head coach, Ken Sparks led the Eagles to the first of five NAIA championships. Since 1980, Sparks has become the longest serving football coach as well as the coach with the most wins in school history. (Photograph by Mike Dubose.)

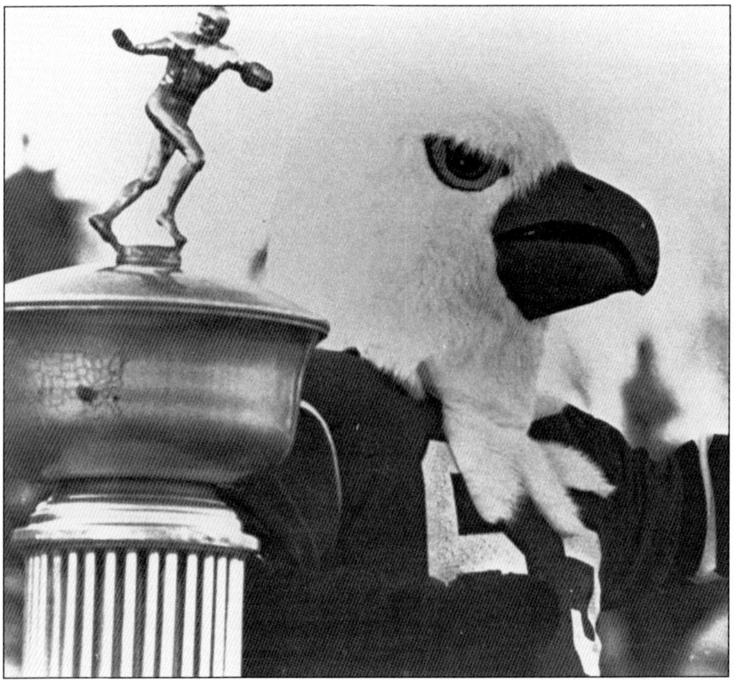

EAGLE MASCOT WITH NAIA CHAMPIONSHIP TROPHY, 1989. In 1989, the Eagles defeated Emporia State 31–20 in Jefferson City for their fifth and final NAIA championship. Talon the mascot stopped long enough from instilling school spirit to pose with the championship trophy.

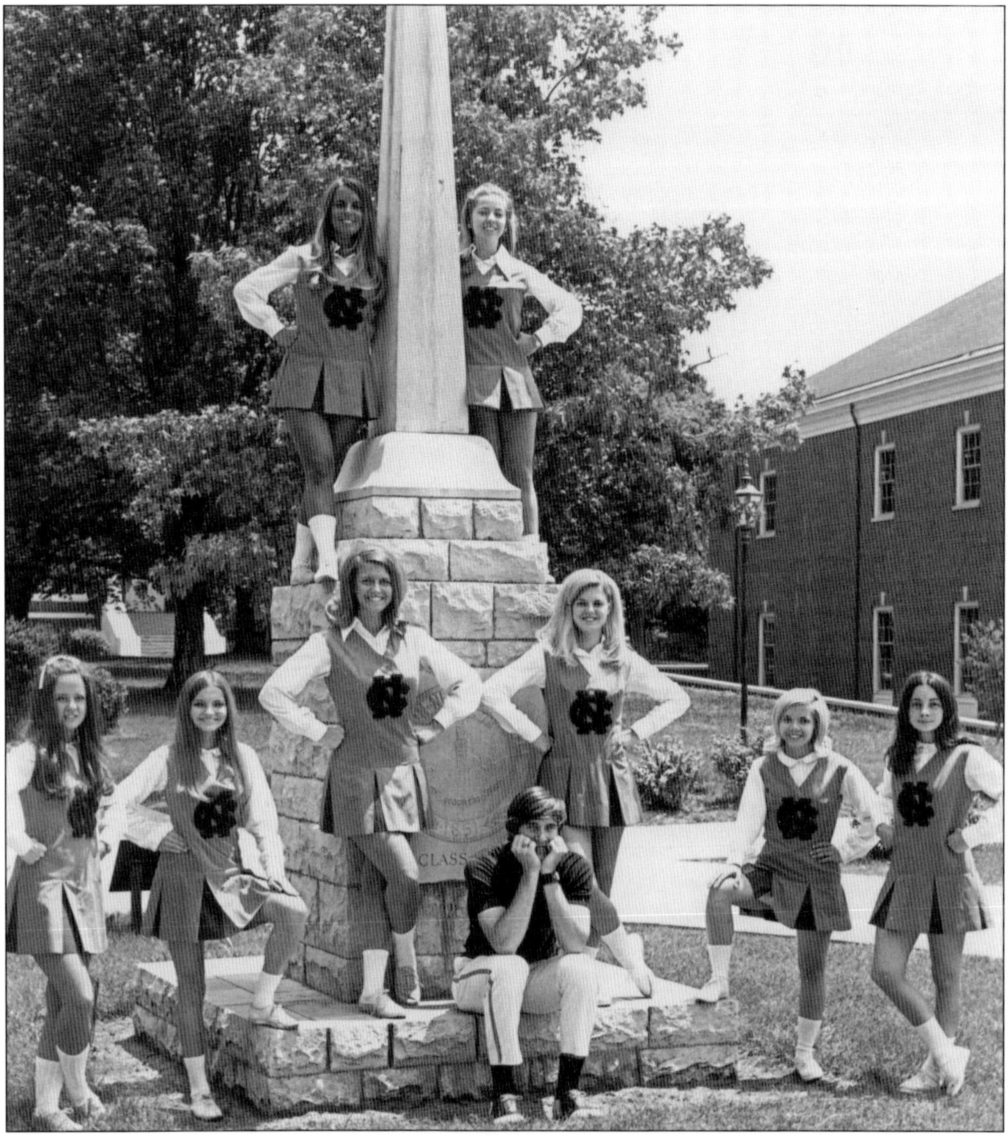

CHEERLEADERS. Over the years, Carson-Newman's cheerleaders have been a constant at athletic events, providing spirit and entertainment. This 1970s squad took time to pose in front of the Eagle Monument, a gift from the class of 1949.

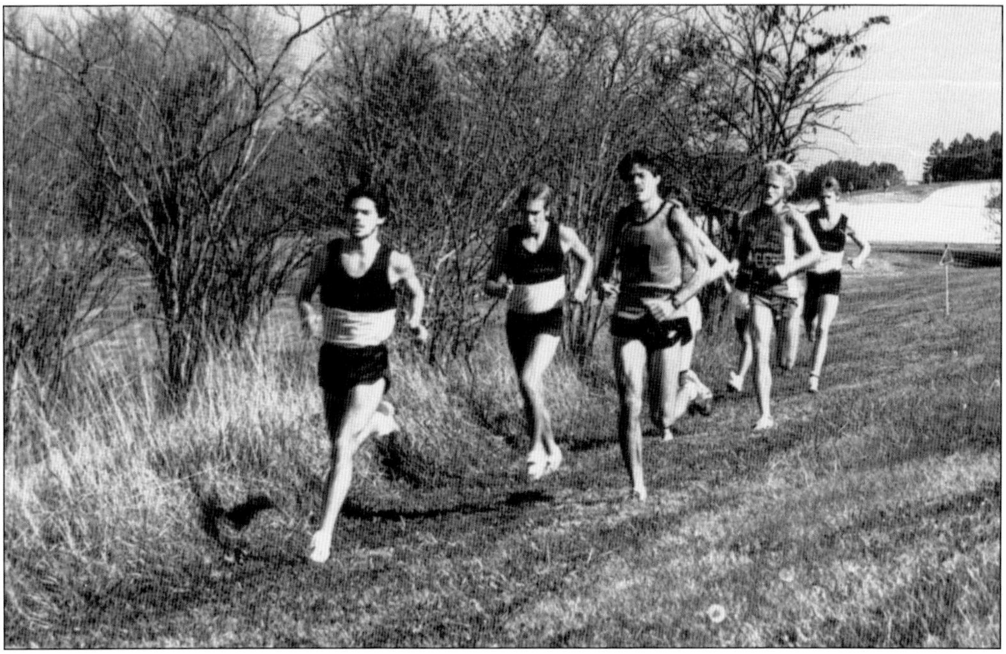

CROSS-COUNTRY. Also coached by "Frosty" Holt, the first organized cross-country team was established in 1962, while the 1963 squad received credit in the *Appalachian* as being the first to actually compete. They won the first of several Volunteer State Athletic Conference Championships in 1970.

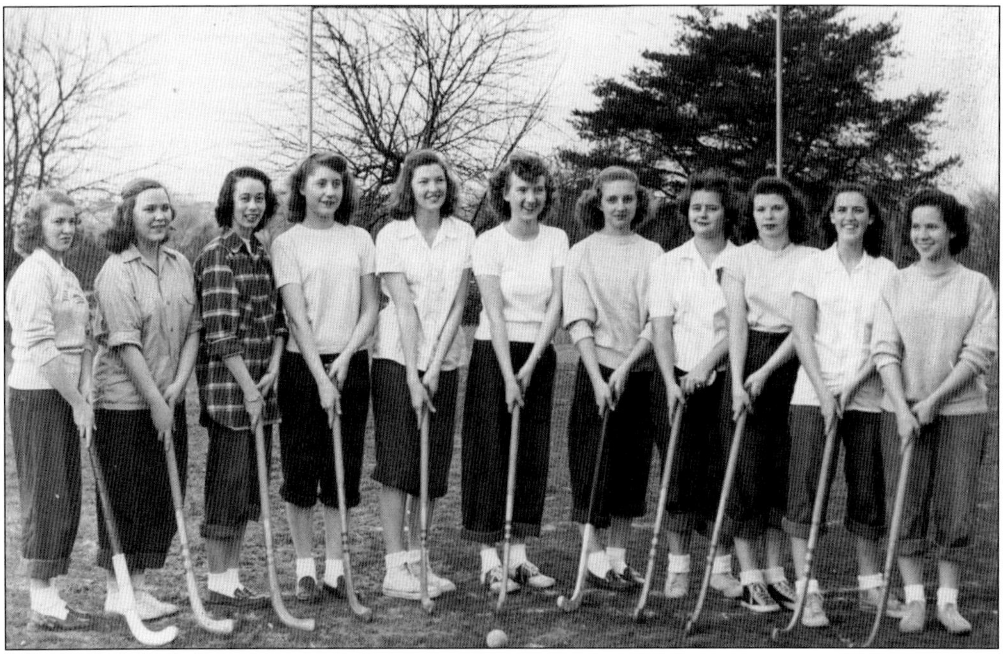

FIELD HOCKEY. During the 1940s, field hockey was one of the sports organized by Mae Iddins for female students. After World War II, Iddins expanded her physical education program and in 1945, a major was added. Other sports for women included basketball, soccer, badminton, tennis, fencing, and touch football.

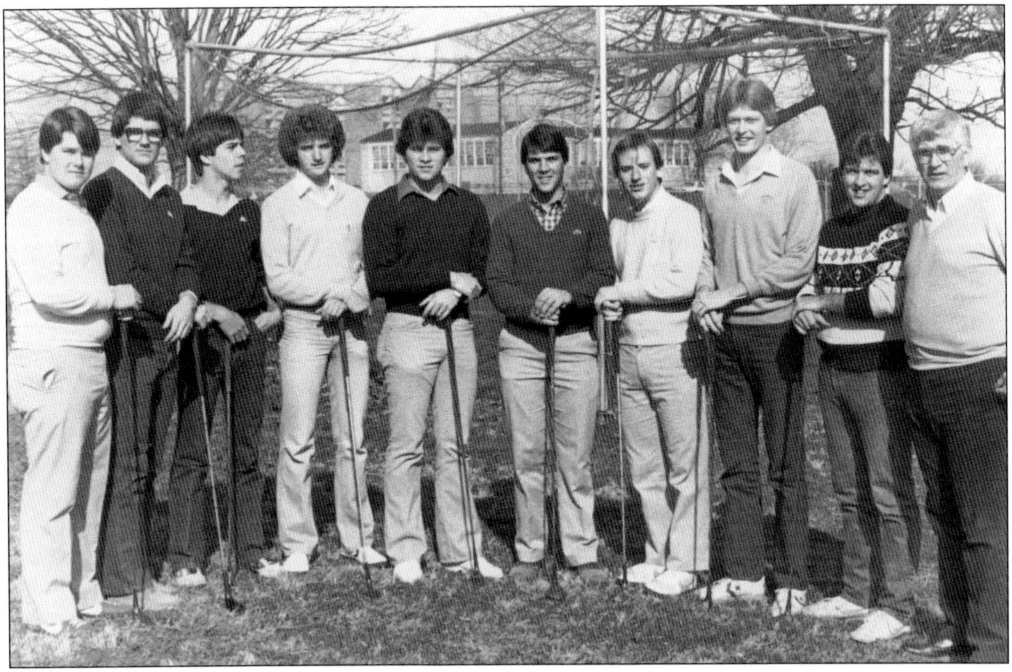

Golf. Established in 1961 under coach Dick Campbell, the golf team was not very competitive its first three years. In 1964, the program was discontinued due to financial reasons but was reinstituted in 1967. Coach Charlie King returned to his alma mater in 1968 and would continue to guide the program for the next few decades. In 2008–2009, the girls' team had its inaugural season.

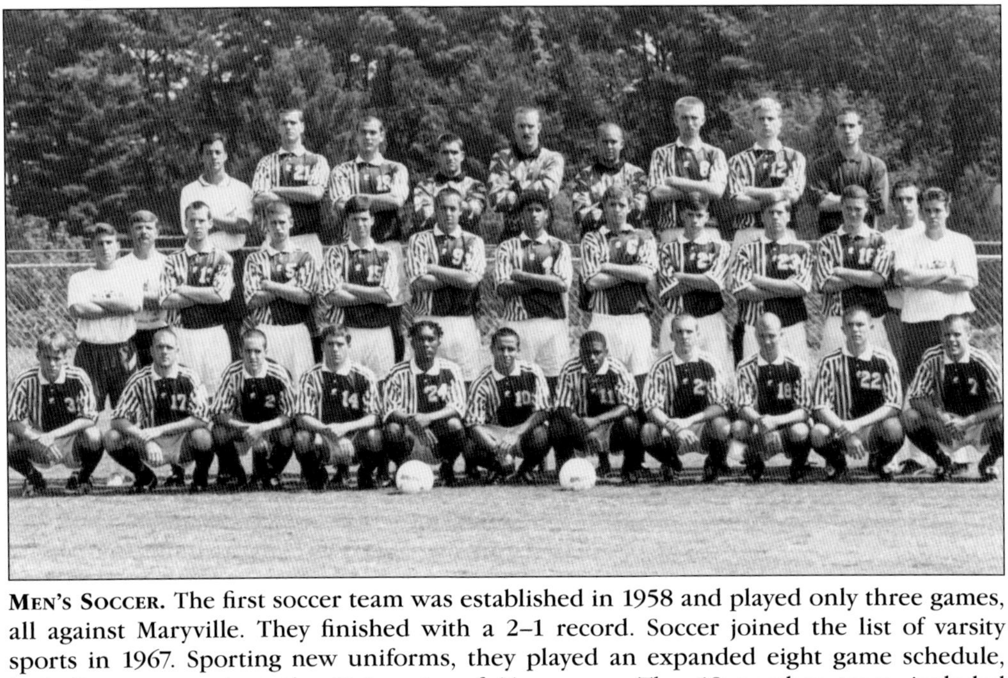

Men's Soccer. The first soccer team was established in 1958 and played only three games, all against Maryville. They finished with a 2–1 record. Soccer joined the list of varsity sports in 1967. Sporting new uniforms, they played an expanded eight game schedule, including two against the University of Tennessee. The 18-member team included six international players.

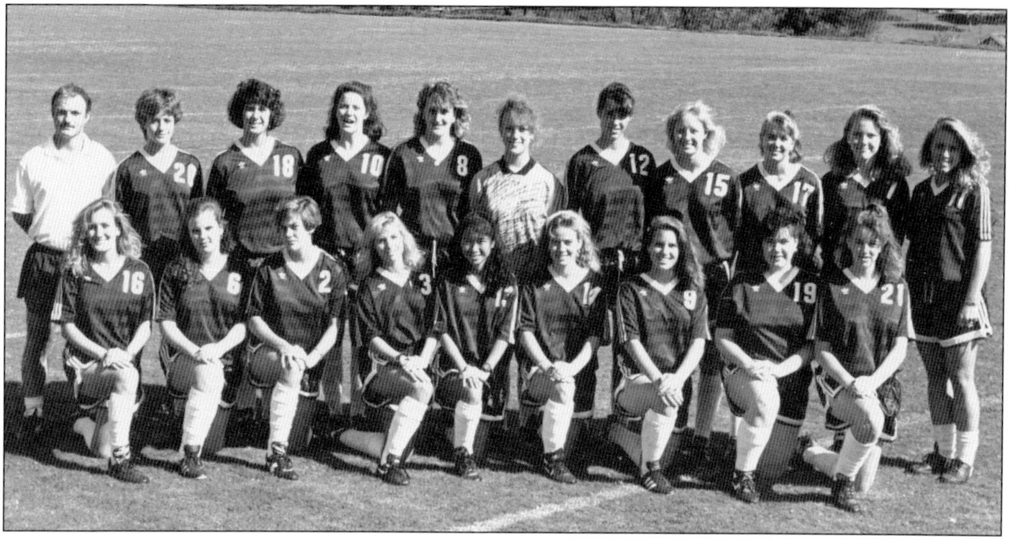

Women's Soccer. The last year for intercollegiate competition for women athletes for several decades was in 1931. Under the direction of Prof. Mae Iddins, an intramural athletic program with a point system was set up so girls could compete on campus in athletic events and earn letters and sweaters. In 1991, Carson-Newman revived the girls' soccer program, allowing them to join the ranks of varsity sports.

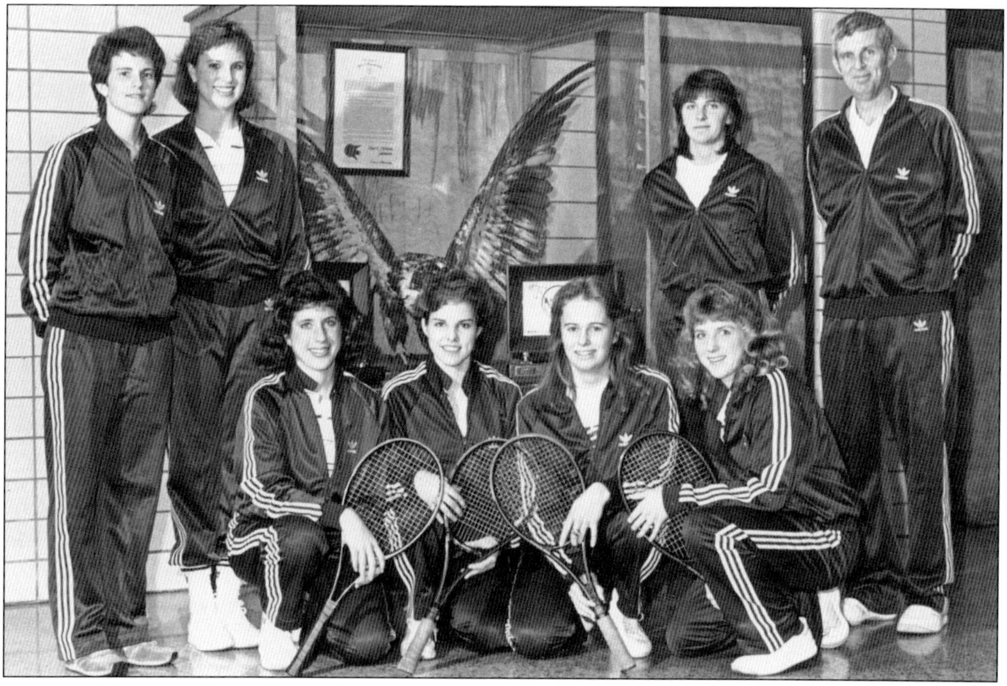

Women's Tennis. The Lady Eagles of the early 1980s featured Jean Love (standing back row left), a two-time NAIA All-American and an Academic All-American. She returned to her alma mater and currently serves as associate professor of health, physical education, and sport science. She is also coach of both the men's and women's tennis teams. Love was inducted into the Carson-Newman Athletic Hall of Fame in 2002. Coach Frank Pinkerton led the successful program for 15 years, stepping down in 1988.

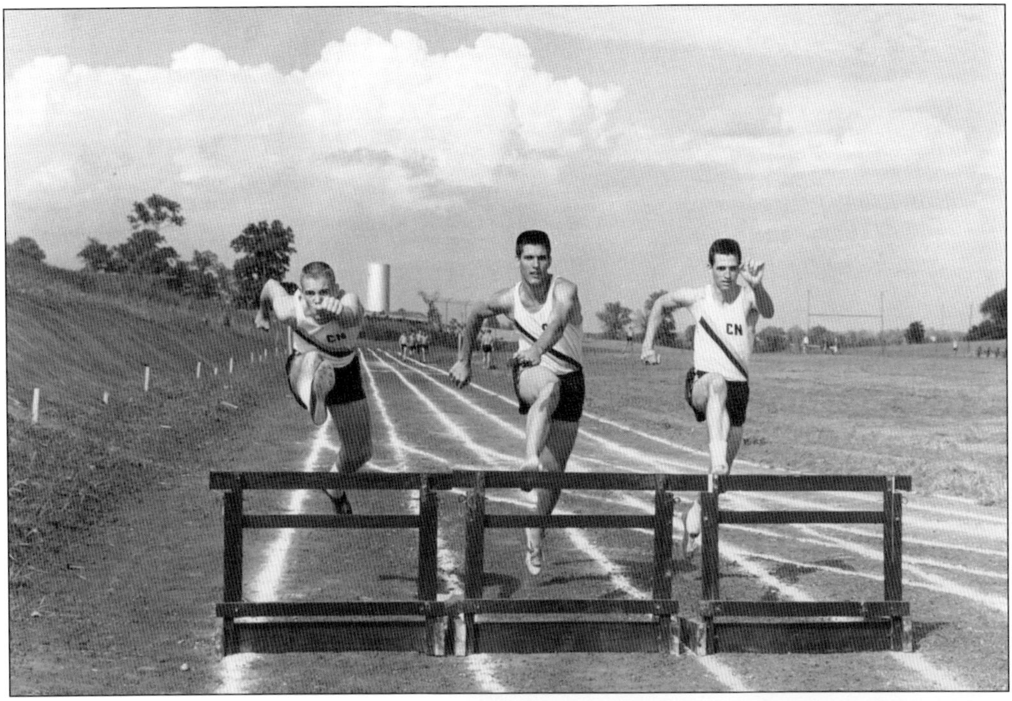

Track. The 1914 group of runners was the first recognized team in school history. After that, competition was sporadic until the development of the first track team in the modern era in 1960 under the direction of Roy Harmon and Charlie Bryant. In 1967, they won their first Volunteer State Athletic Conference Championship.

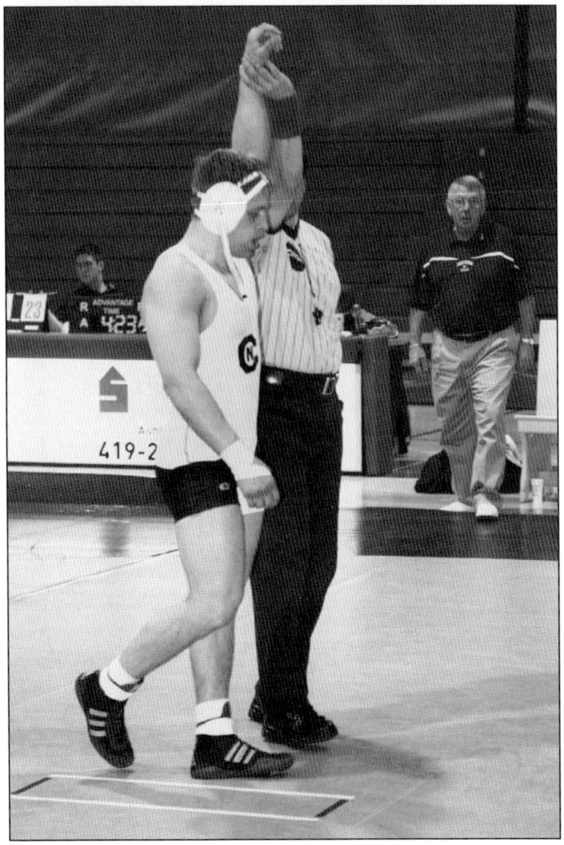

Wrestling. The year 1963 saw the first Carson-Newman wrestling team participate in intercollegiate competition under coach Bob Davis. Richard May took over for the 1967–1968 season, but that proved to be the end of varsity competition for several years. The program was revived in 1978 when coach Don Elia (back right) was hired. He guided the program for the next 31 years. One of the college's standouts was 2007 All-American Nate Jones (front left). The program was discontinued in 2009. (Courtesy of Don Elia.)

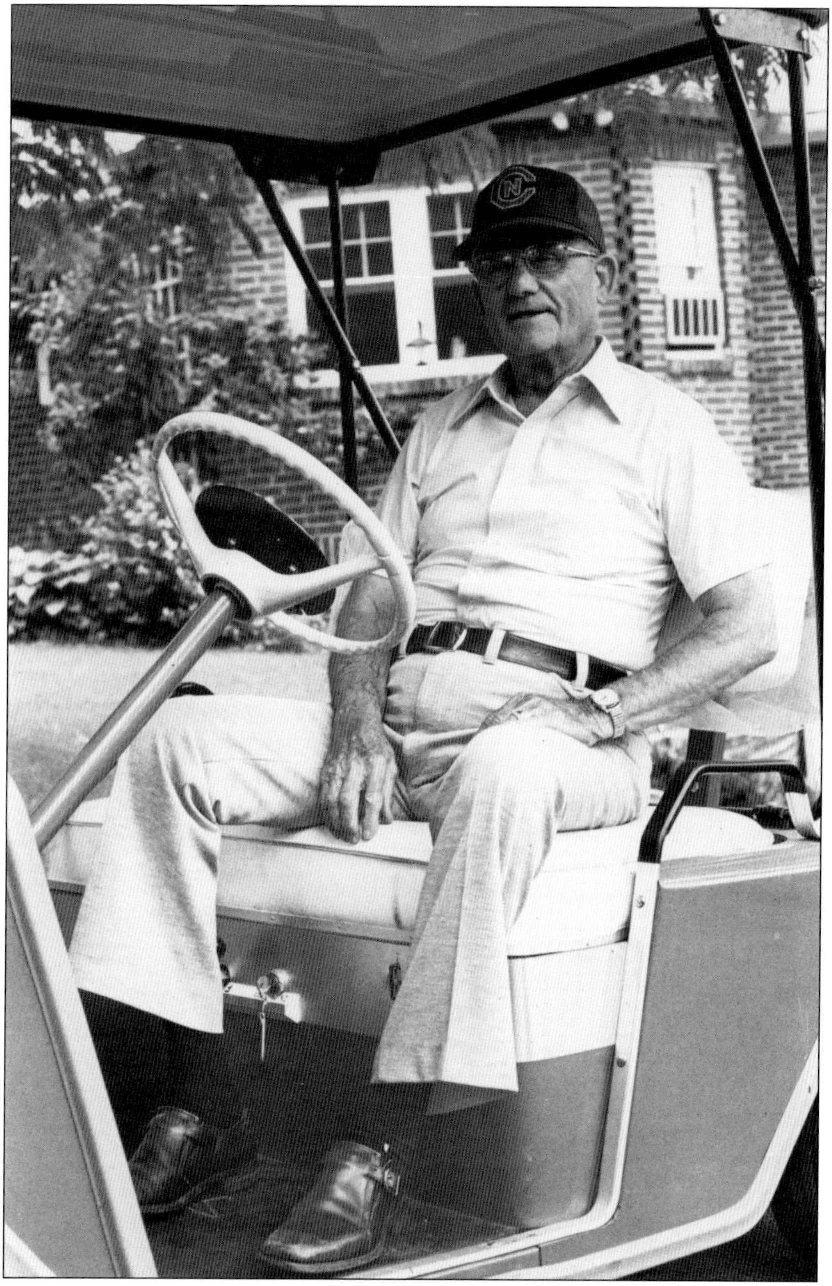

Sam B. "Frosty" Holt. Holt enrolled at Carson-Newman in 1921, lettering in three sports. He returned to his alma mater in 1929. Assuming athletic director and coaching responsibilities, "Frosty" went on to become a Carson-Newman legend. He skippered football, basketball, and baseball teams, including the Navy V-12 personnel during World War II. From 1946 until his retirement in 1968, he was elected to the Helms National Baseball Hall of Fame, received the 25- Year Service Award by the American Baseball Coaches Association, and was named to both the Tennessee Division of the National Football Hall of Fame and Tennessee Sports Hall of Fame, as well as the NAIA Coaches Hall of Fame. In 1961, the field house was named in his honor. "Frosty" died in 1986 at the age of 83.

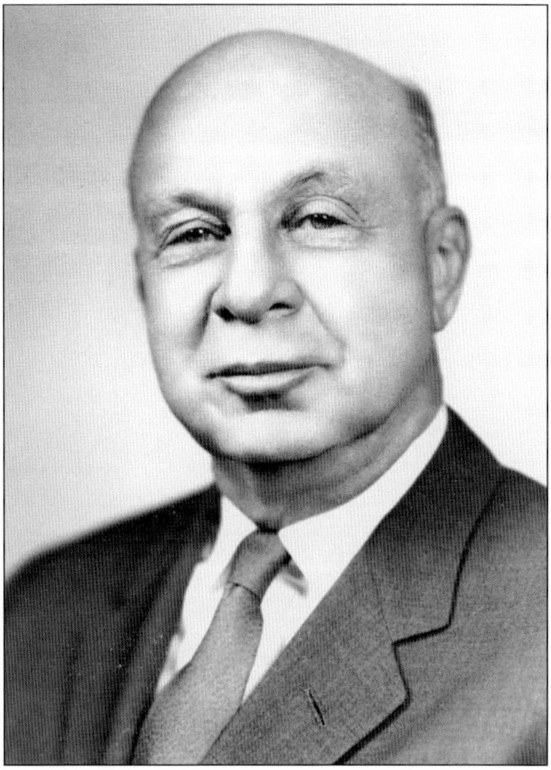

Dana X. Bible. Dana X. Bible was born in Jefferson City, Tennessee, went to local public schools, and attended Carson-Newman College where he graduated in 1912. He was awarded an honorary doctorate of divinity degree in 1951. During his 34 years of coaching football, his teams won 14 major conference championships, including five at Texas A&M, six at Nebraska, and three at Texas. He also led the Longhorns to the 1941 national championship. After 33 years of coaching, Bible finished with a 198–72–23 record. He was elected into the College Football Hall of Fame in 1951. (Photograph by University Studio.)

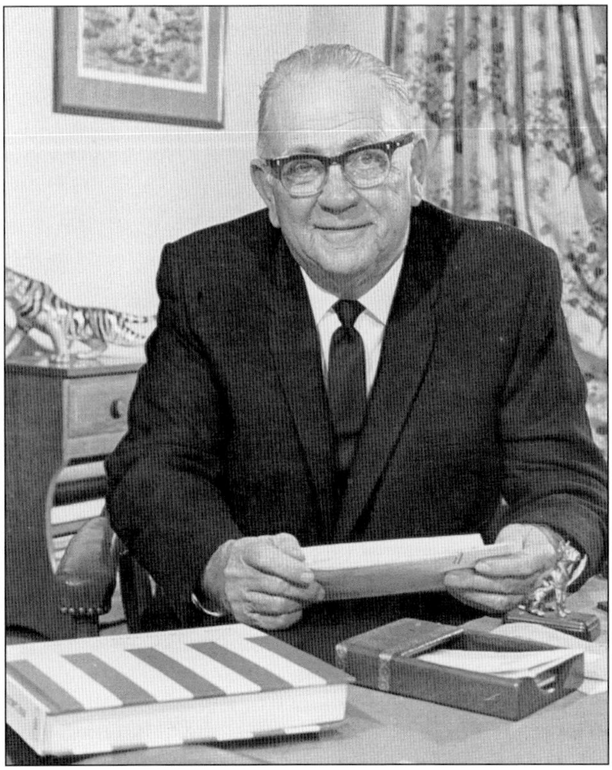

Bernie Hawthorne Moore. Born in Jonesboro, Tennessee, Moore graduated from Carson-Newman in 1917. He coached football at Mercer and LSU. During his 12-year coaching career, he won 73 games, lost 36, and tied five. He became commissioner of the Southeastern Conference in 1948, serving until his retirement in 1966. Moore was inducted into the College Football Hall of Fame in 1954. (Courtesy of the Southeastern Conference.)

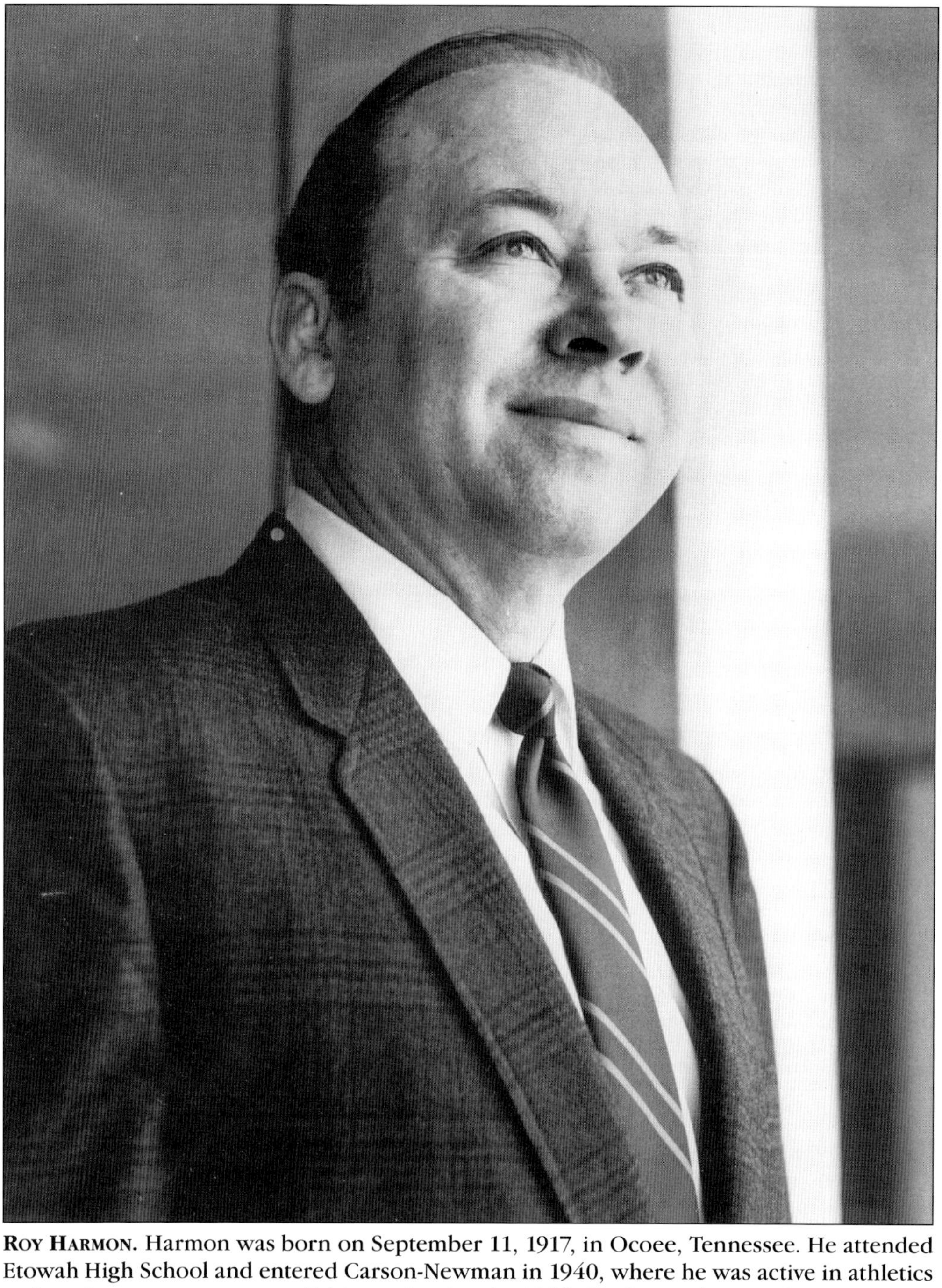

Roy Harmon. Harmon was born on September 11, 1917, in Ocoee, Tennessee. He attended Etowah High School and entered Carson-Newman in 1940, where he was active in athletics and student government until his graduation in 1944. He began his coaching career at Knoxville's Young High School and later moved to Lenoir City. In the fall of 1951, he returned to Carson-Newman as head football coach, succeeding "Frosty" Holt. During that time, he obtained a master's degree from the University of Tennessee and was chairman of the physical education department. In 1964, he relinquished his coaching duties but continued as department chair. (Courtesy of Tom Harmon.)

Six

Structures of Learning

Campus Buildings

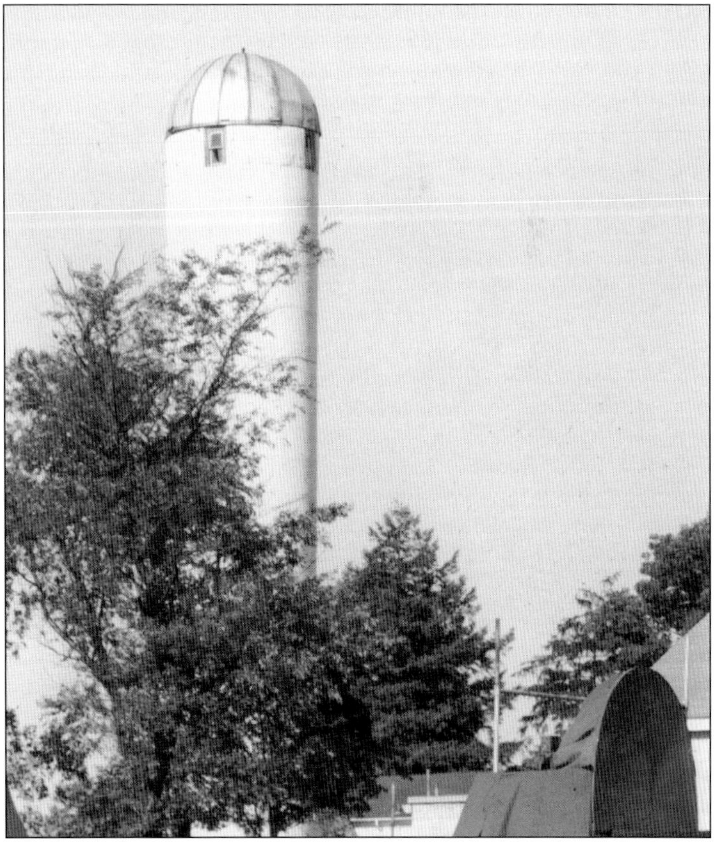

Observatory. When Col. A.R. Swann constructed the Sarah Swann Home in 1904, he also built a 10,000-gallon tank to supply water from a local spring to the campus. With the encouragement of former physics professor Alexander Chavis, this structure was converted to an observatory in 1933 as a gift from the class of 1926. In 1948, a 52-inch refracting telescope was added and accompanied a Foucault pendulum. It was torn down in 1966 to allow room for an additional wing for Butler Residence Hall. (Courtesy of Thompson Photograph Products.)

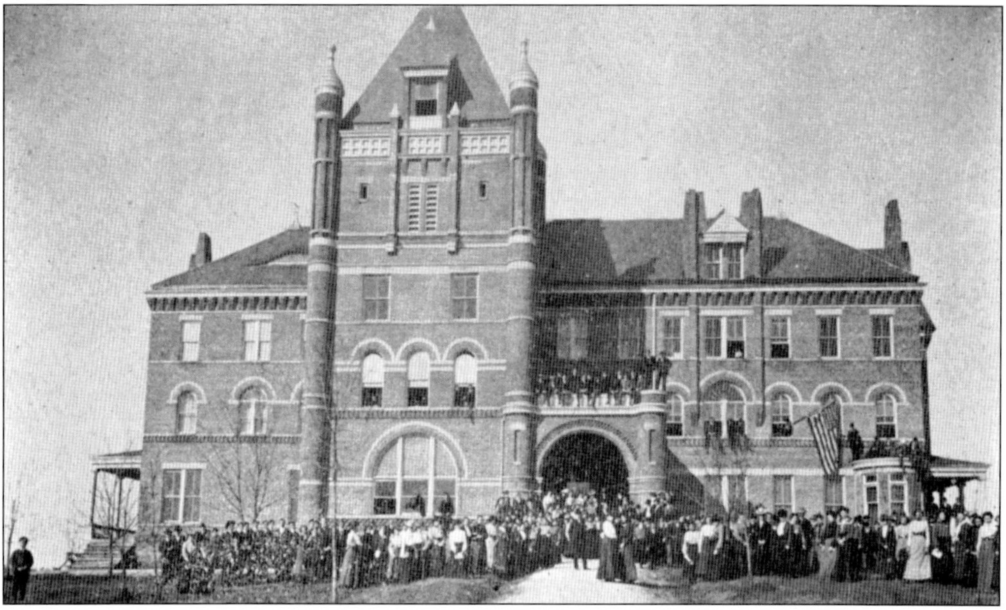

ADMINISTRATION BUILDING. After the consolidation of Carson and Newman Colleges, the school moved to its present location. Work was begun on the administration building in the spring of 1890 and by 1892 the first two floors were completed. The third floor was finished in 1897. Serving as the main campus building, this structure was home to administrative offices, classrooms, and library, as well as the literary societies' halls. The auditorium stage was used for a basketball court. On December 13, 1916, fire completely destroyed the building. (Courtesy of John Crosby.)

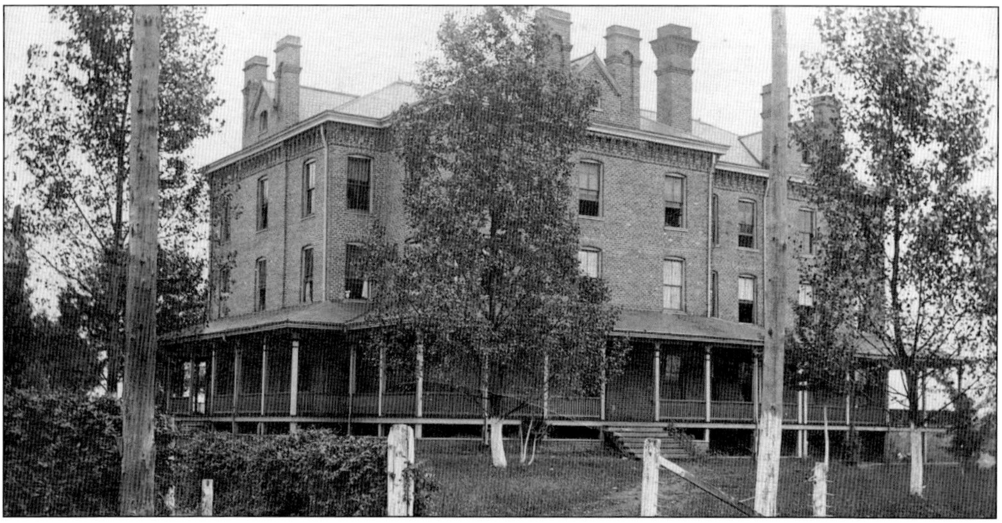

HENDERSON HOME FOR YOUNG LADIES. Located where the library now stands, this building was constructed in 1899 as a women's dormitory. Bricks from the original campus building and two Newman dormitories were used in its construction. It contained a kitchen and housed 50 women. Steam heat was introduced in 1901, making the 13 fireplaces and chimneys somewhat obsolete. At the recommendation of Pres. O.E. Sams, the name was changed to Henderson Hall in honor of C.W. Henderson, a large financial contributor to the school. It was razed in 1968. (Courtesy of John Crosby.)

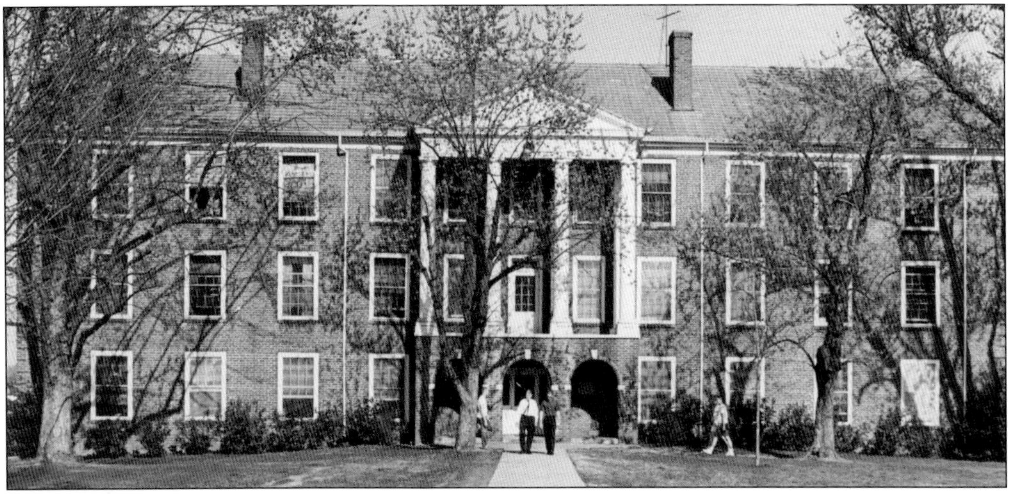

BLANC-DAVIS HALL. Completed in 1906, Davis Hall was funded by Mrs. W.L. Davis of Knoxville and named in honor of her husband. Accommodating 80 young men, it was operated on the club plan with meals being cooked and served in the hall's own kitchen. In 1924, Henry D. Blanc's generous gift and supervision of construction allowed Blanc Hall to be built in front of and attached to Davis Hall. Fondly referred to as "The Barn," this residence provided a home and innumerable memories for hundreds of students. It was razed in 1967, with the students writing an obituary in the *Orange and Blue*.

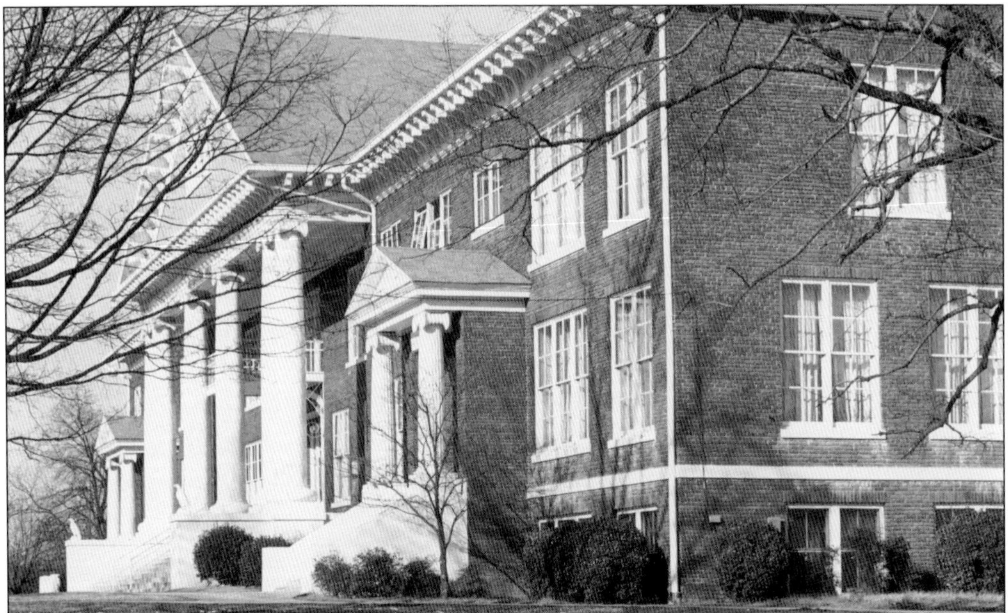

JOHN T. HENDERSON MEMORIAL HALL ADMINISTRATION BUILDING. Located on the site of the administration building destroyed by fire in 1916, the new structure was completed in 1919. It contained space for classrooms as well as faculty and administrative offices. The library was located on the first floor from 1919 to 1949, and the literary societies also had their halls there. It was known simply as the administration building until 1942, when it was named in honor of Pres. John T. Henderson (1892–1903). On January 16, 1974, the structure was completely destroyed by fire. The Henderson Humanities Building stands in its place today.

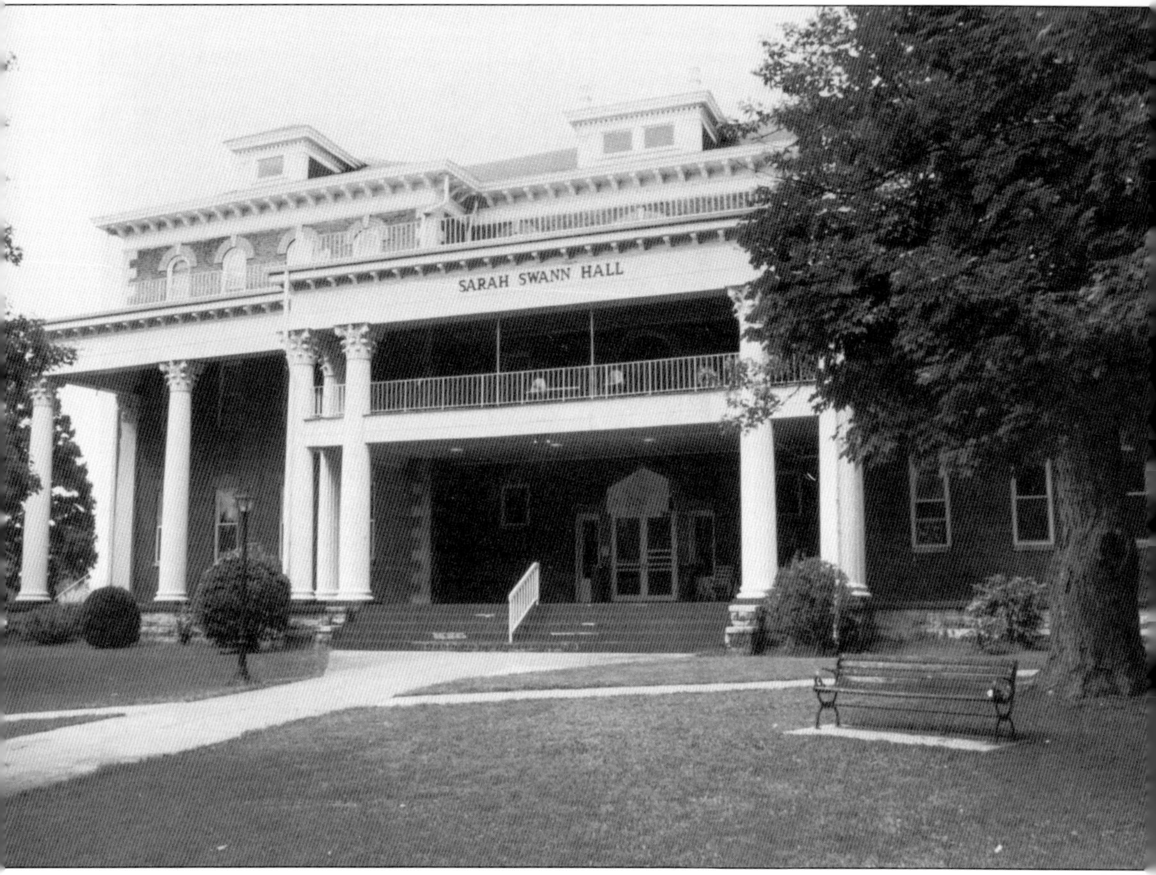

SARAH SWANN HALL. In 1904, Col. A.R. Swann responded to the need for an additional women's dormitory, naming it in honor of his mother. Initially, the young women participated in "the club plan of boarding [with] the young ladies assisting in the work and paying only the actual expenses of provisions," ranging from $6.00 to $6.50 per month for board, fuel, and lighting. It is the oldest building on campus and home to 120 women. It initially contained a kitchen and dining hall that were later converted into rooms. At one time, the Hypatian and Calliopean Literary Societies maintained their elegant halls there. Swann was renovated in 1965 and again in 2002.

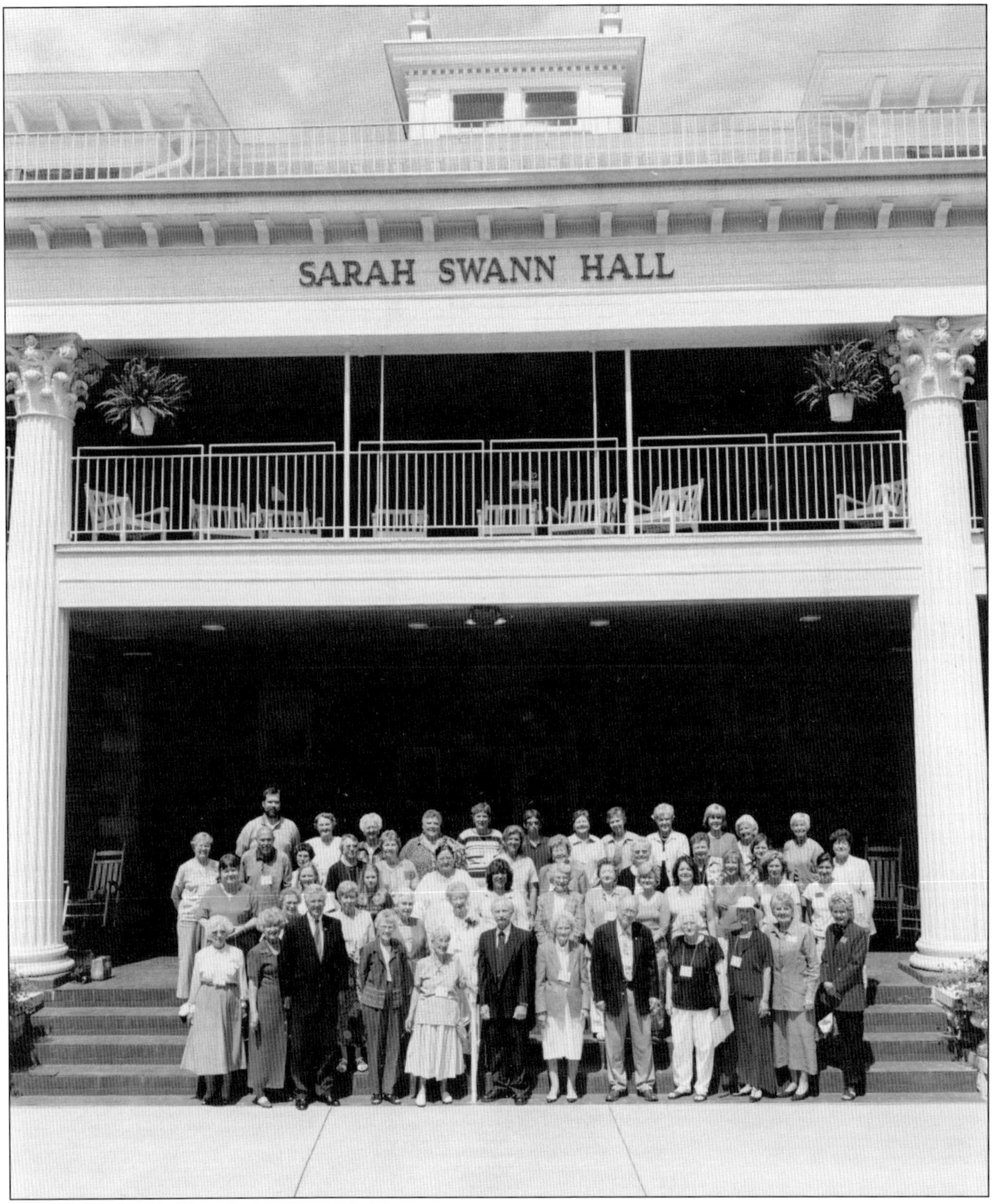

SARAH SWANN CENTENNIAL. In 2004, Sarah Swann celebrated 100 years of providing a home to female students. On June 17 and 18, 40 alumnae were invited to stay in the residence hall. They were treated to an afternoon tea on the front lawn, a family-style dinner in one of the parlors, an invitation to attend class sessions, and the chance to relive all those wonderful memories. (Photograph by Ricke Hester.)

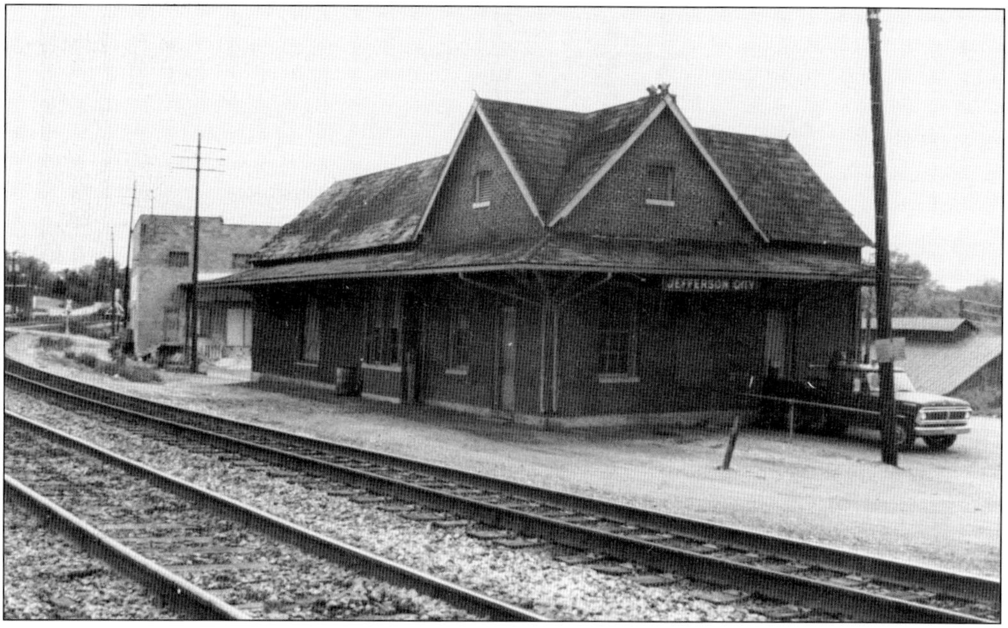

Jefferson City Railroad Station. In 1858, the railroad was completed through Mossy Creek. For the next 110 years, trains brought students to the campus. They were often met by staff who would help bring their luggage up Russell Avenue by buggy. In 1968, Southern Railroad discontinued passenger service to Memphis, thus ending a chapter in the history of Jefferson City and Carson-Newman.

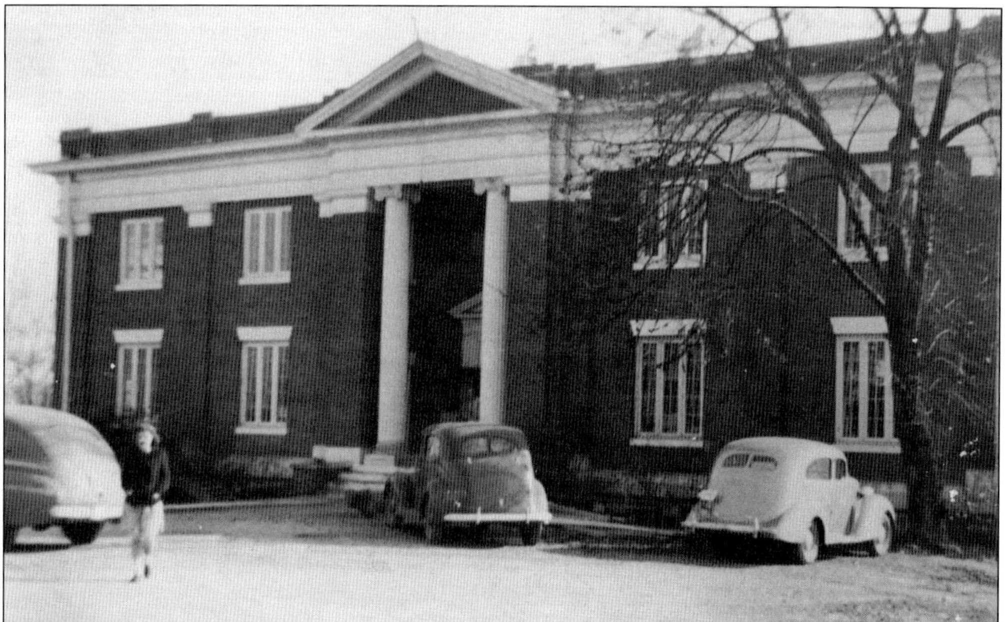

Butler Blanc Gymnasium. Generous contributors and trustees of the college, D.L. Butler and Henry D. Blanc helped fund the construction of the gym in the spring of 1923. It once contained a swimming pool in the basement that has since been filled in. It currently contains a gymnasium, fitness loft, offices, and classrooms.

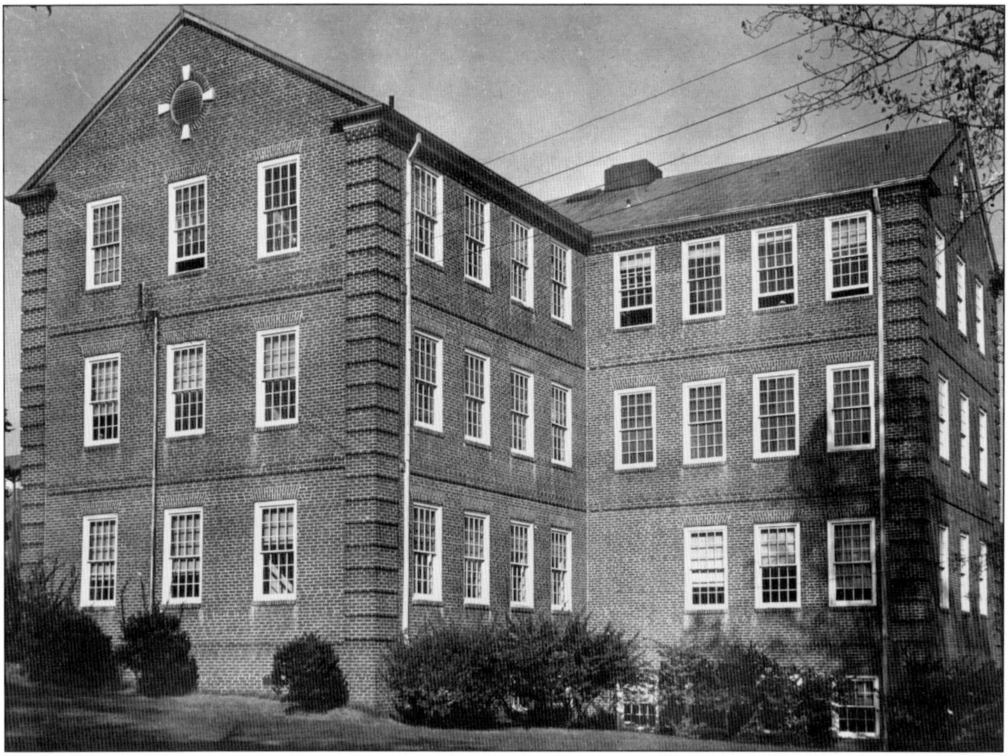

James T. Warren Art Building. Built in 1939, the building was named in memory of former president Dr. James T. Warren and was originally used for the science department. In the fall of 1972, renovations took place converting the building into classrooms, studios, and the Omega Gallery.

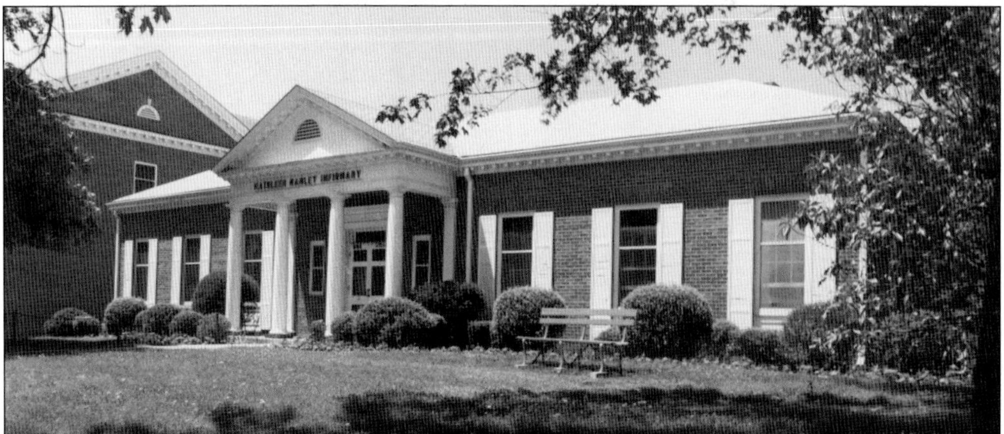

Kathleen Manley Facility. In 1940, with a gift from D.L. Butler and a bequest from Ida Lawrence Murray, Carson-Newman acquired a large two-story residence near the main campus to be used for an infirmary. This first infirmary opened in August of that year under the direction of a graduate nurse. Later, a local doctor made daily calls. In cooperation with the Kresge Foundation, the Nolachucky Baptist Association undertook the present infirmary's construction, dedicating it in 1961 to Kathleen Manley and six other Baptist missionaries. It houses student counseling and health services.

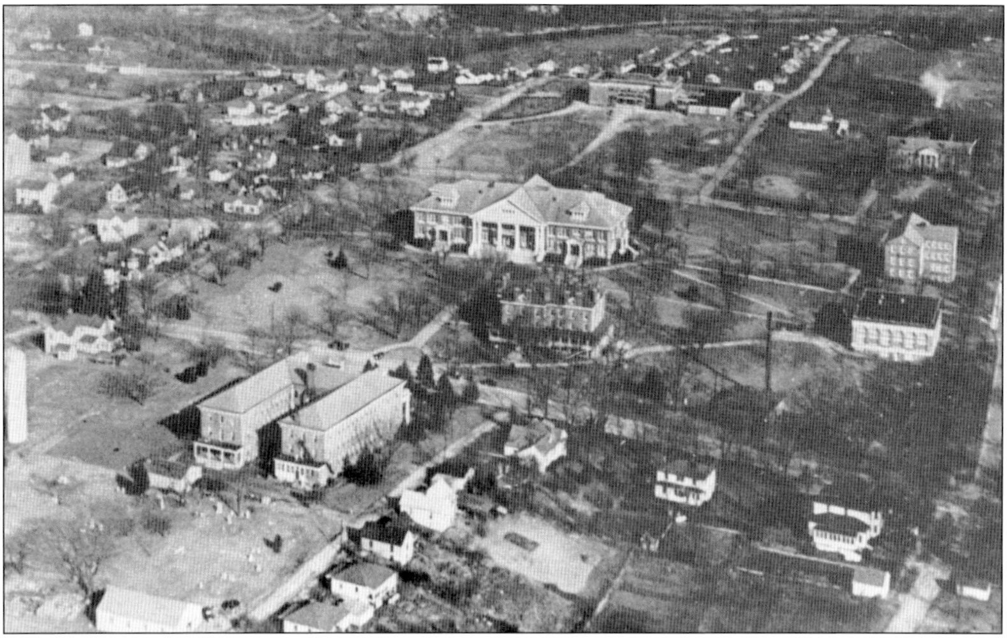

Aerial View, 1940s. The founding fathers would have been impressed by campus growth. By the mid-1940s, total enrollment was just over 400 students. Total cost for room, board, tuition, and fees was $300 to $360 per year, depending on course of study. (Courtesy of Jim Pethel.)

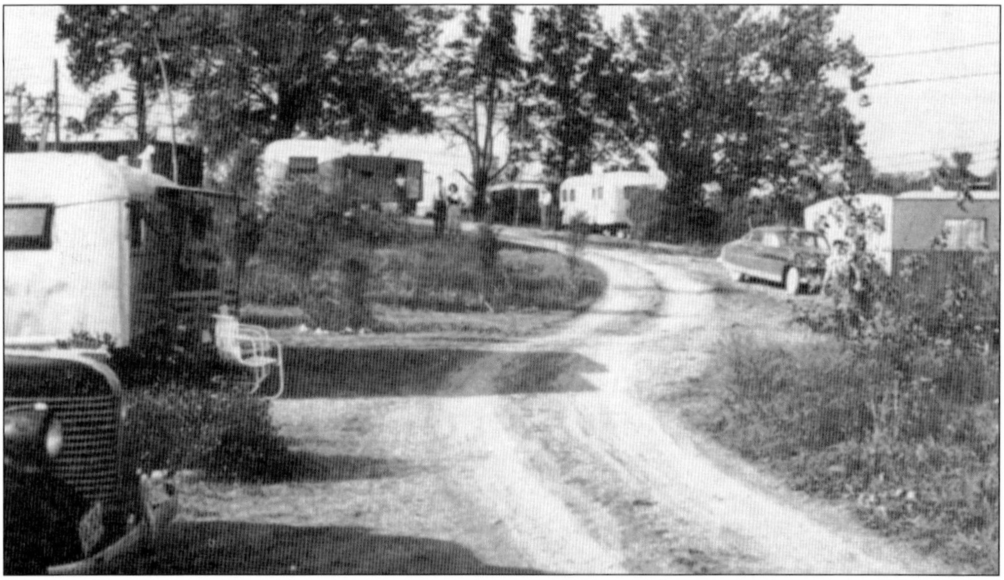

Eagle Village. The campus trailer park known as Eagle Village stood on the site of the current Silver Diamond Baseball Complex. The first trailer was placed there in 1946 and served as home for numerous students until the early 1970s. The 1949–1950 catalog noted that a rent-free area "sufficient to accommodate fifty trailers is reserved for married students." Students owned their own trailers and paid utilities plus a nominal fee for maintenance. The school also provided a bath house and laundry facilities. The little community elected its own mayor, rent collector, custodian, and social chairman.

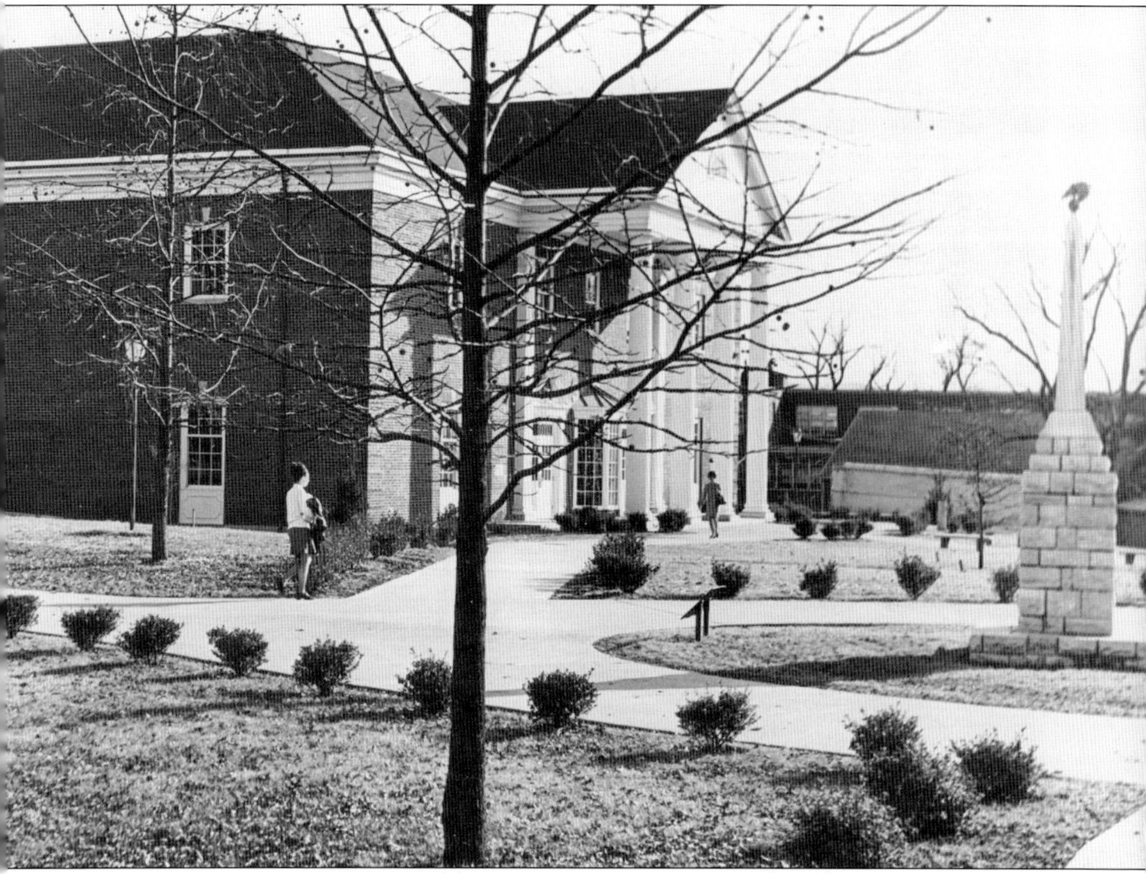

STEPHENS-BURNETT MEMORIAL LIBRARY. The Maples Library was dedicated during homecoming 1949, a gift of longtime trustee D.L. Butler to honor his wife's family. The staff moved into a new structure on December 7, 1970, while renovations of the Maples building were completed in 1971, connecting the two buildings. In May 1989 it was named for Charles Burnett Stephens, a longtime supporter of the institution and the Stephens-Burnett family, whose connection with the school dated back to the 1800s.

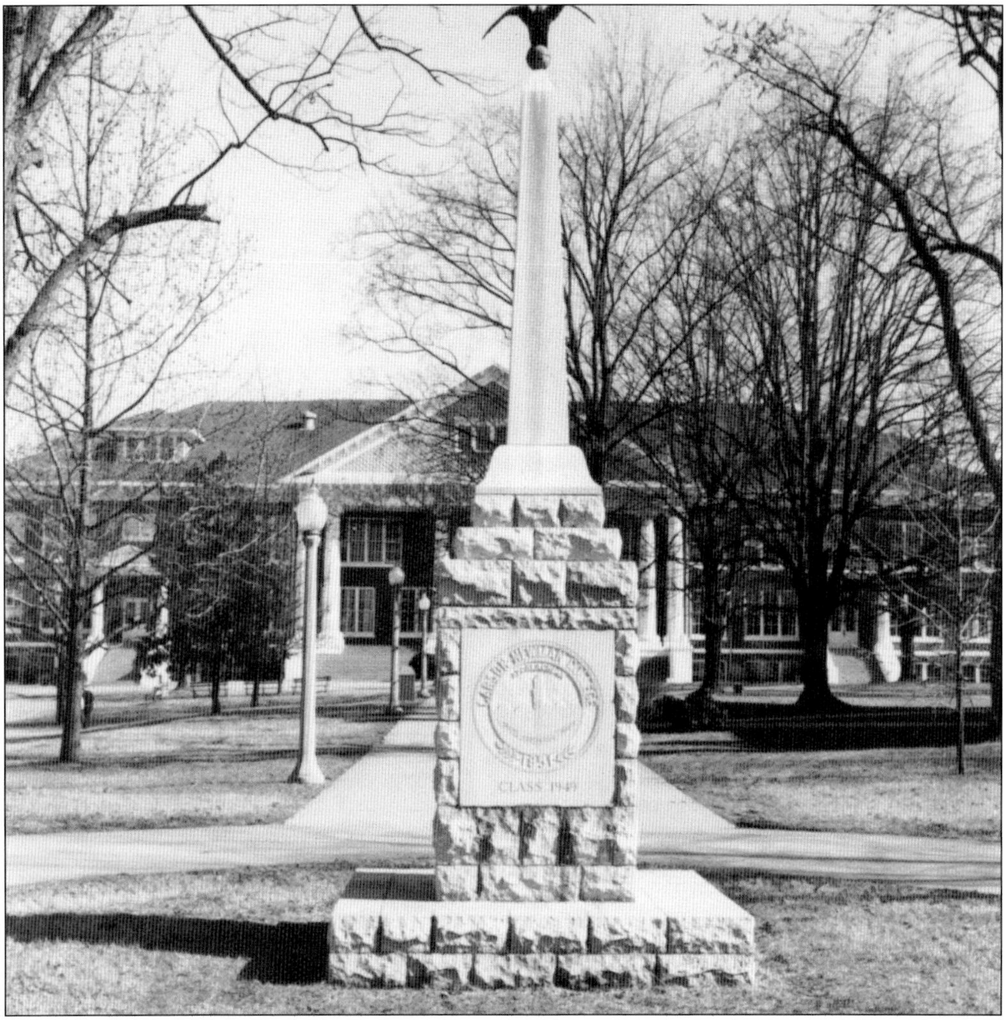

EAGLE MONUMENT. A gift from the class of 1949, the monument was a focal point on campus, but during the next decade it also became the target of rival schools such as LMU, Maryville, and Tusculum. In the late 1960s, the eagle disappeared for good. In 1987, the alumni association raised funds for a replacement and replaced it during a special homecoming ceremony.

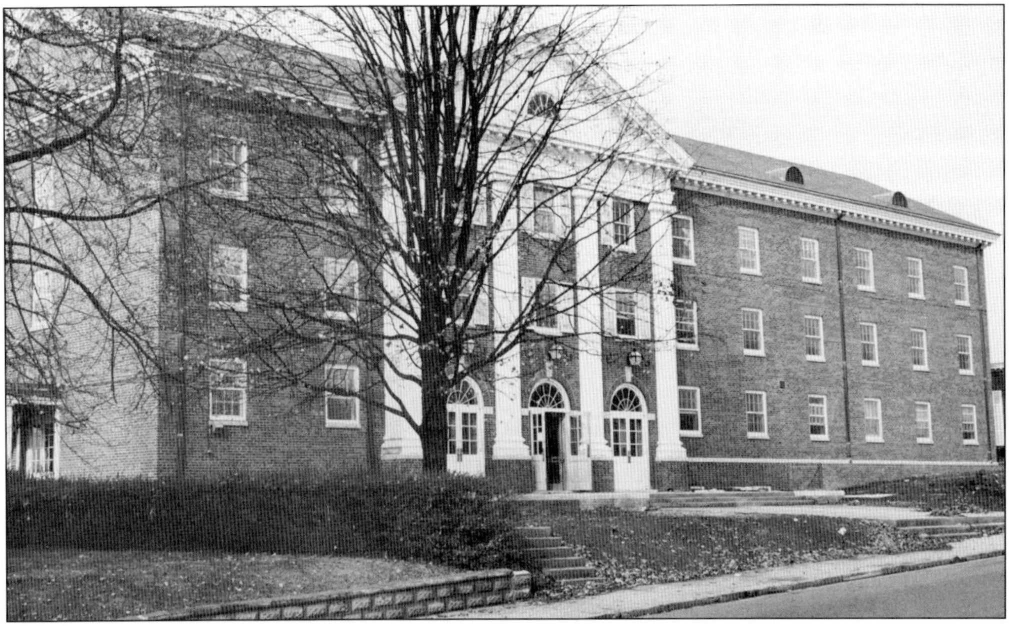

Burnett Hall. One of three current female residence halls, Burnett Hall was originally the home of former president J.M. Burnett. It underwent additions in 1949 and 1952. In 1963, the original section was removed along with the home of former professor John D. Everett and the current structure was built. The parlor is named in honor of donor Mrs. A.J. Foster. It houses approximately 300 women.

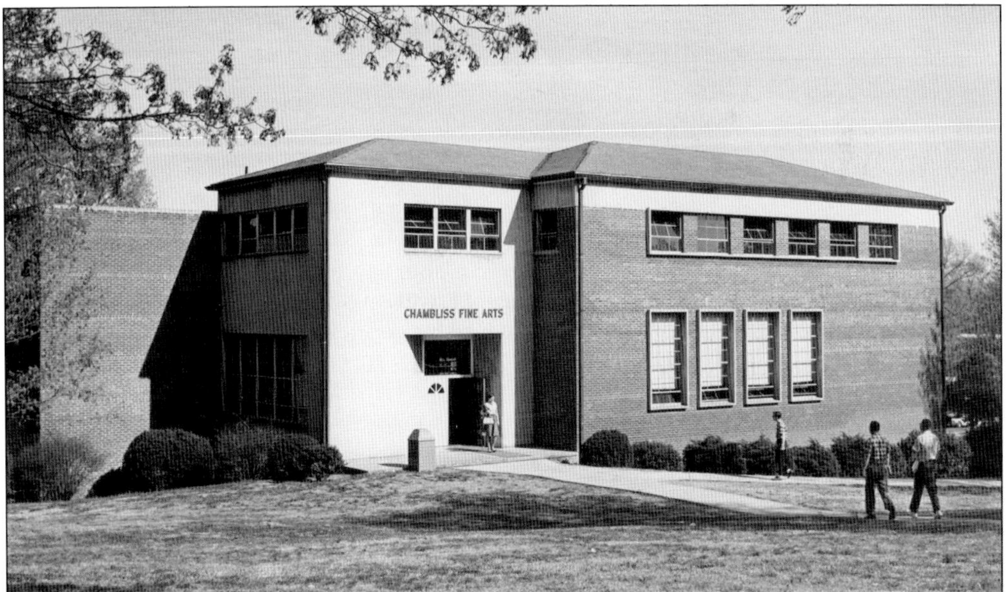

Chambliss Building. Originally known as the Chambliss Fine Arts Building, it opened in 1950 and was designed for music and art courses. It was given by the Ocoee Baptist Association and Justice A.W. Chambliss. Named for his father, Rev. John Alexander Chambliss, it stands as a memorial to the school's first full-time Bible professor. In 1981, it was renovated for use by the psychology and sociology departments.

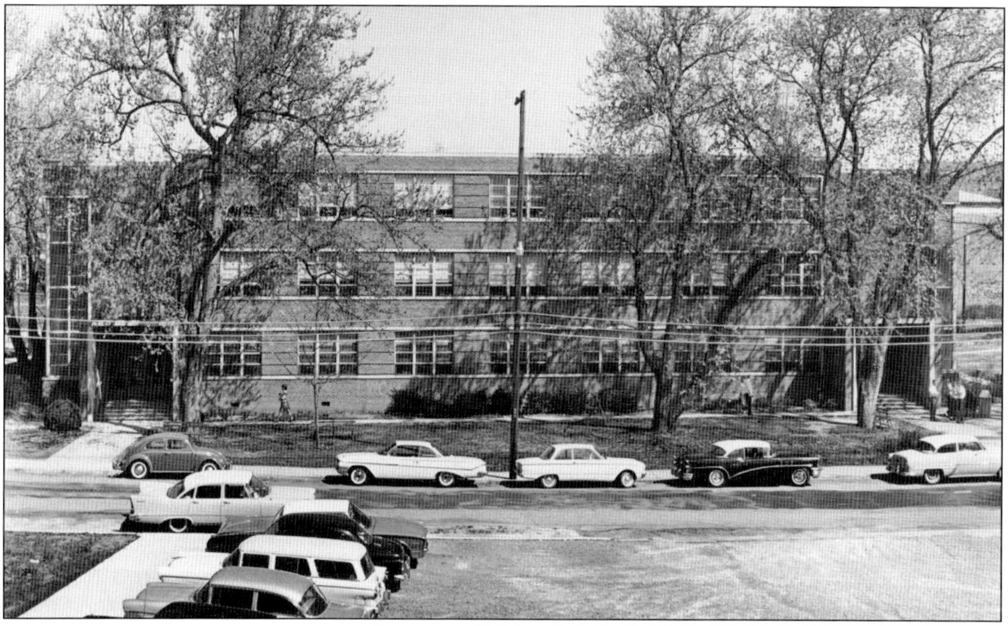

Baker Building. Money from the Knox County Baptist Association supplemented a building campaign to provide funds for this building. It opened in 1951 and was named for Cecil Hurst Baker, who served as chairman of the board of trustees and as the association's moderator. Baker was once home to the family and consumer science division and the offices of the *Orange & Blue* and the *Appalachian*, as well as the cafeteria and student center.

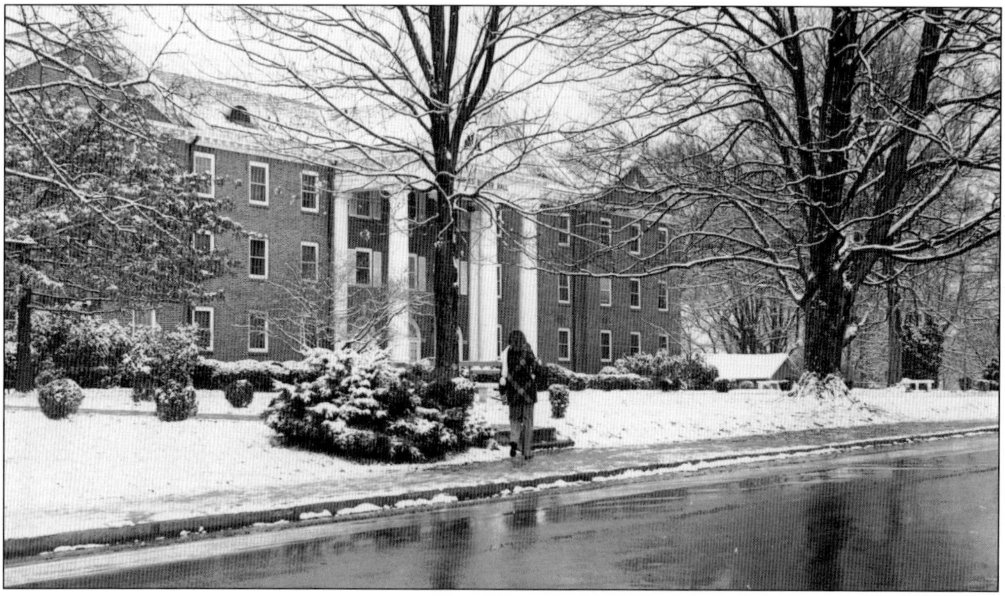

Bertie Maples Butler Hall. A graduate and former music professor, Butler's generous gift enabled this residence hall's construction. The main part of the hall was opened in 1954. Two additional wings were added in 1958 and a third addition was built in 1968. Butler was home to over 300 young ladies until 2007, when it was closed for renovations. It now houses three floors of male students, and as the Butler Hall Welcome Center, it houses the offices of admissions and financial assistance.

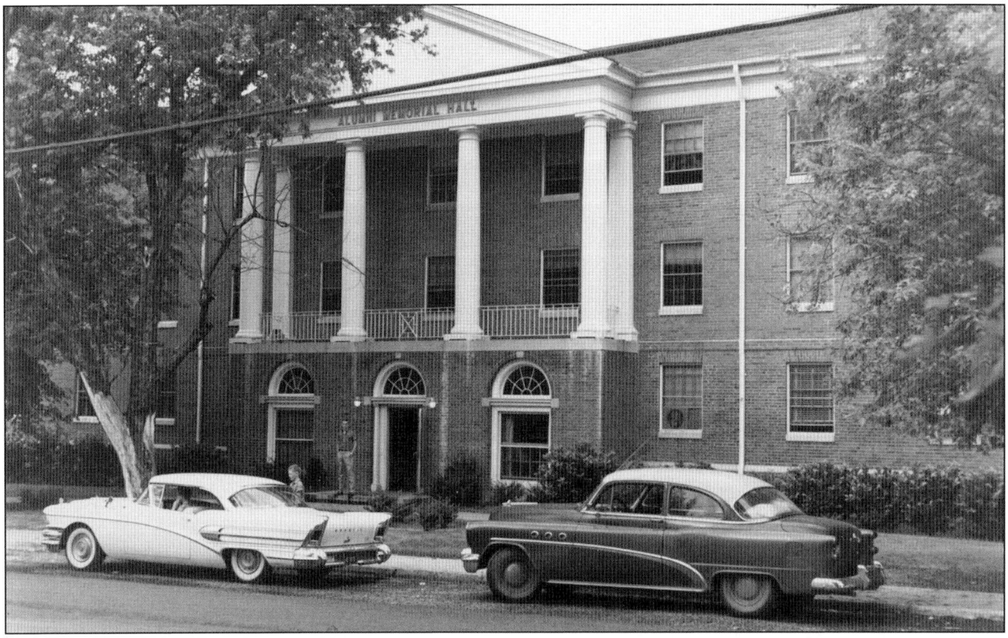

ALUMNI MEMORIAL HALL. In September 1956, Alumni Residence Hall was opened in the fall semester for male students. Named for the alumni and friends of the school who helped finance its construction, it housed approximately 150 men. It was renovated in 2002. The military science department and ROTC program were also located there until their relocation in 2001. Since 2008, the building is now home to female students. (Photograph by Rees Photo Center.)

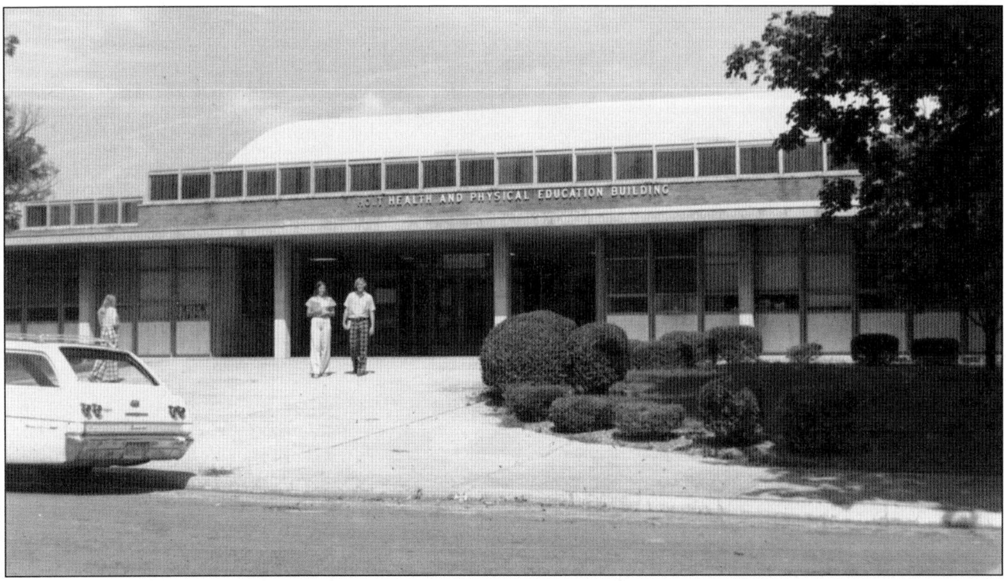

HOLT FIELDHOUSE. The building was completed in 1959 and two years later, it was named in honor of one of the school's most cherished alumni and coaches, Sam B. "Frosty" Holt. Renovated and incorporated into the Maddox Student Activities Center, it contains a gymnasium, athletic offices, a training room, a weight room, locker rooms, and Carson-Newman College Hall of Fame. Dana X. Bible was the guest speaker at the building's dedication.

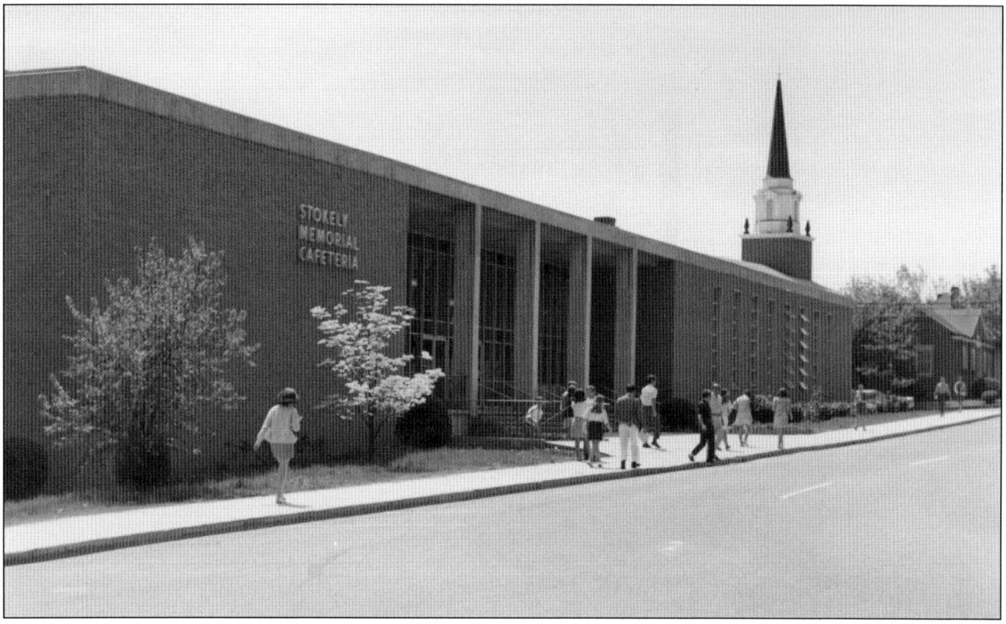

STOKELY MEMORIAL BUILDING. Constructed in 1963 and named for W.B. Stokely Jr. and his family, the first floor contains the cafeteria and several dining rooms. The cafeteria was remodeled in 2005 and again in 2010. The basement houses both the undergraduate and graduate education departments, classrooms, and the newly renovated resource center, the Cole-Little Curriculum Laboratory, a gift of alumni Joe and Louise Little.

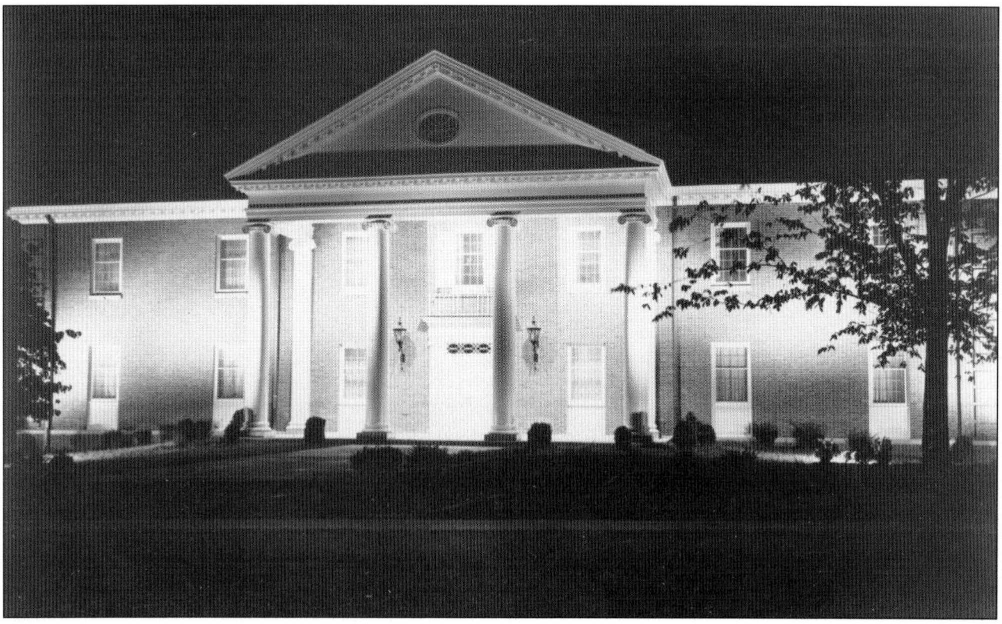

FITE ADMINISTRATION BUILDING. Named for former president D. Harley Fite and his wife Esther, the building was completed in 1967. Built during the "Decade of Development," the building was one of many completed during Dr. Fite's administration. After its construction, administrative offices were moved from the John T. Henderson Memorial Hall Administration Building, which then housed academic offices and classrooms.

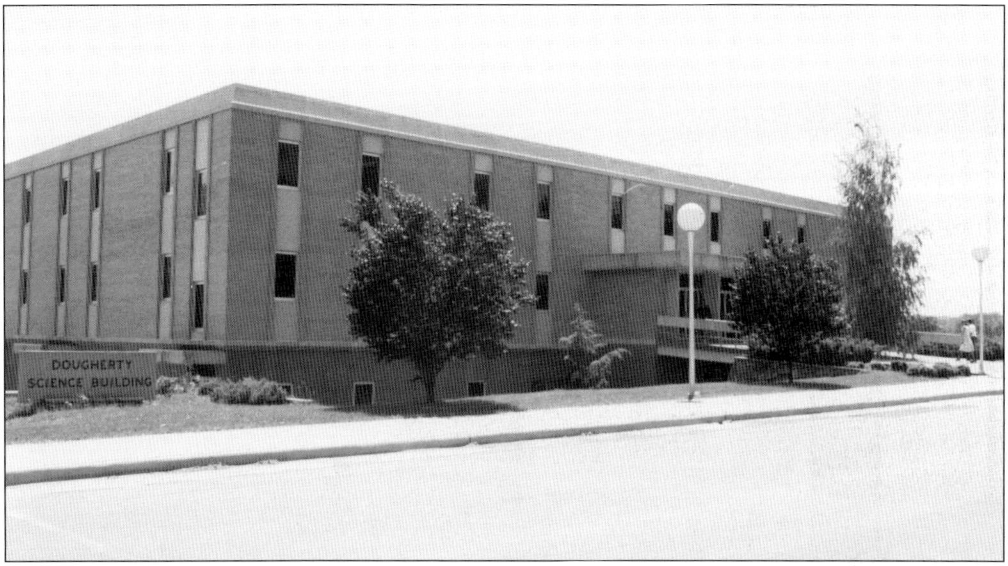

Dougherty Science Center. Named for Mr. and Mrs. Thomas Hunter Dougherty, this much-needed facility was completed in 1972 and dedicated on May 11, 1973. It houses the physics, geology, mathematics, biology, and chemistry departments. A greenhouse and animal facility are located on the roof and a computer lab was added in 1988. It provided updated facilities to replace those of the Warren Science Building that would serve as the new art building.

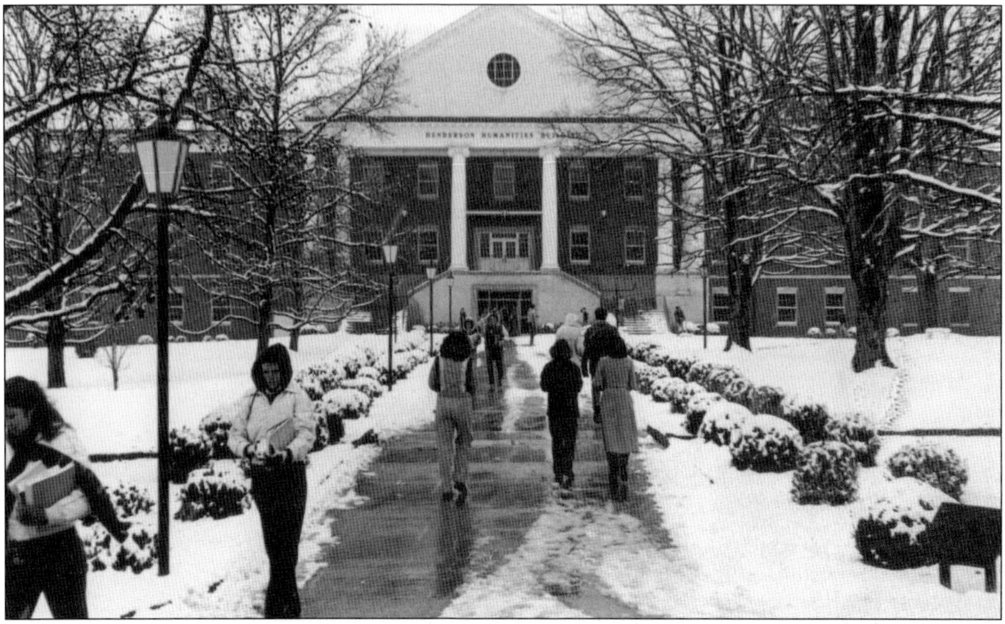

Henderson Humanities Building. The new Henderson was ready by the start of spring semester 1977 and dedicated on April 21. With exterior construction to resemble the previous building, it contains the English, religion, foreign language, philosophy, and communication departments. It also contains Gentry Auditorium, named for former president W.L. Gentry (1917–1919), and the Phoenix Theatre. It is an ongoing testimony that God can bring beauty from ashes.

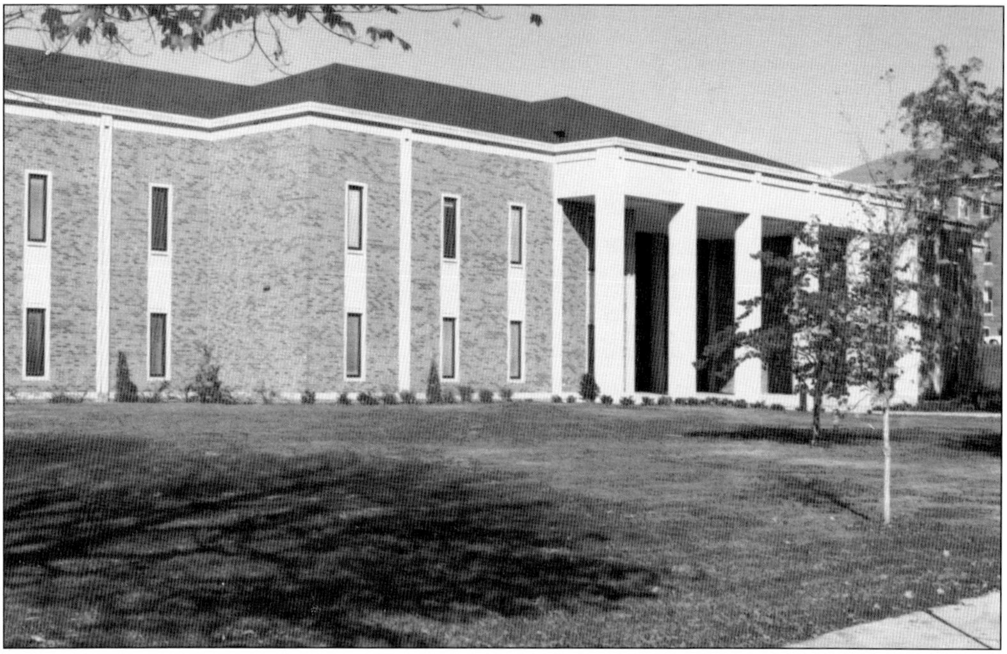

Mabel Lewallen Tarr Music Building. Ground was broken on September 9, 1978, and the new building allowed the music department to move into a state-of-the-art facility. Dr. Wesley Forbis, the secretary of the Department of Church Music, Baptist Sunday School Board, gave the address at the May 7, 1981, dedication. In 1983, the recital hall was named for J.D. and Mildred McNees Thomas, generous supporters of the school. The building was named for Mabel Tarr in 2003 during homecoming festivities.

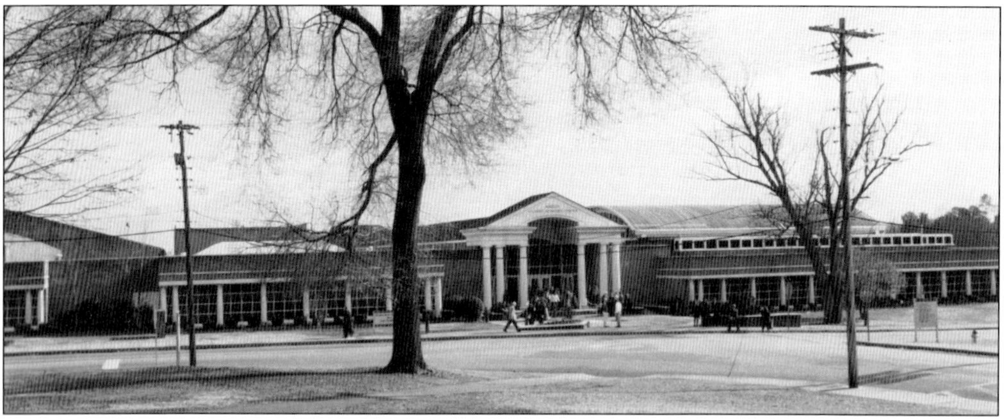

Maddox Student Activities Center. The realization of a longtime dream, this facility was completed in June 1993 after six years of planning and building. On October 15, the building was dedicated "to the glory of God and the service of humanity." In 1994, *Athletic Business* cited the facility as one of the year's top 10 Facilities of Merit along with Arrowhead Pond of Anaheim and Oriole Park at Camden Yards. During the June 4, 1999, retirement dinner for Pres. J. Cordell Maddox, his name was dramatically added to the front of the building.

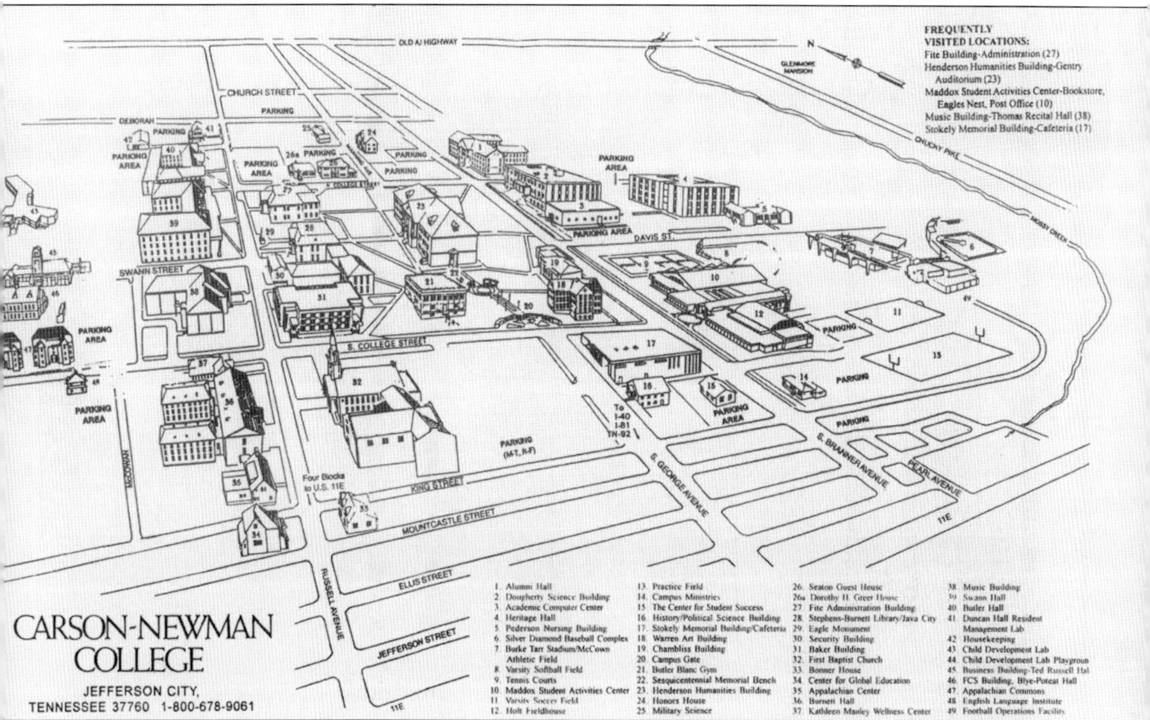

THE CAMPUS. After several name and venue changes since its 1851 founding, Carson-Newman settled into its present location after Carson and Newman Colleges merged in 1889. Through the help of generous gifts and building projects, the college exhibited exciting growth over the next 160 years, expanding into the current campus. (Courtesy of East Tennessee Printing.)

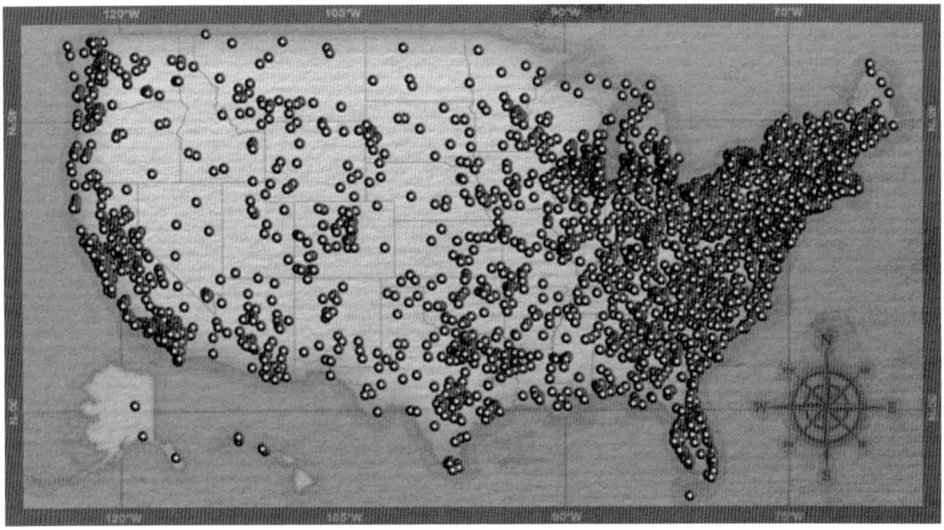